NOTHING

BLANK

Words, Graphics
and Photography
of GREG MILLS

EMPTY

DEDICATED TO MY CHILDREN;
Amanda Marie, Kayla Mariah, Megan
Elizabeth and Garrett Matthew,
"Always dare to dream for only
then are you truly free beware of
those who do not for they are blind
and can not see."
Also to Grandma Walker who always
believed in me and my dreams.

Published by Spiritwind Book and Filmworks, San Francisco, California
Words, Graphic Design and Photography by Greg Mills
ISBN#

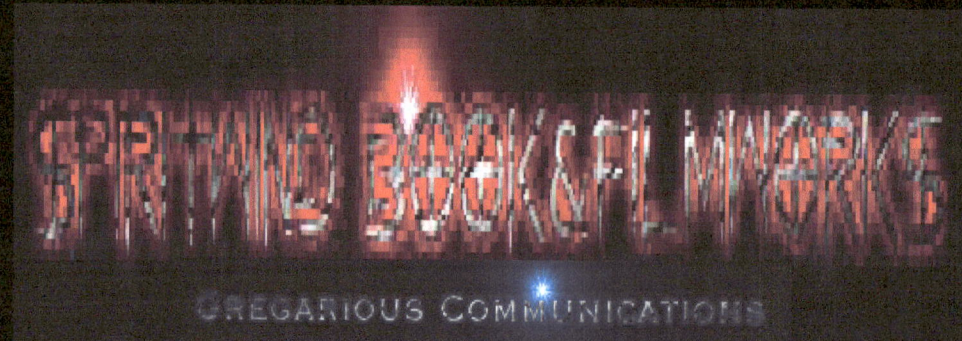

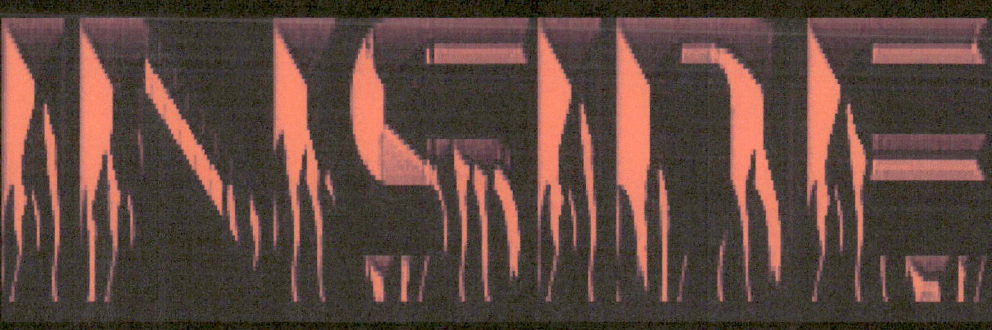

INSIDE

DREAMOTION:

Black and White.............next to Nada page – last page
Sunrises,Sunsets and Moonrises........sun of a page – la page
In the Crowd...................................26 – 47
Trainmotion........Shortfilm....Take 1 – Cut...that's a Rap
Angles,Curves and Shadows............ Plate 1 – Plate 27
Dances with Light.......................No 1 – No. 8
Clouds......................................111 –107
Odds & Ends.....................Hello – Goodbye

NADA

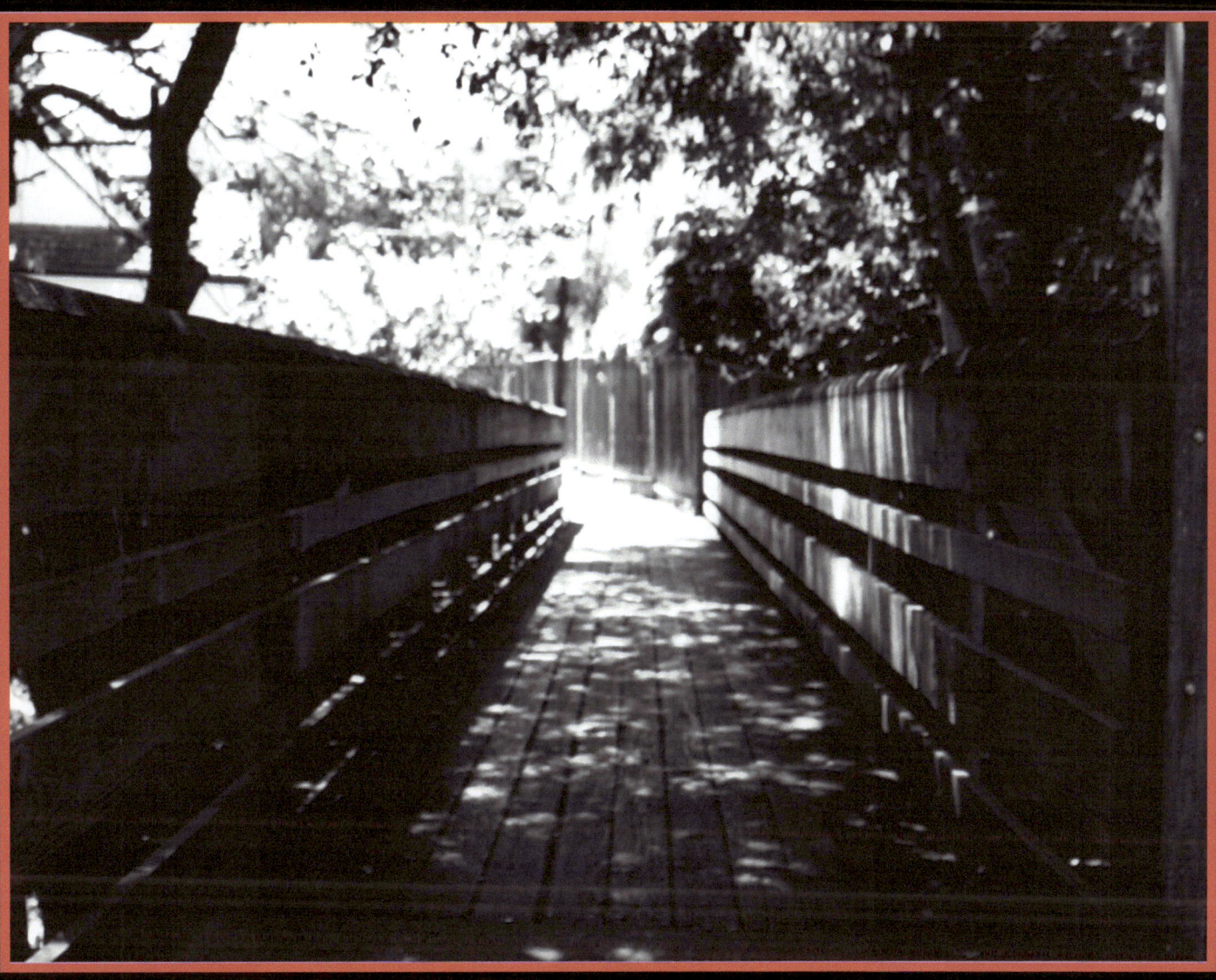

the Bridge   Belmont, California

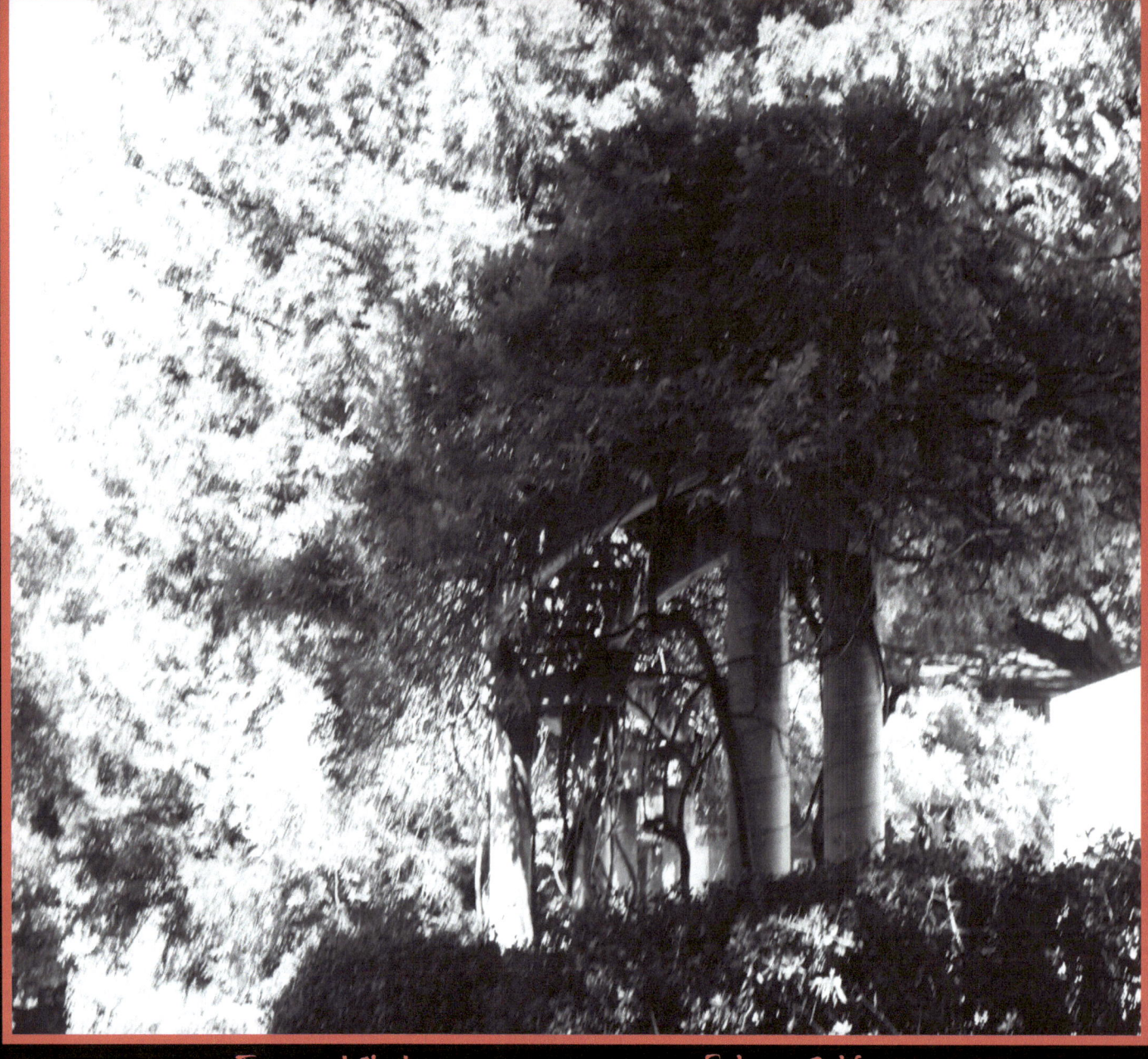

Trees and Shadows   Belmont, California

This Page

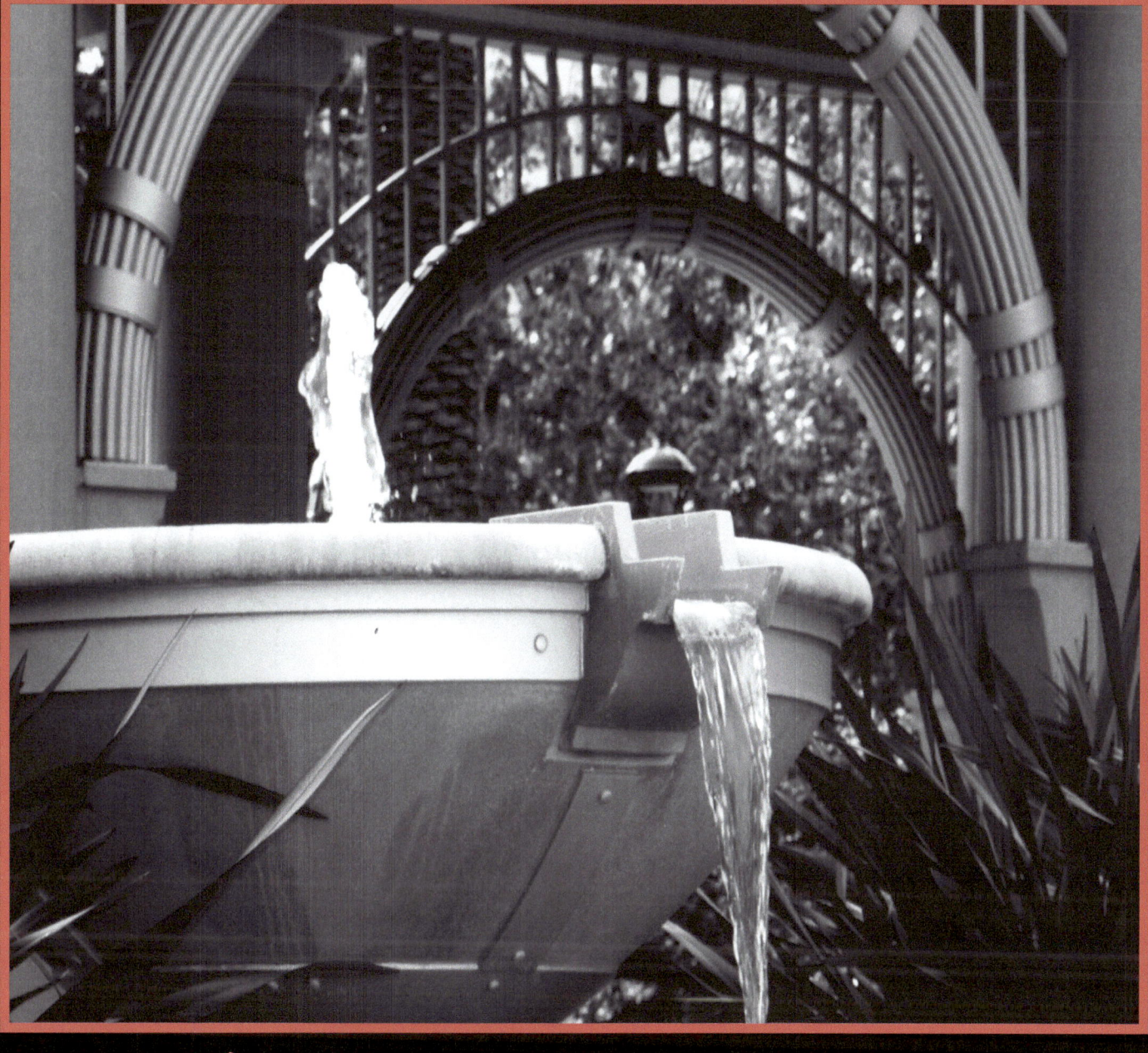

Fountain Arches   Redwood City, California

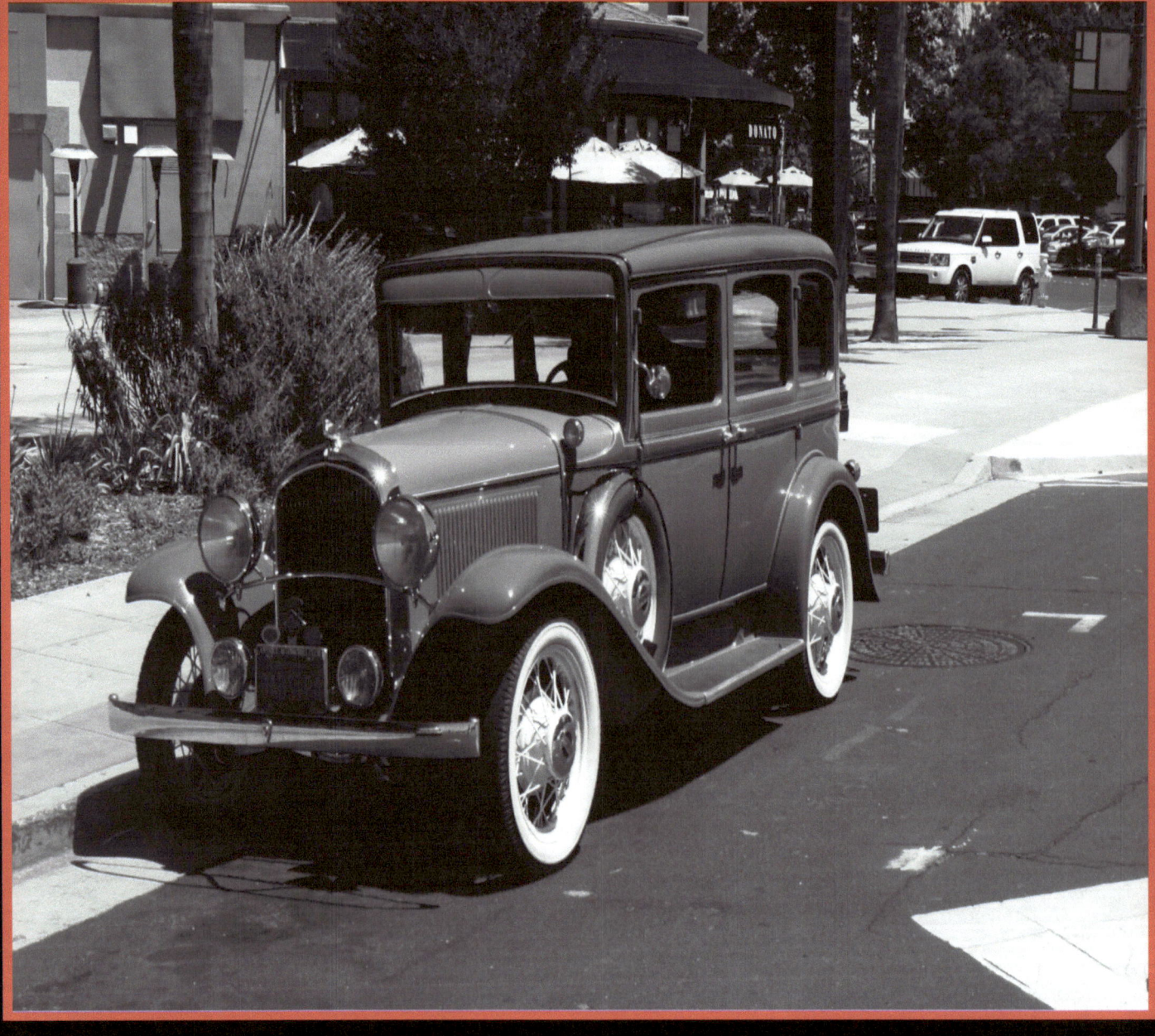

Classic Plymoth   Redwood City, California

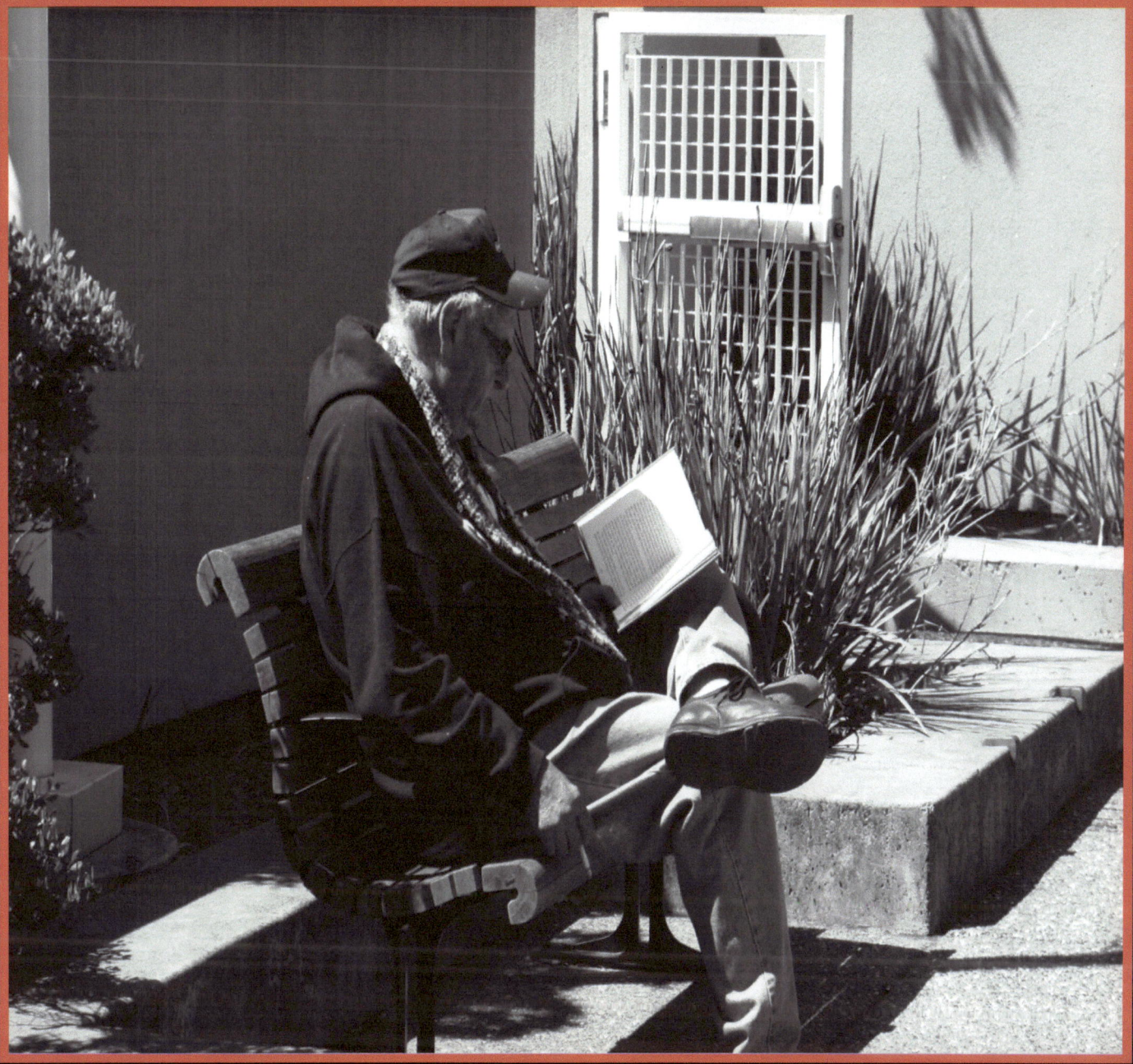

John the Actor   San Carlos, California

Johns Page

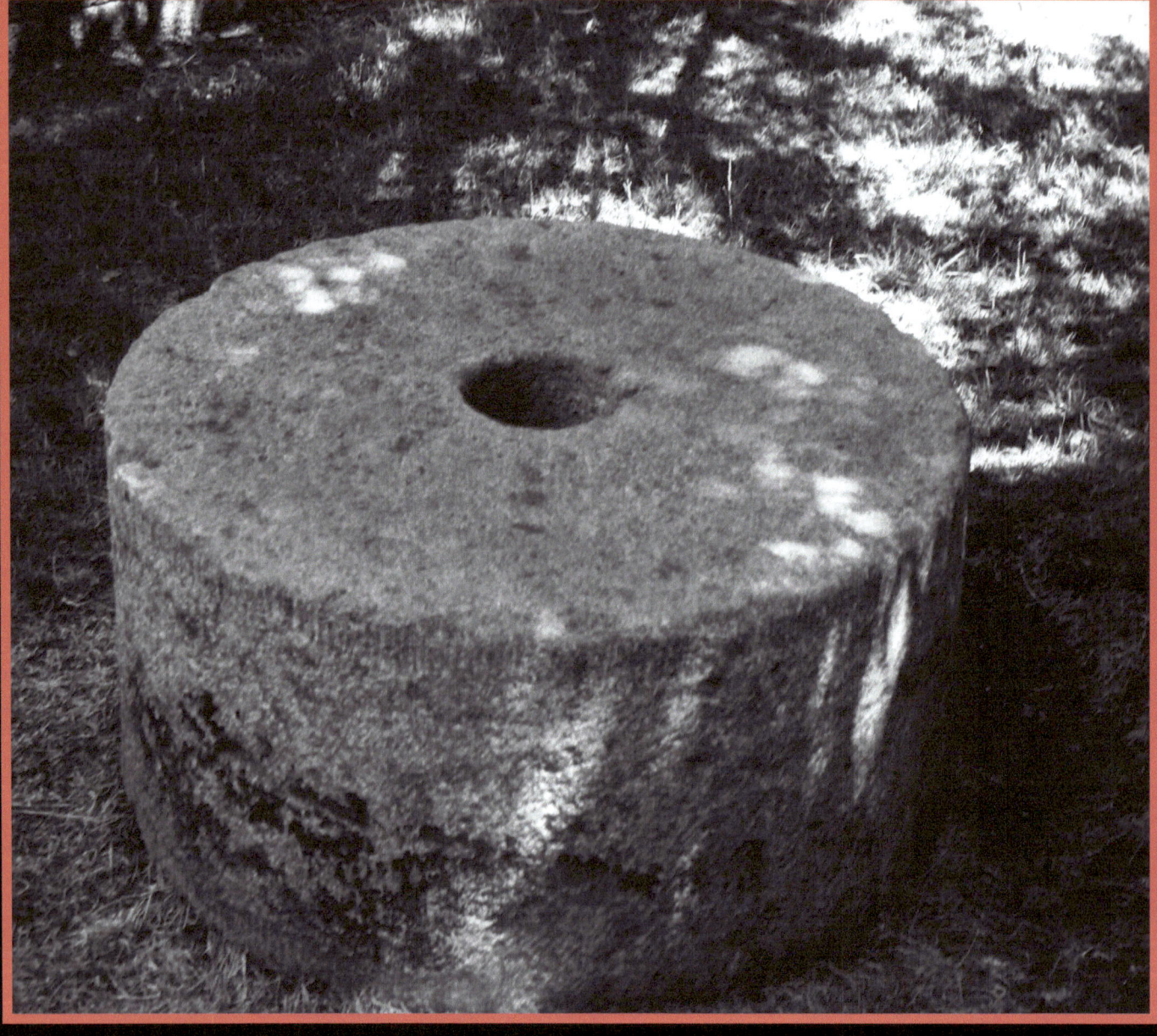

Grinding Stone   Belmont, California

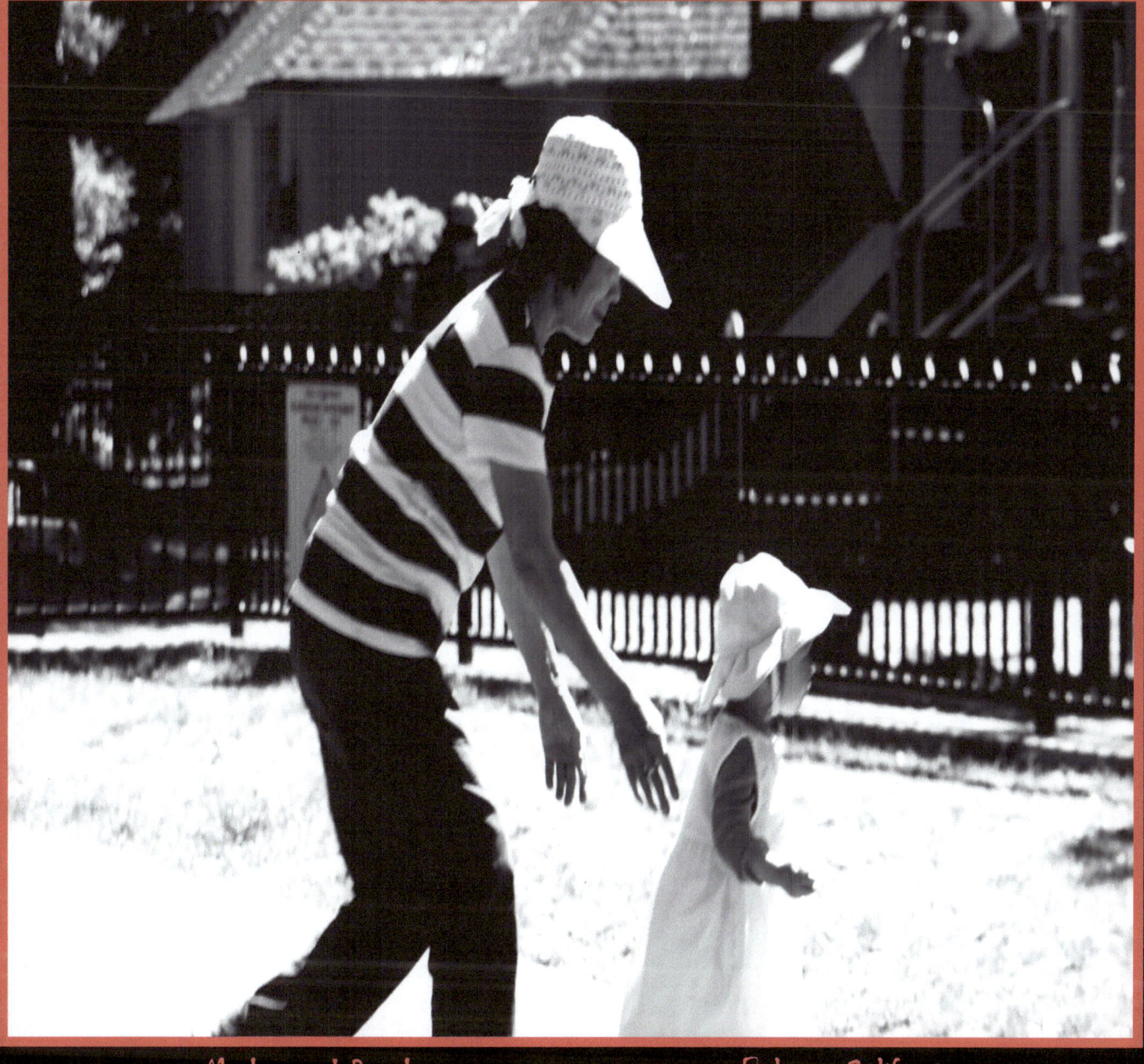

Mother and Daughter   Belmont,California

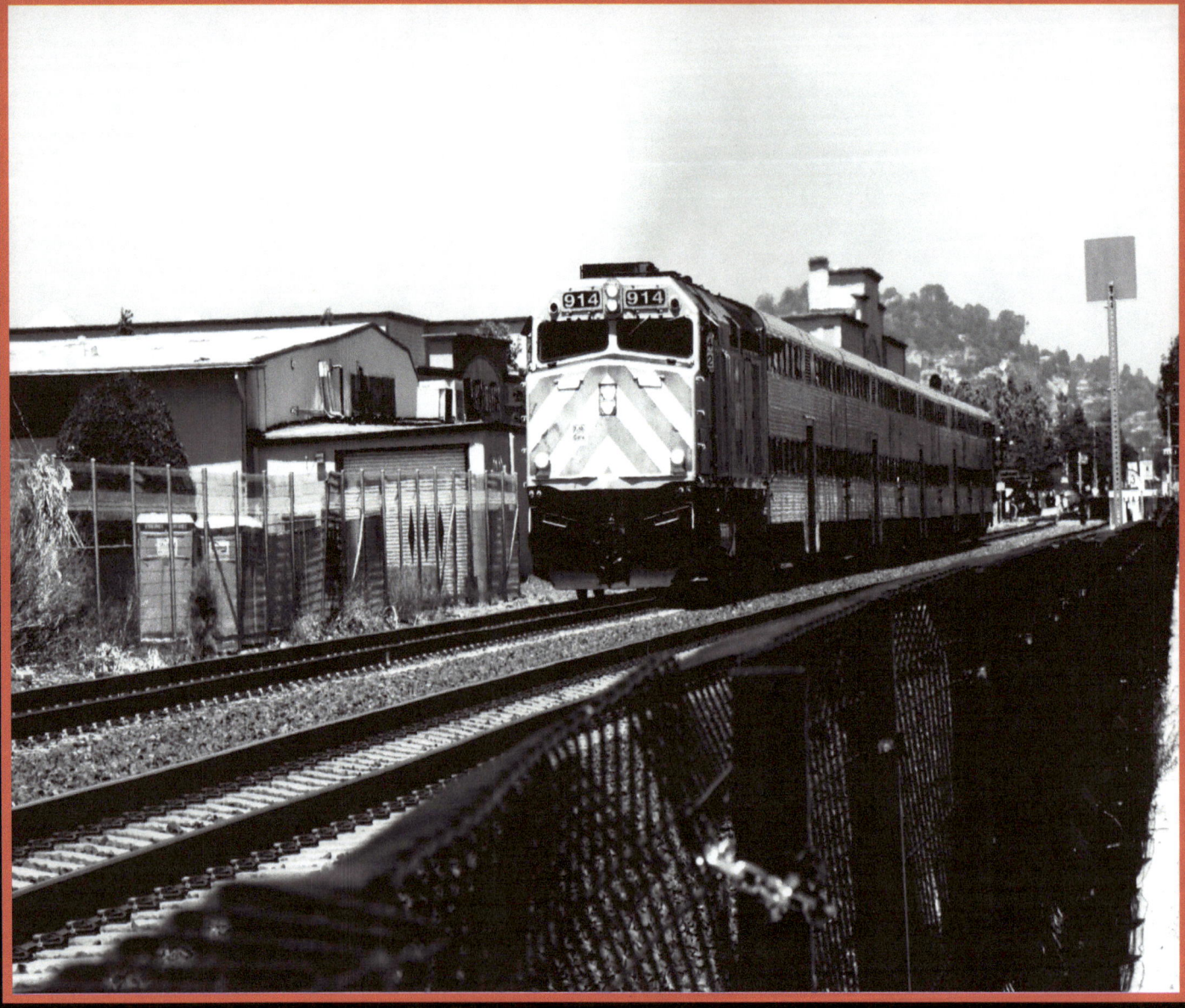

Train on trestle   Redwood City, Califonia

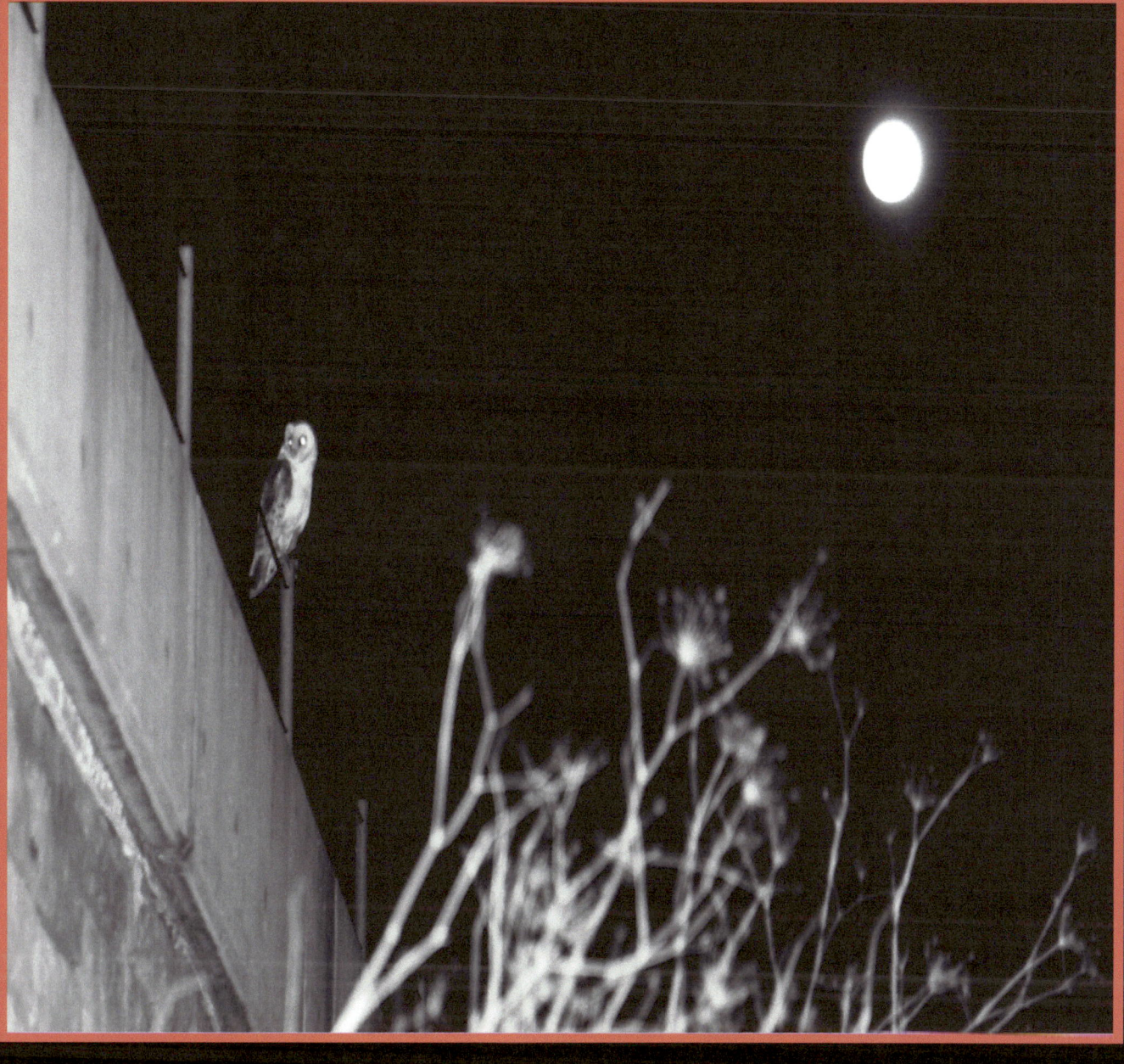

Owling at the Moon   Belmont, Califonia

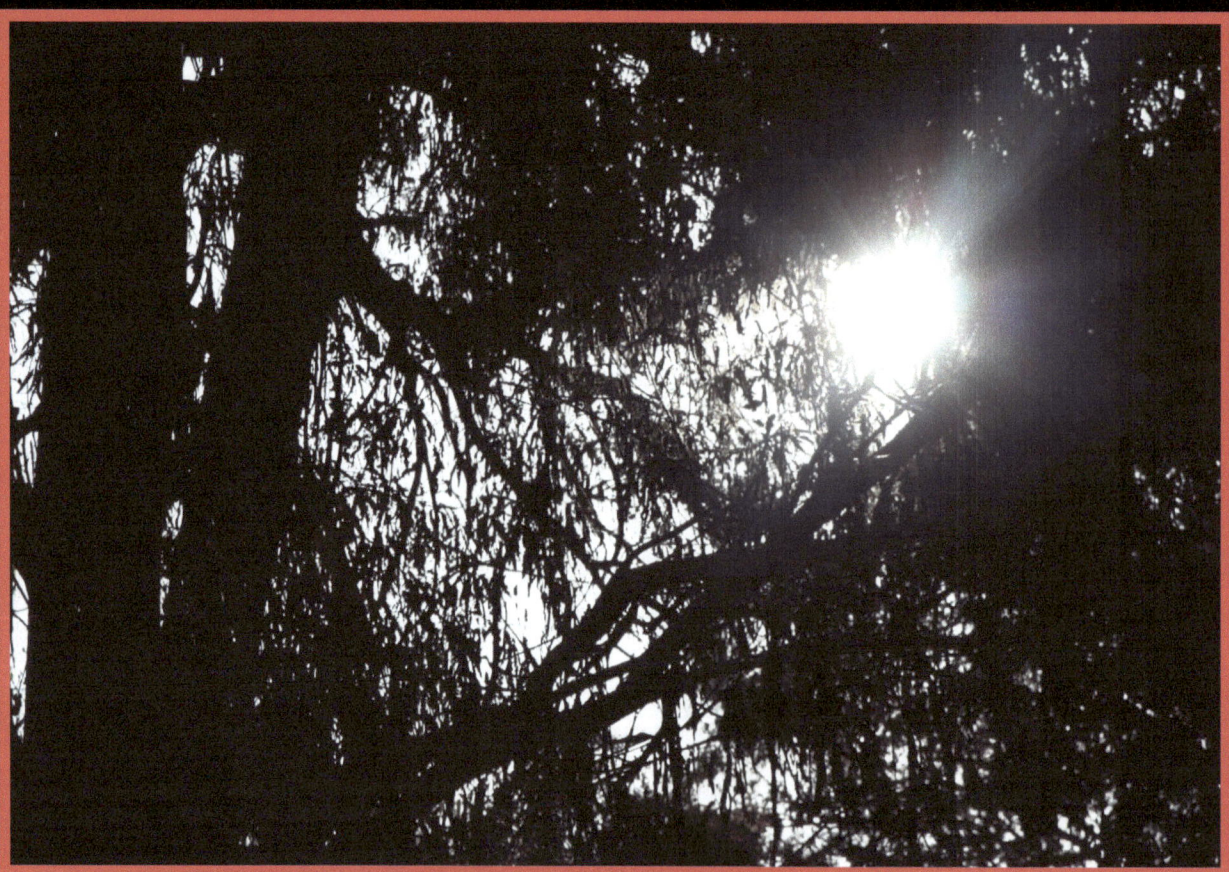

Sunrise through the trees   Belmont, California

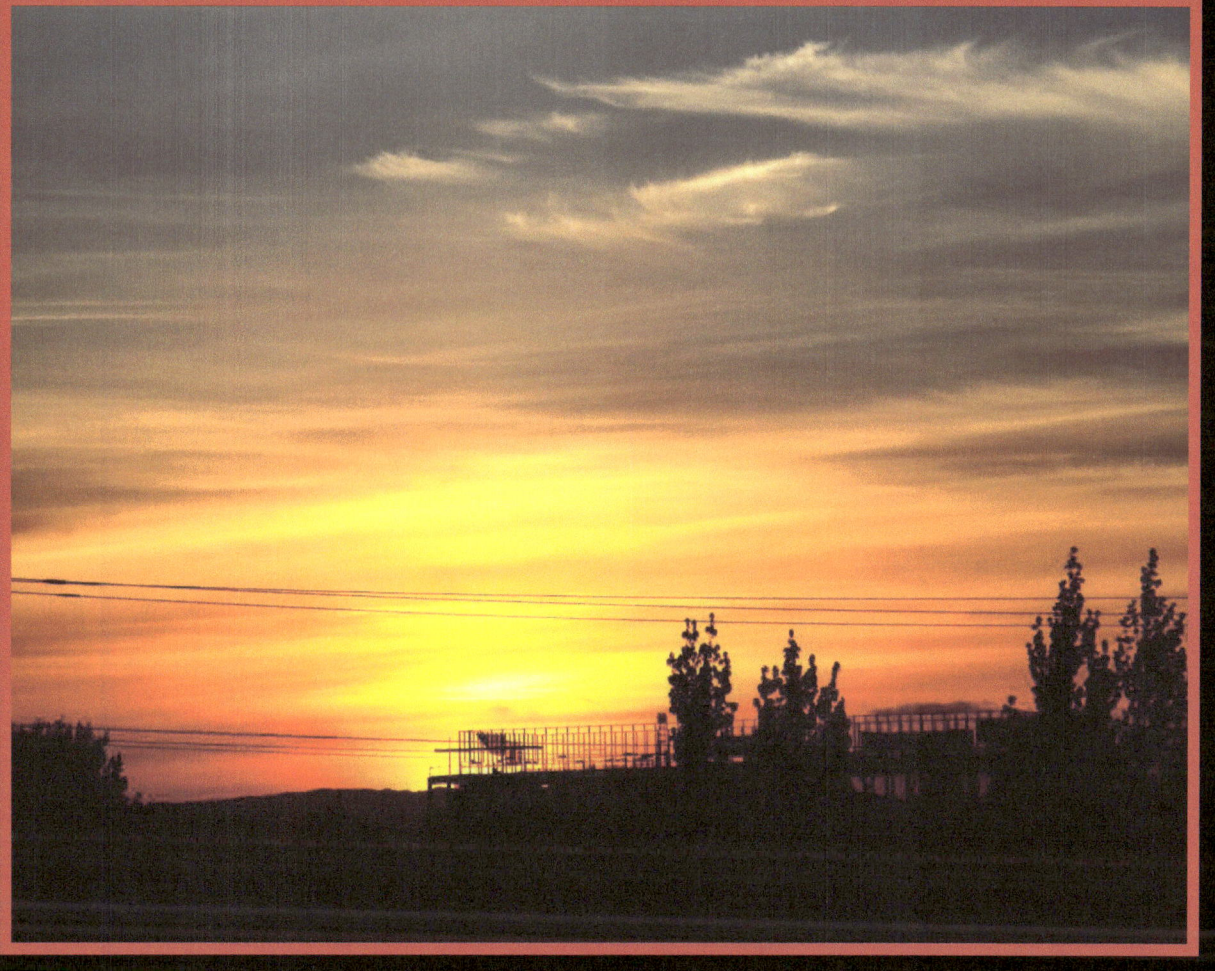

Patio Sunrise   San Carlos, California

Sunny Page

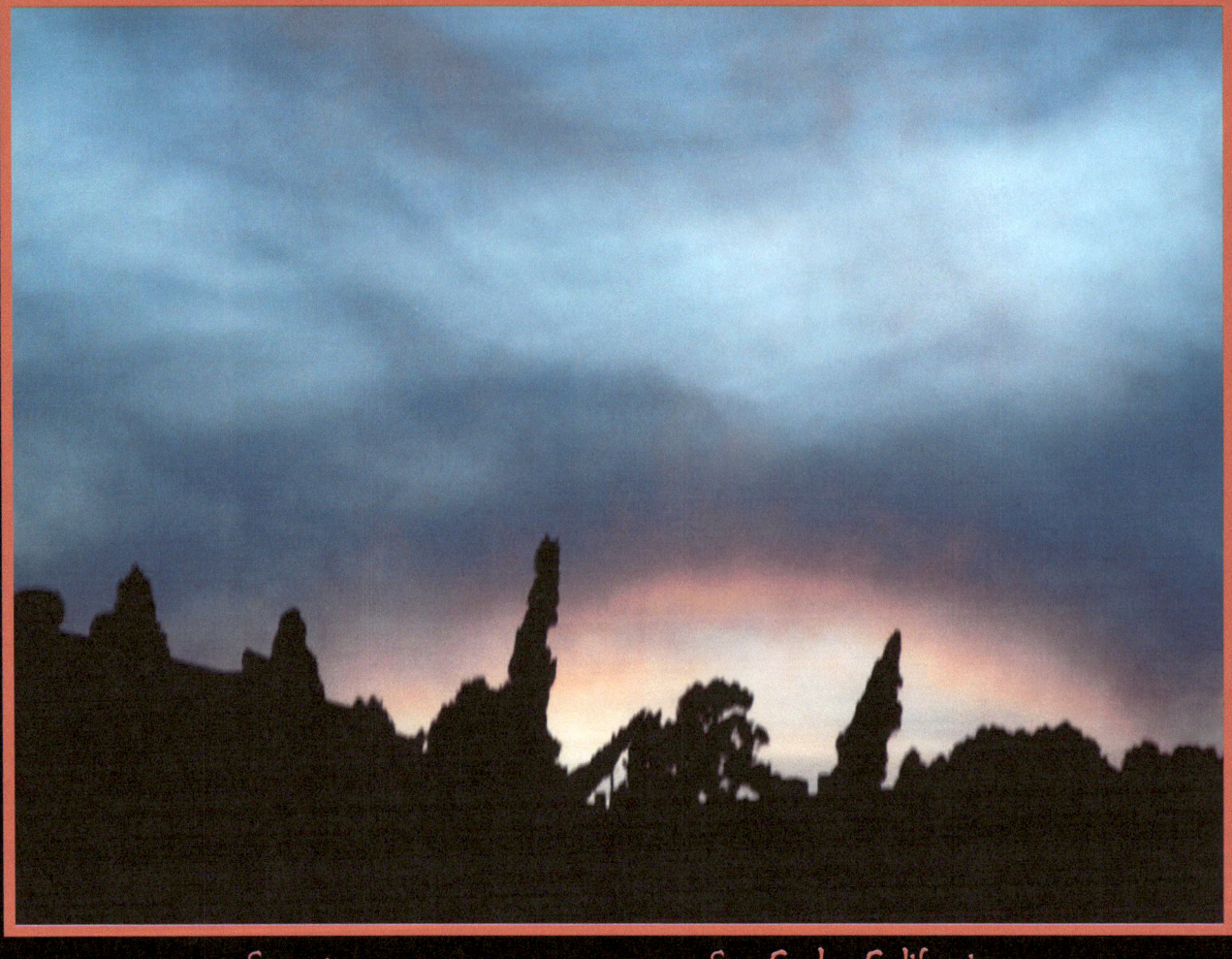

Sunset over cypress   San Carlos, California

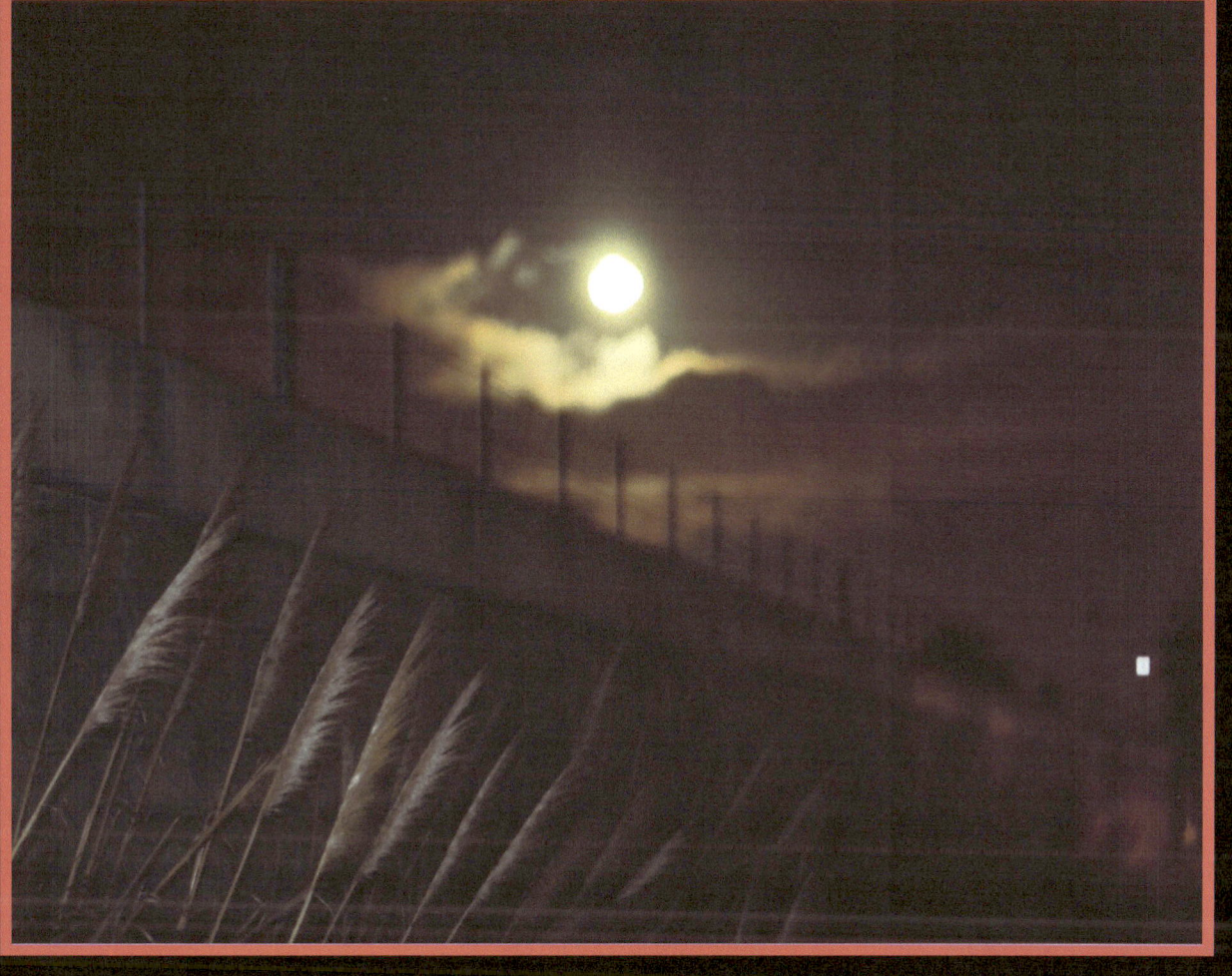

Dreamotion–the Original   Belmont, California

Dream Page

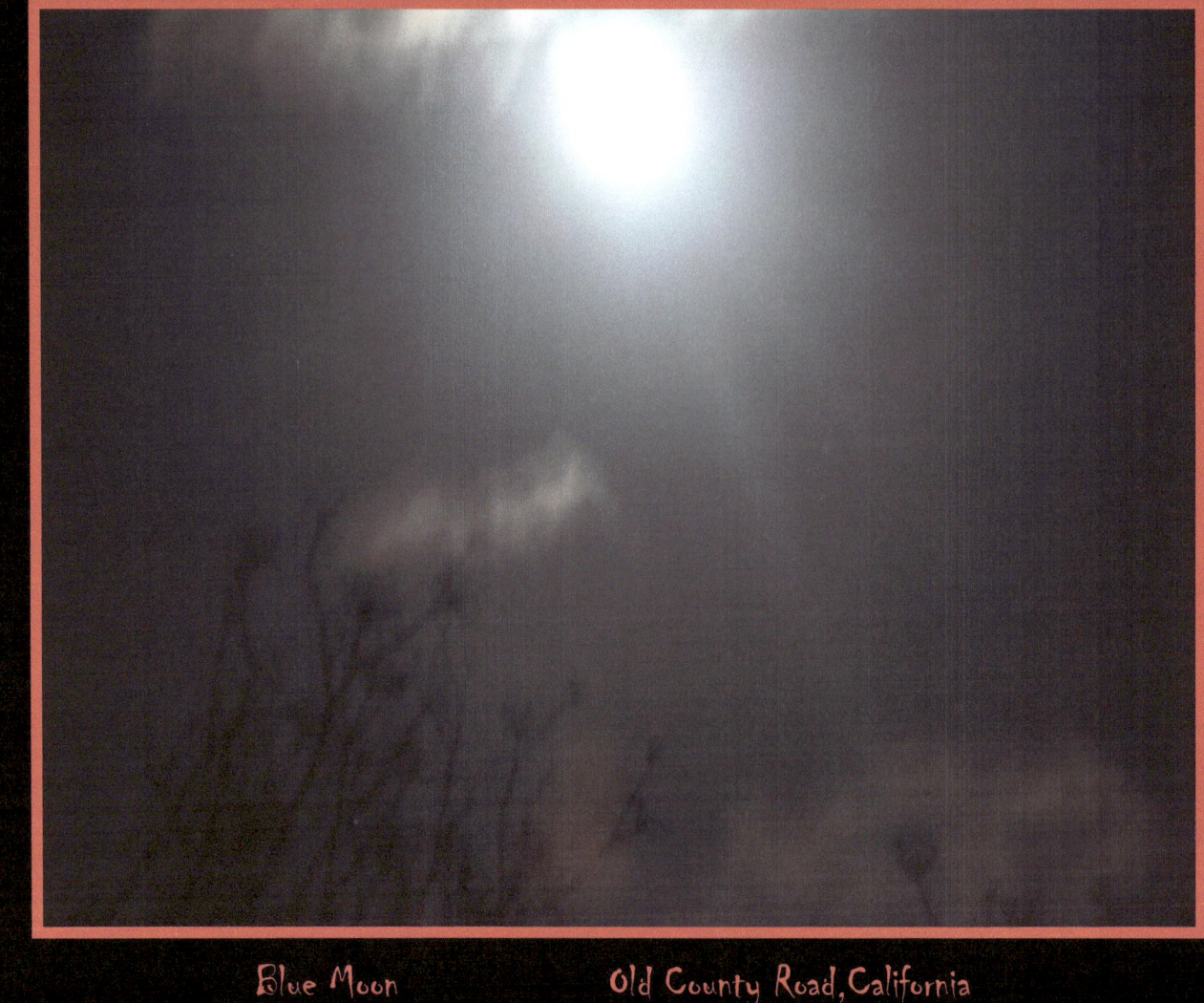

Blue Moon   Old County Road, California

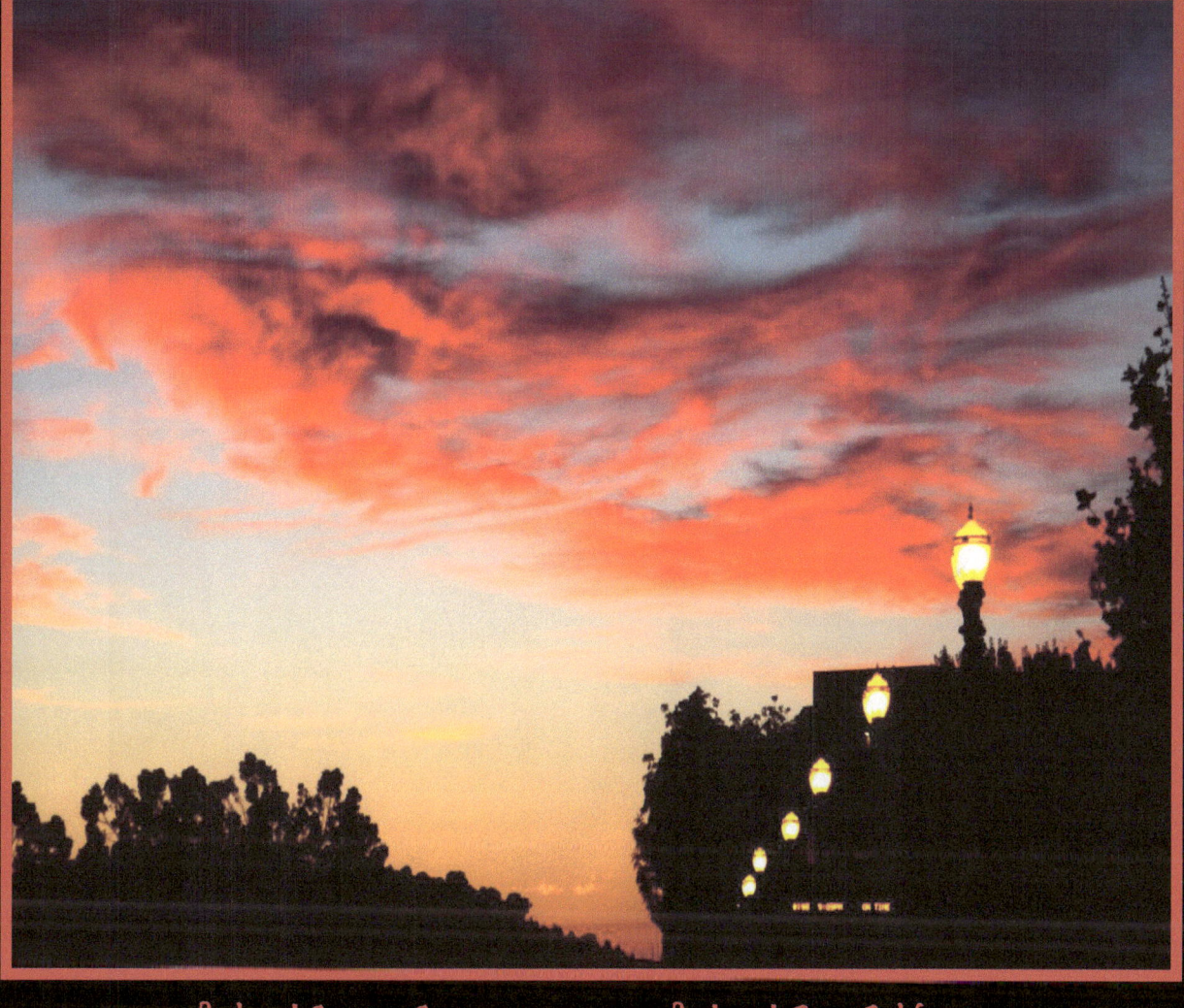

Railroad Station Sunset   Redwood City, California

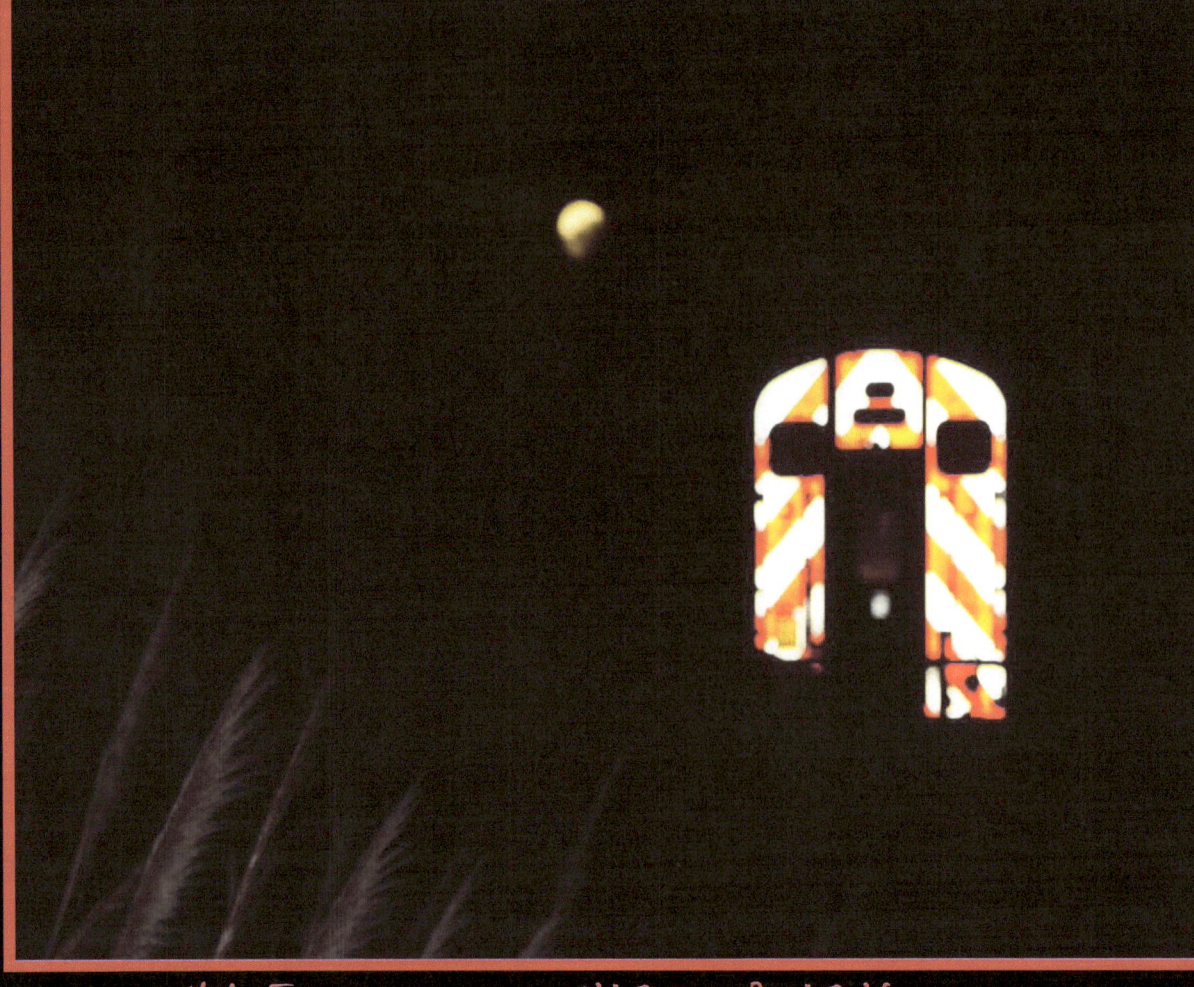

Night Train   Old County Road, California

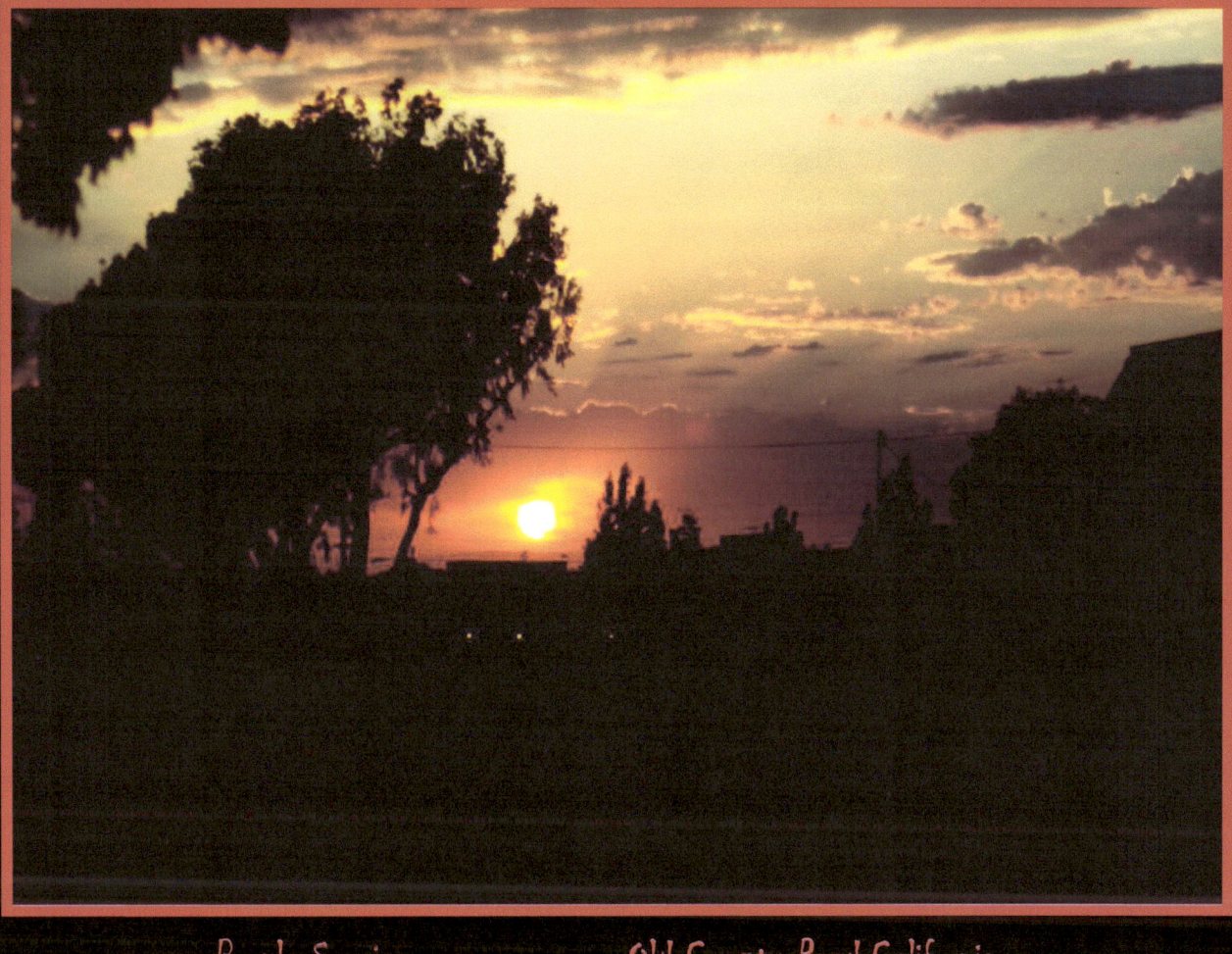

Purple Sunrise   Old County Road, California

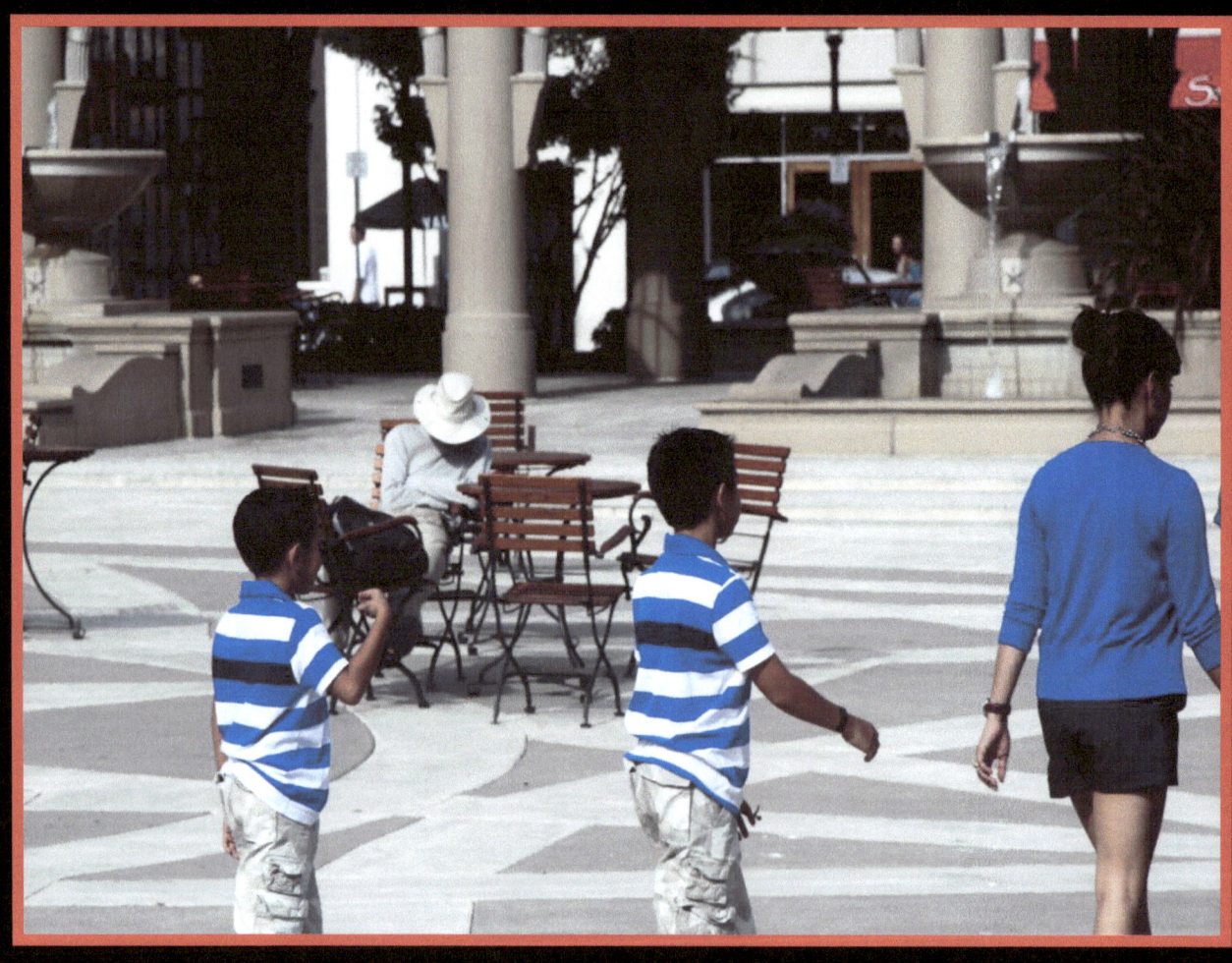

Walk this Way   Redwood City, California

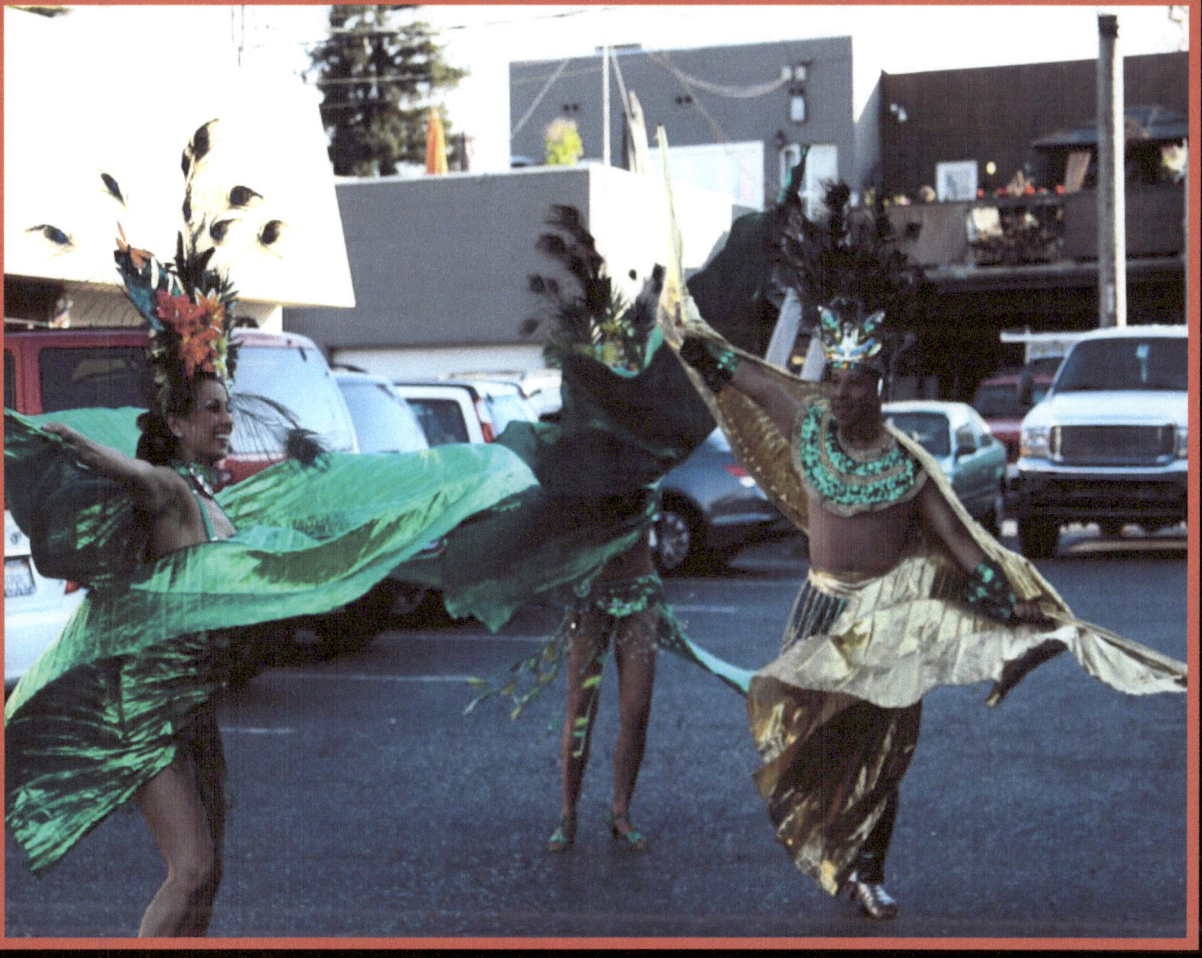

Dance this Way   San Carlos, California

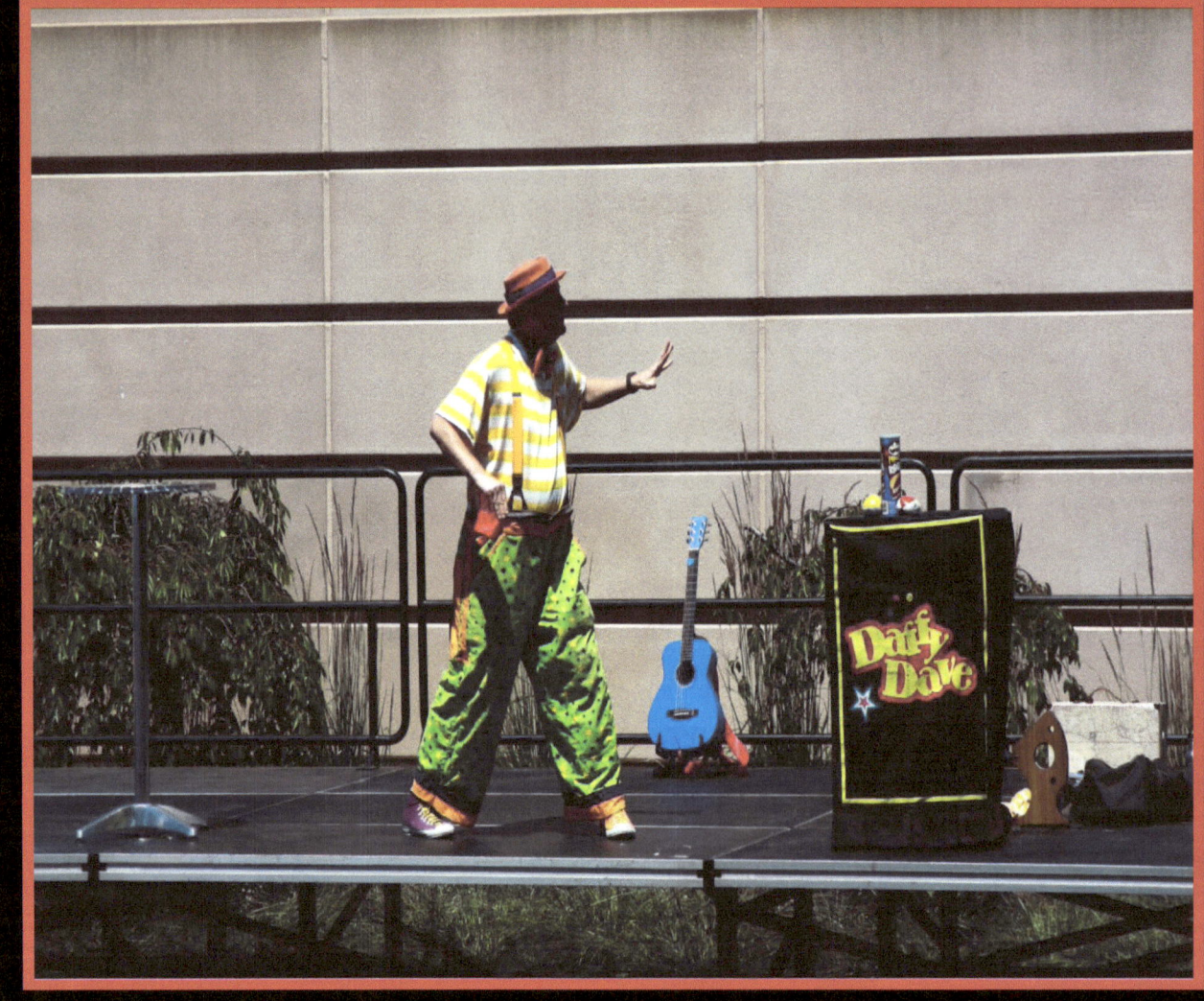

Daffy Dave   Redwood City, California

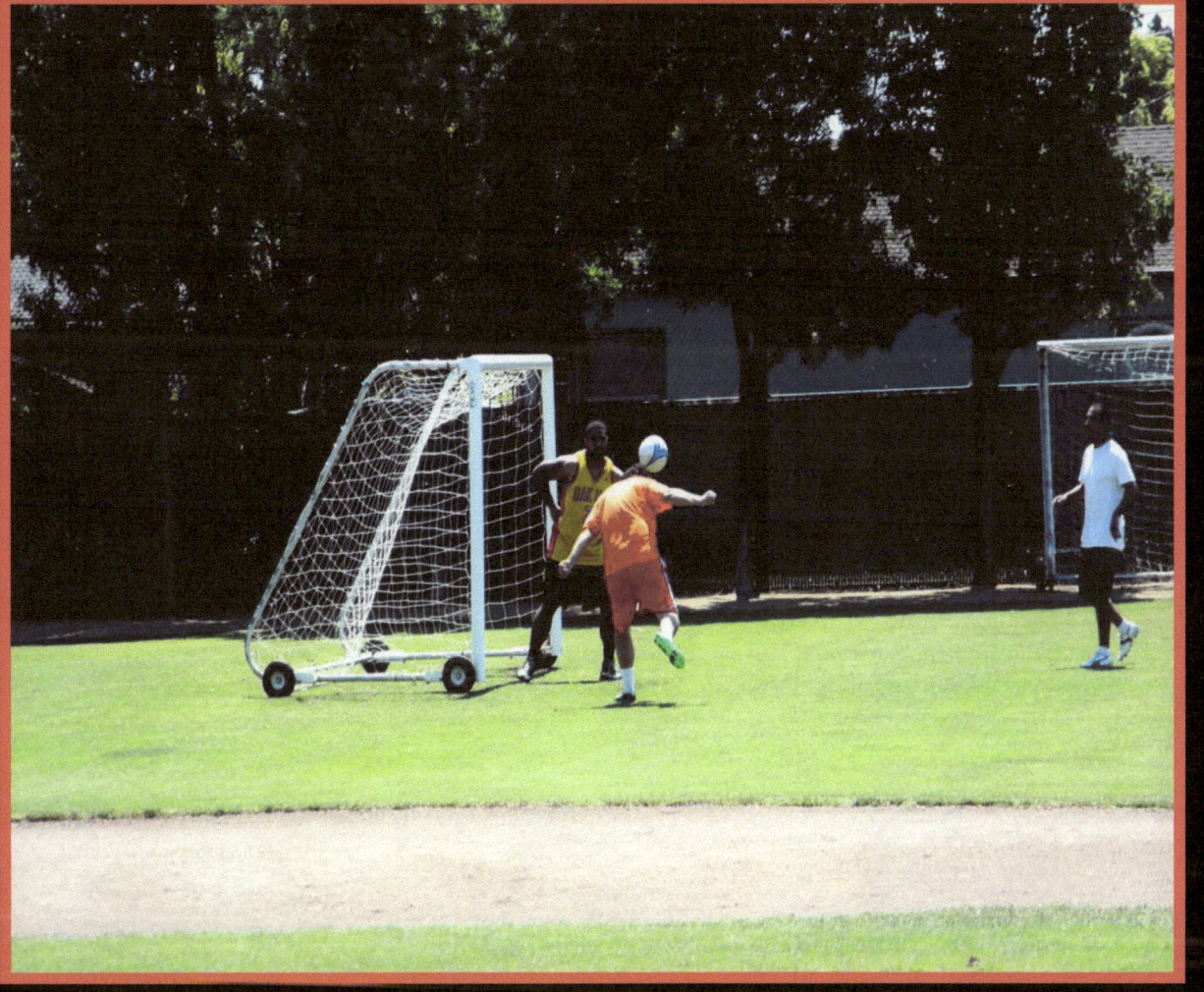

Volley Ball   San Carlos, California

PAGE 29

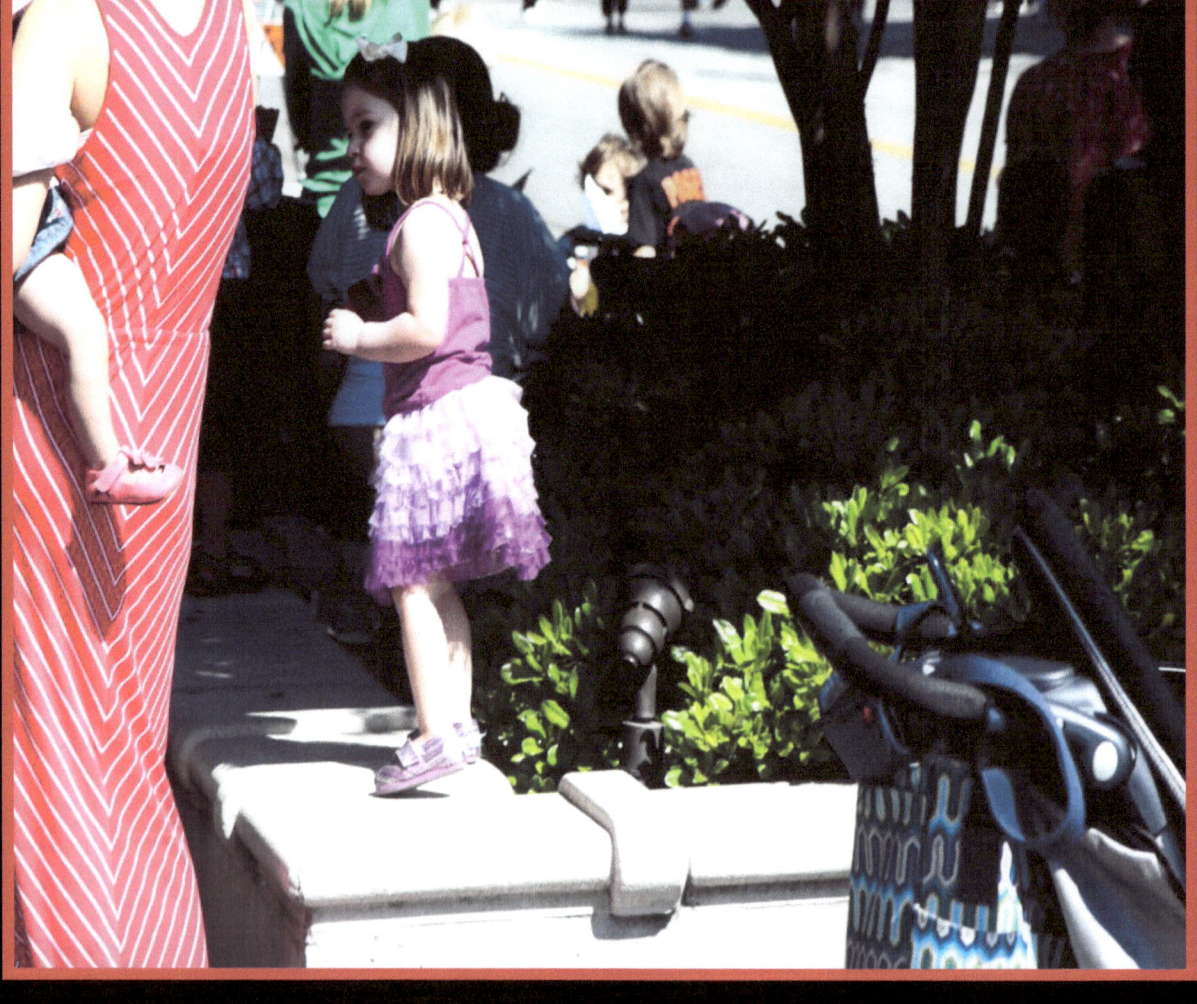

Curious   San Carlos, California

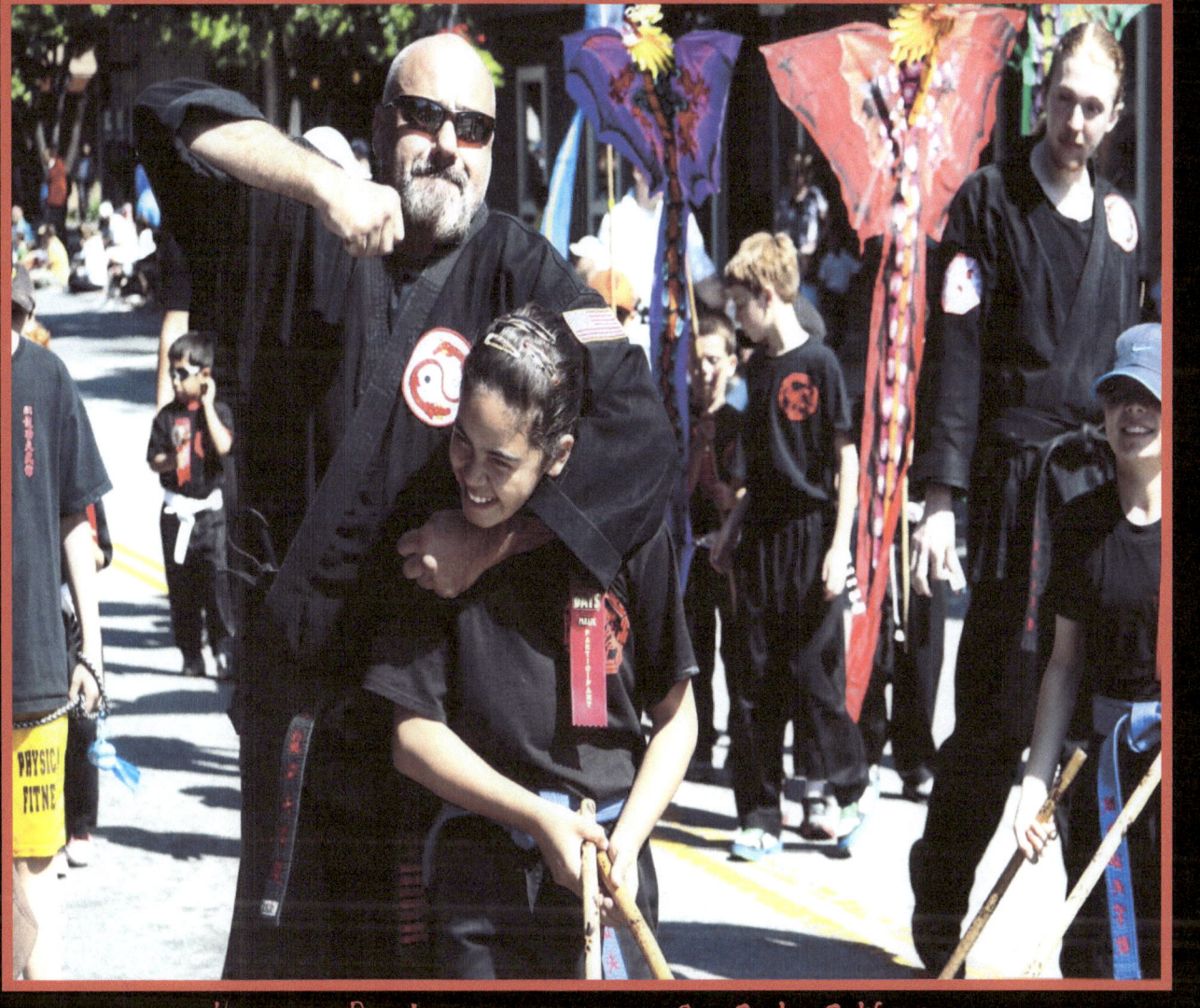

Hometown Parade   San Carlos, California

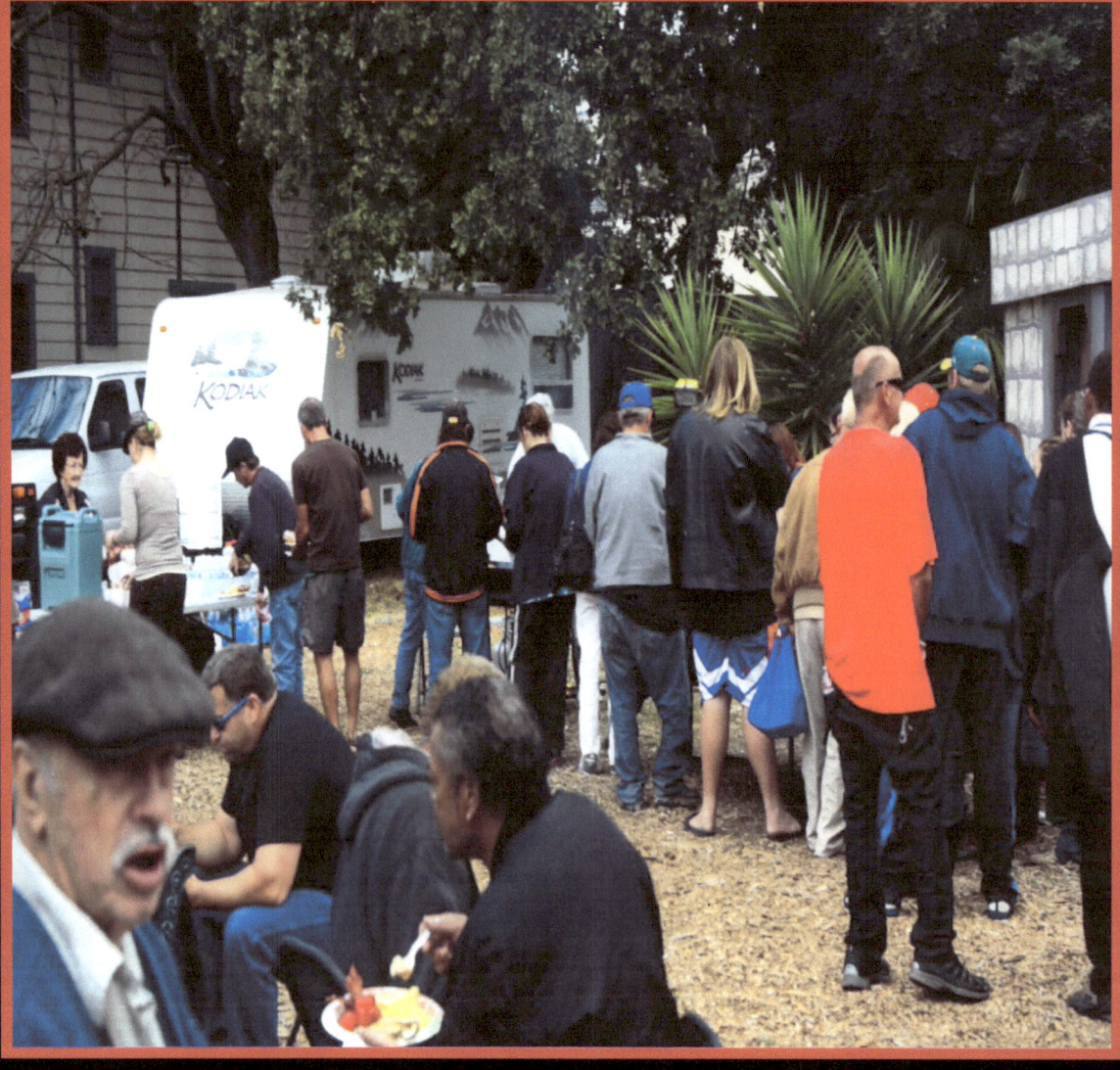

Street Church   Redwood City, California

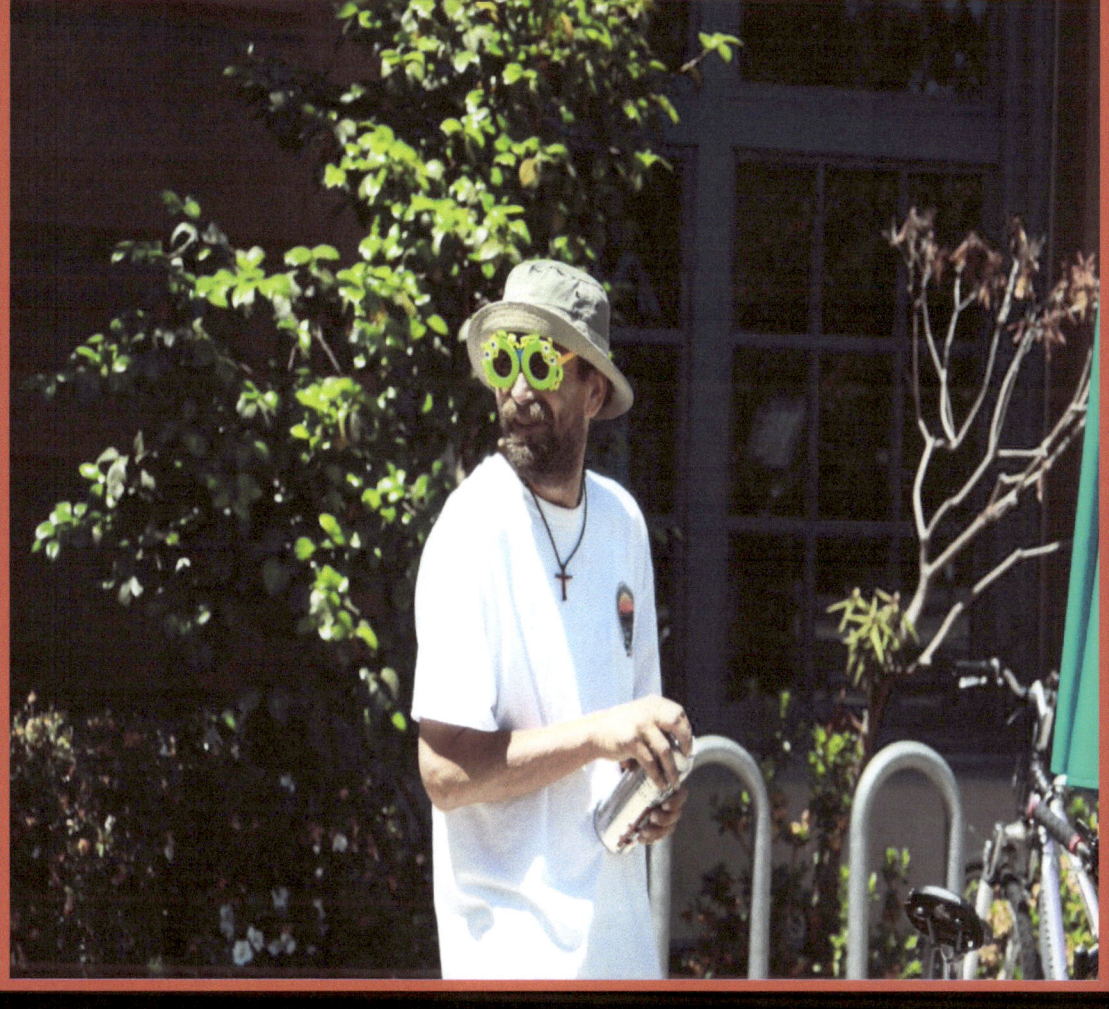

If I had a Piano   Redwood City, California

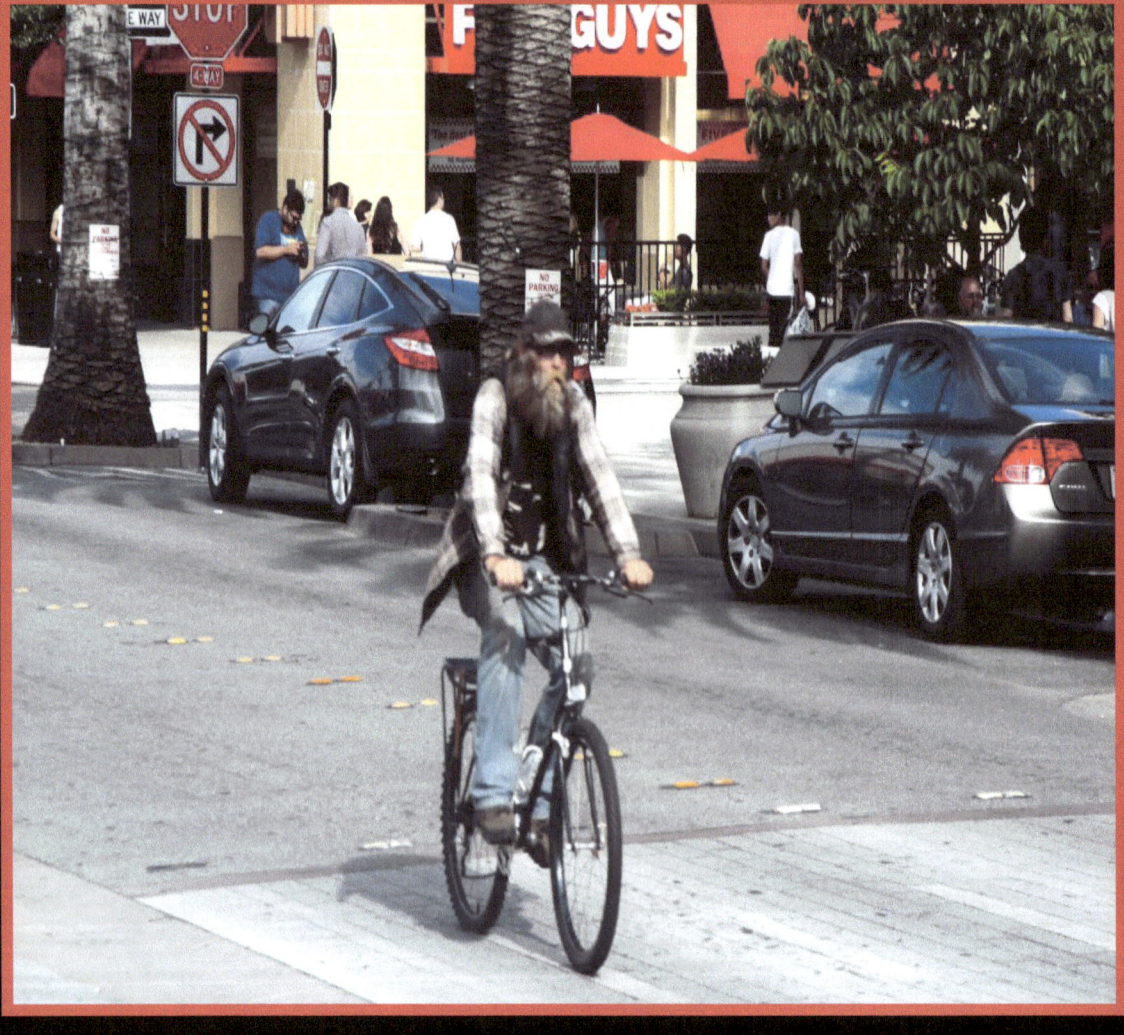

Ride this Way   Redwood City, California

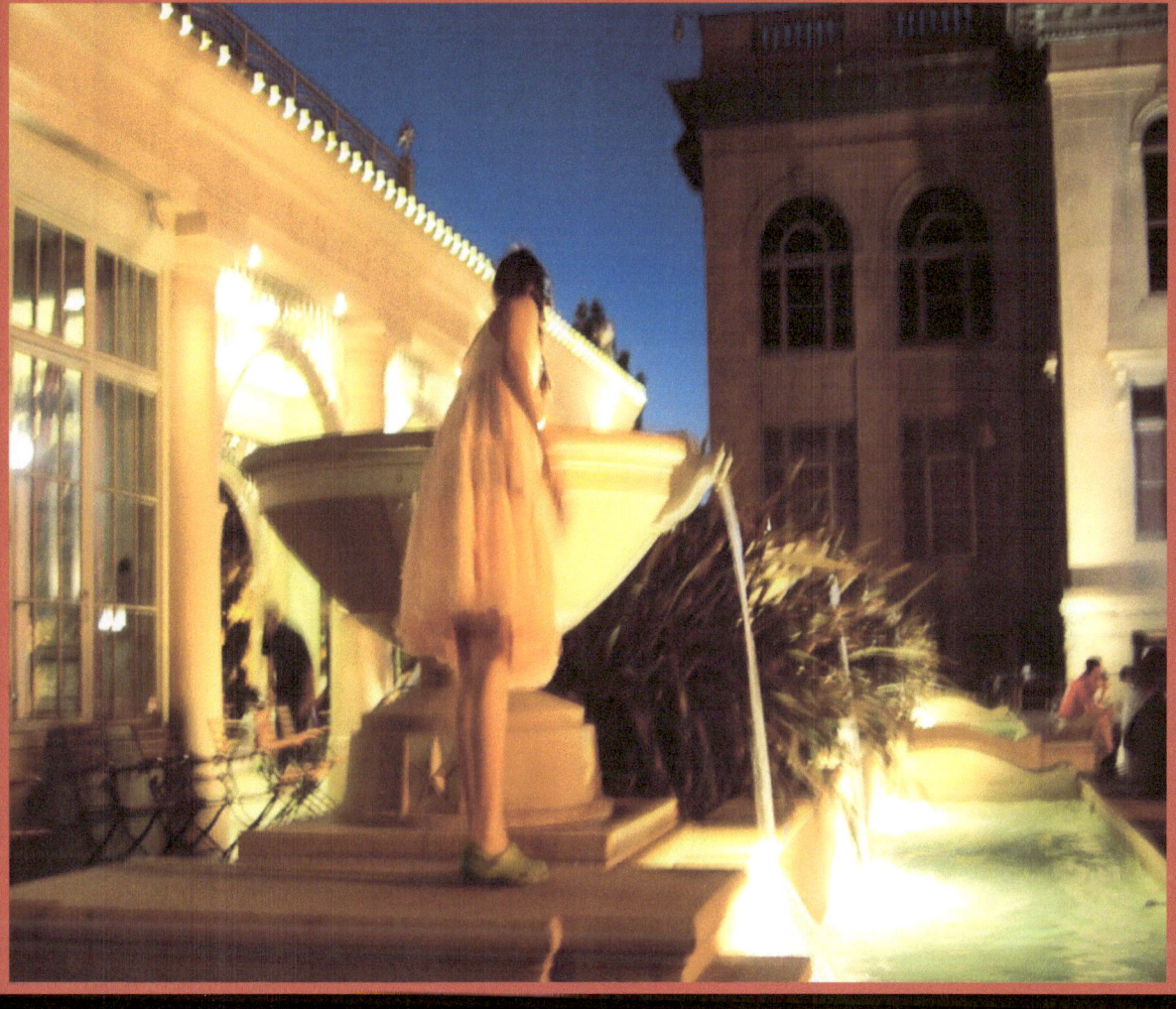

Is that a Quarter?   Redwood City, California

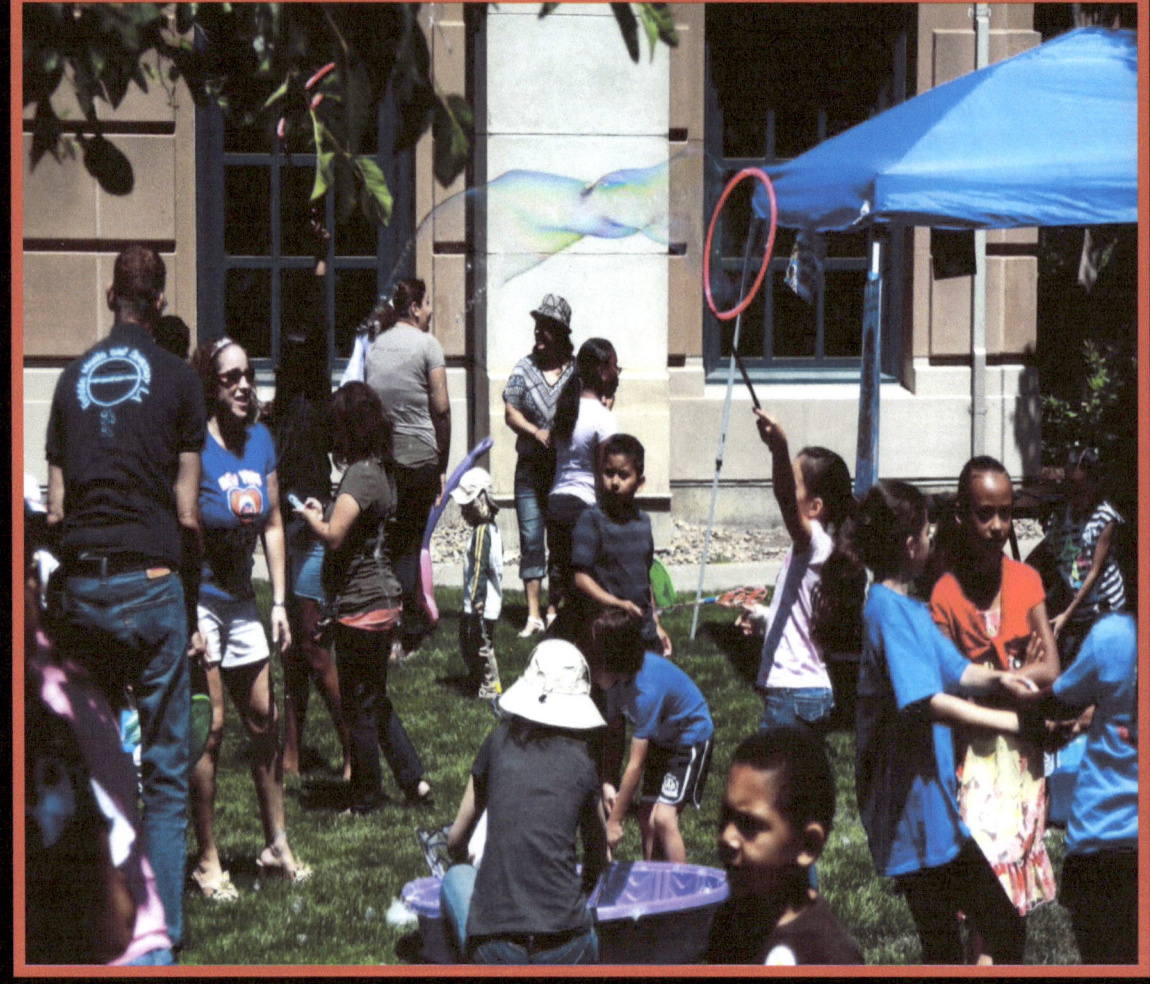

Kids and Bubbles   Redwood City, California

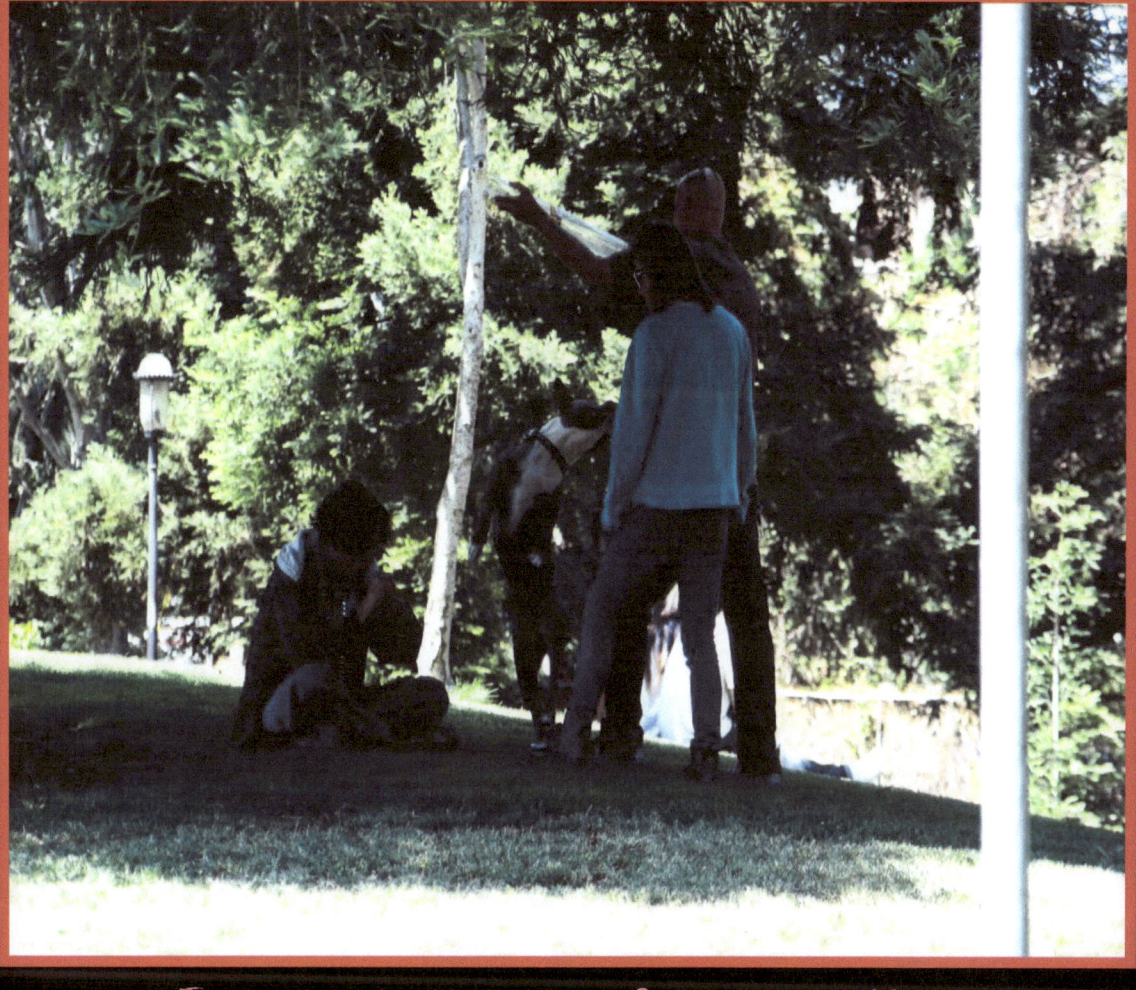

Jump and Smoke   Redwood City, California

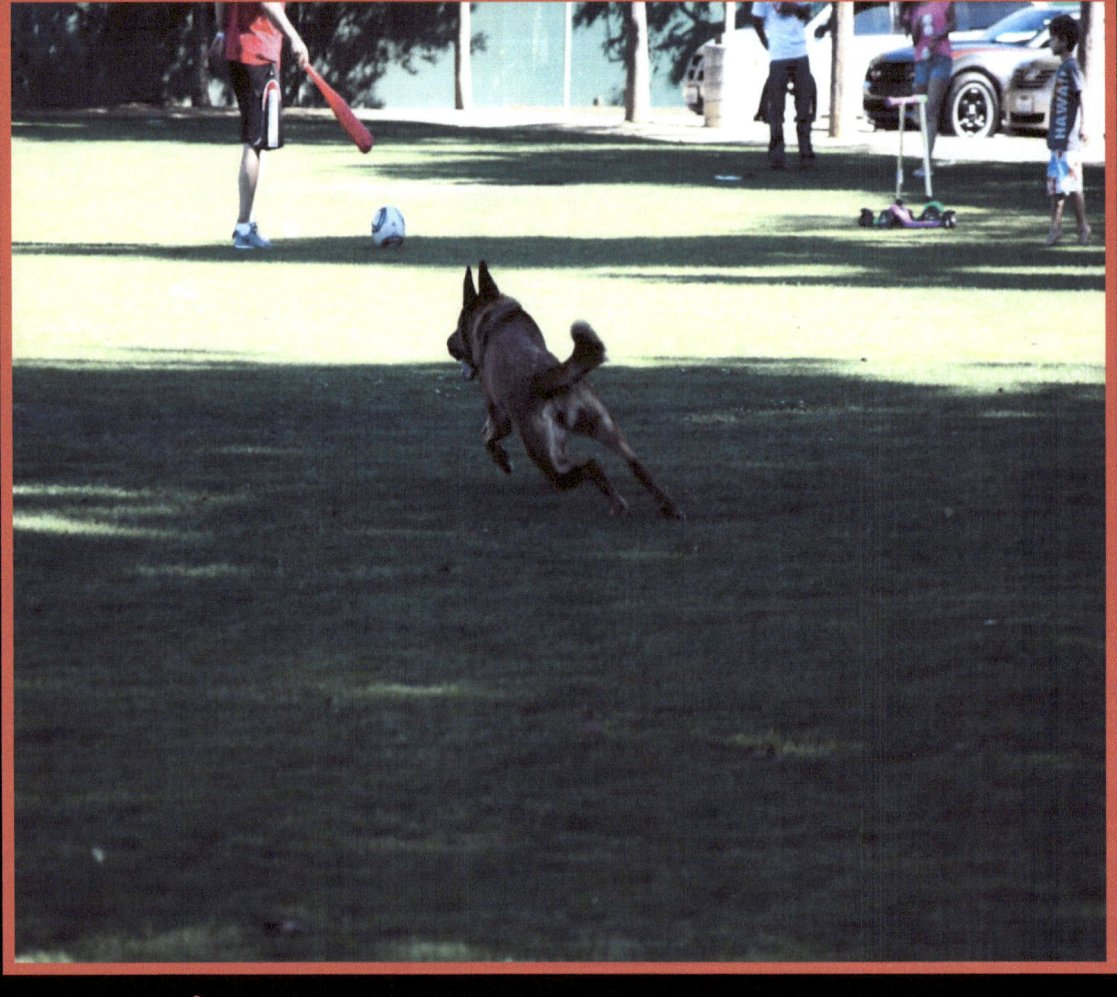

Fast Dog   San Carlos, California

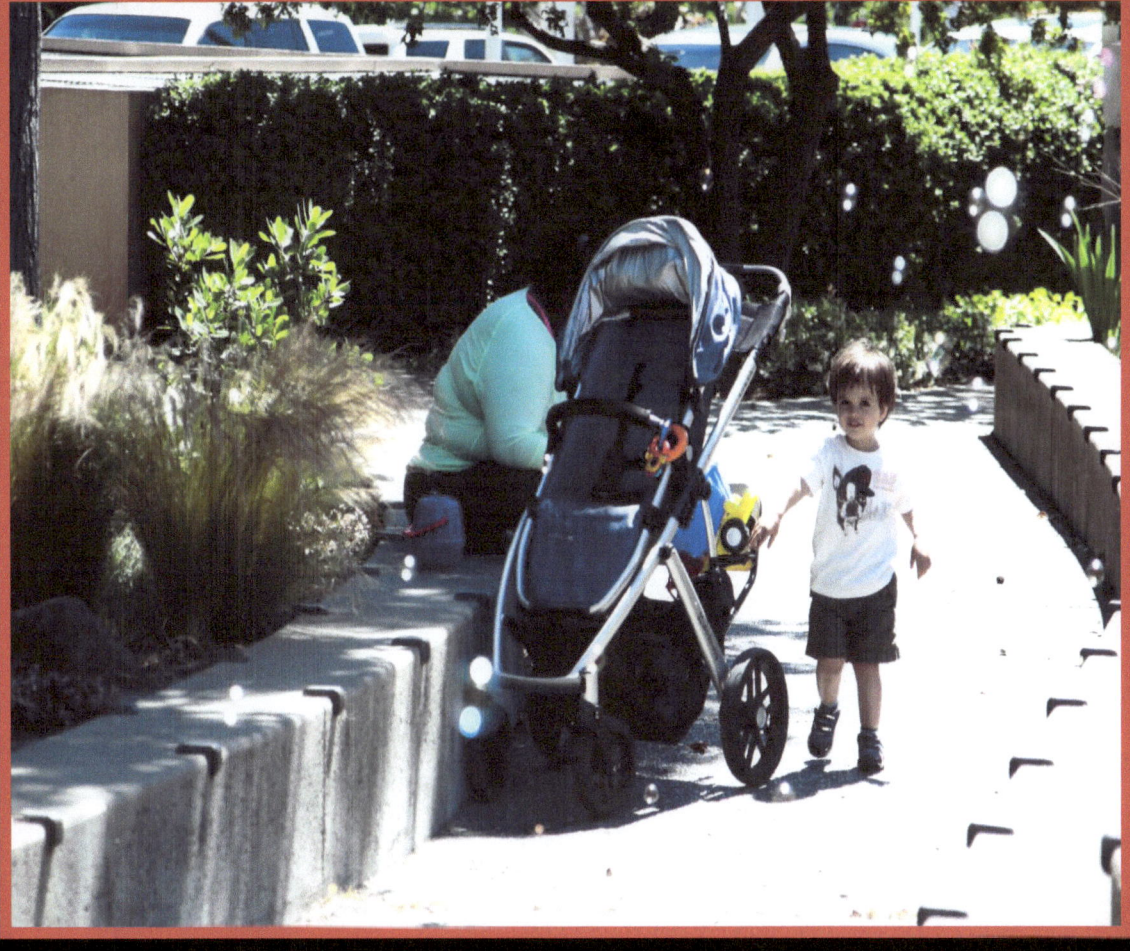

Bubbles are Cool !   San Carlos, California

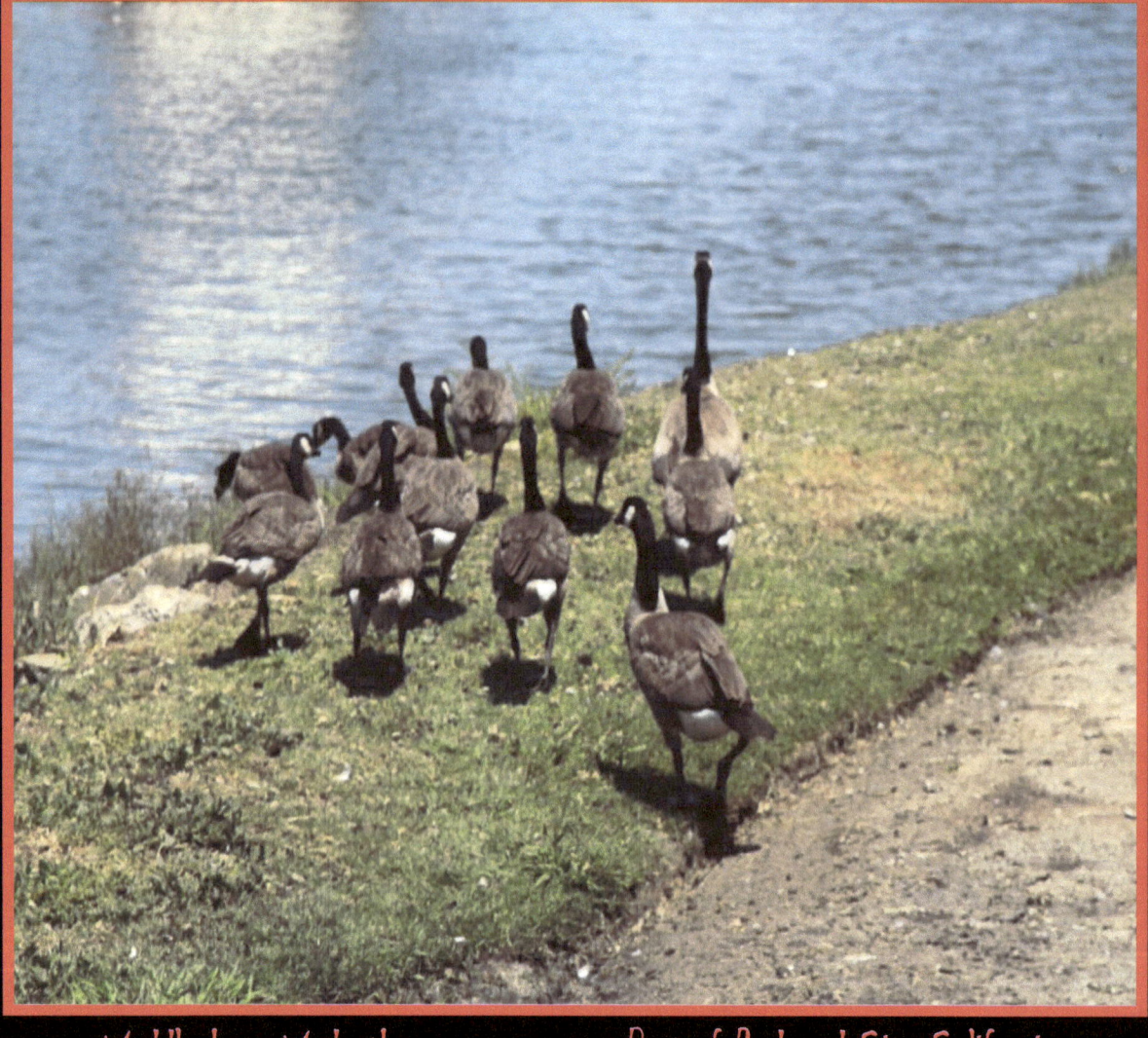

Waddle here Wade there   Port of Redwood City, California

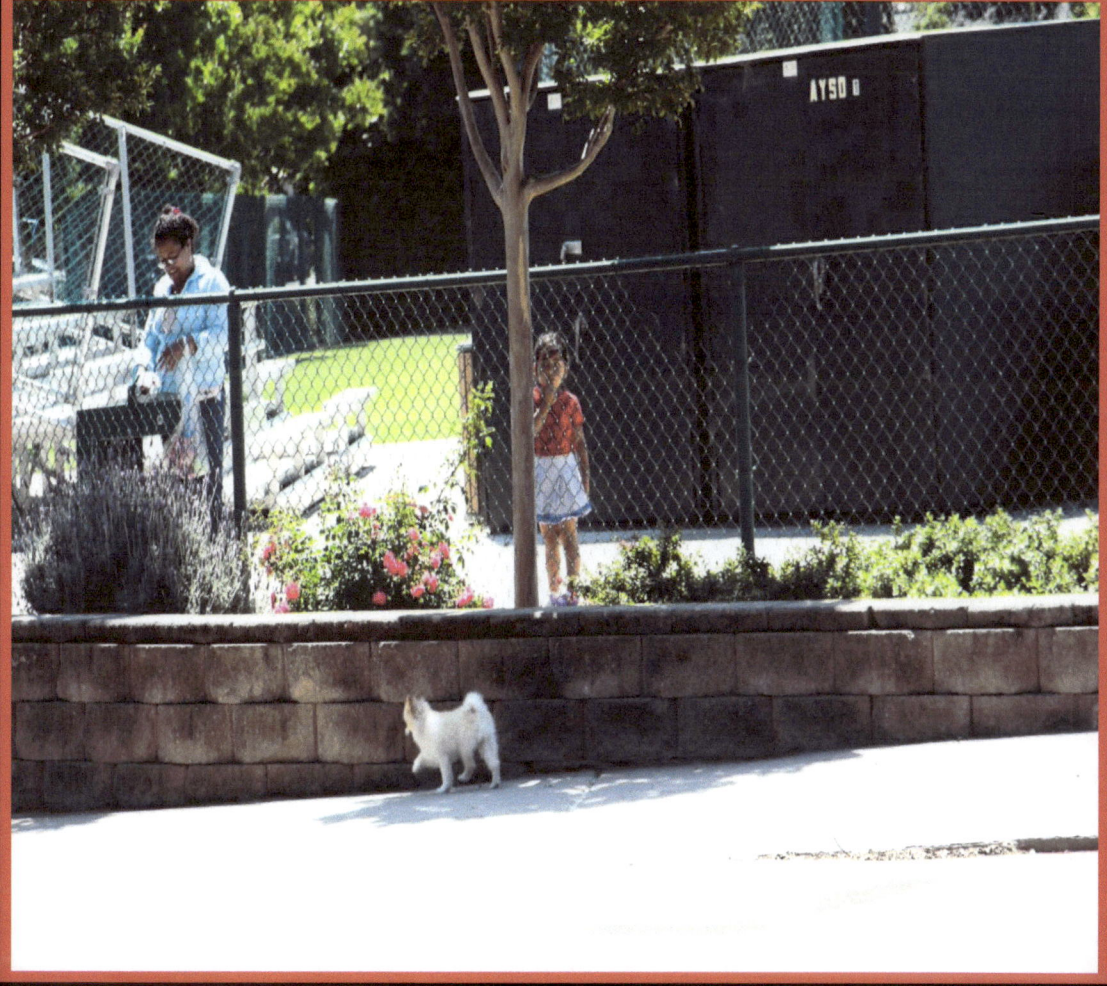

Little Dog Walk   San Carlos, California

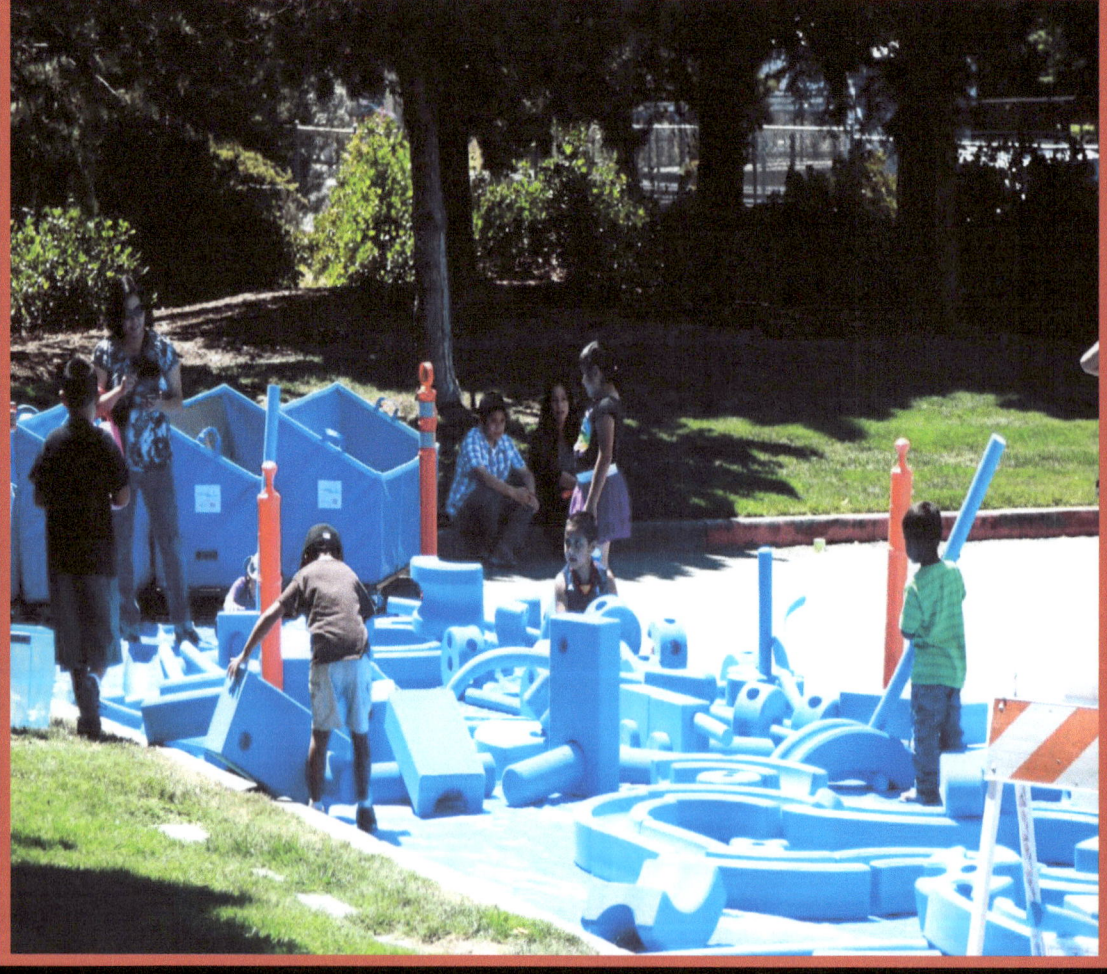

Blue Kid Group   Redwood City, California

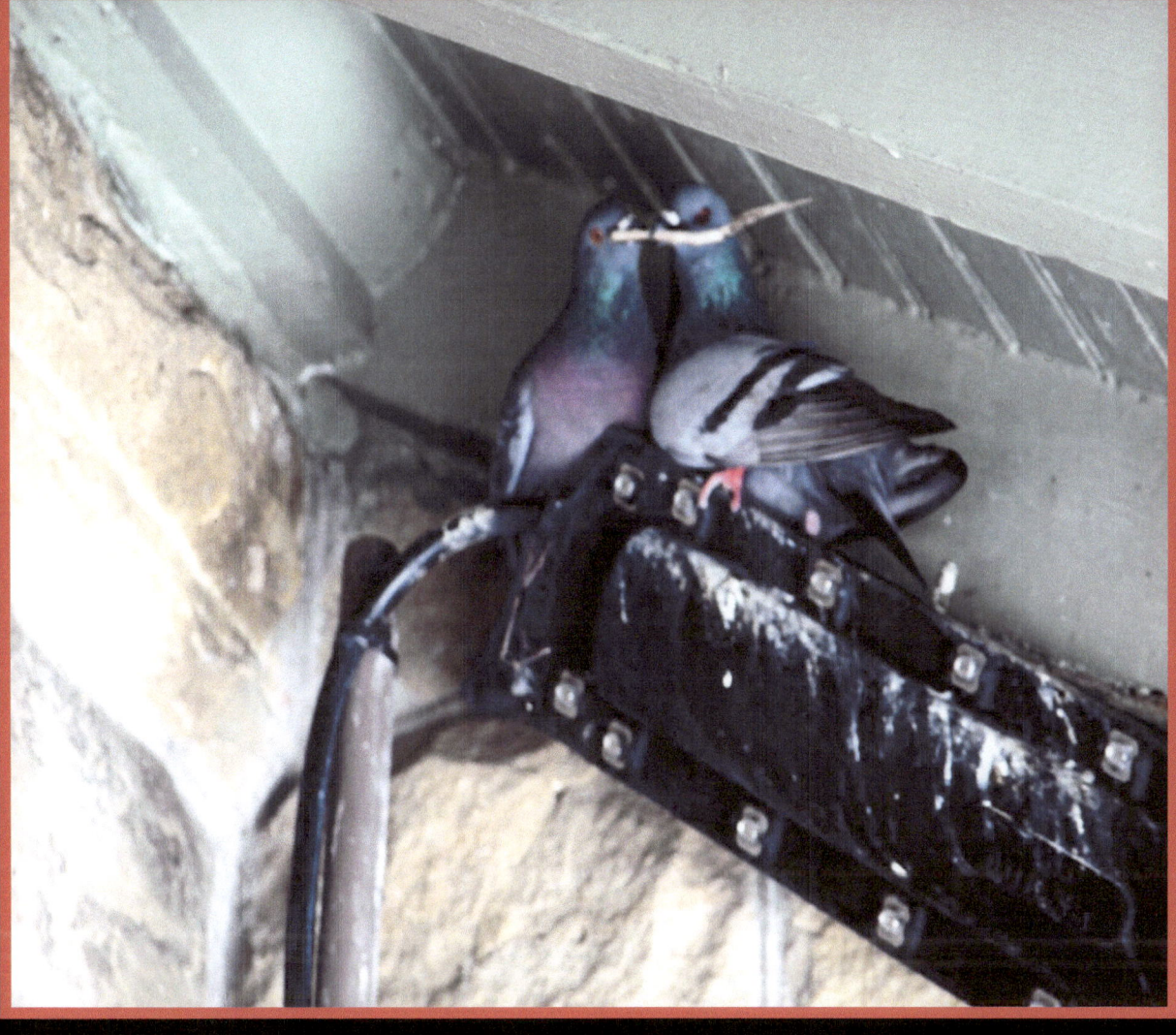

Two's Company Threes a Crowd   San Carlos,California

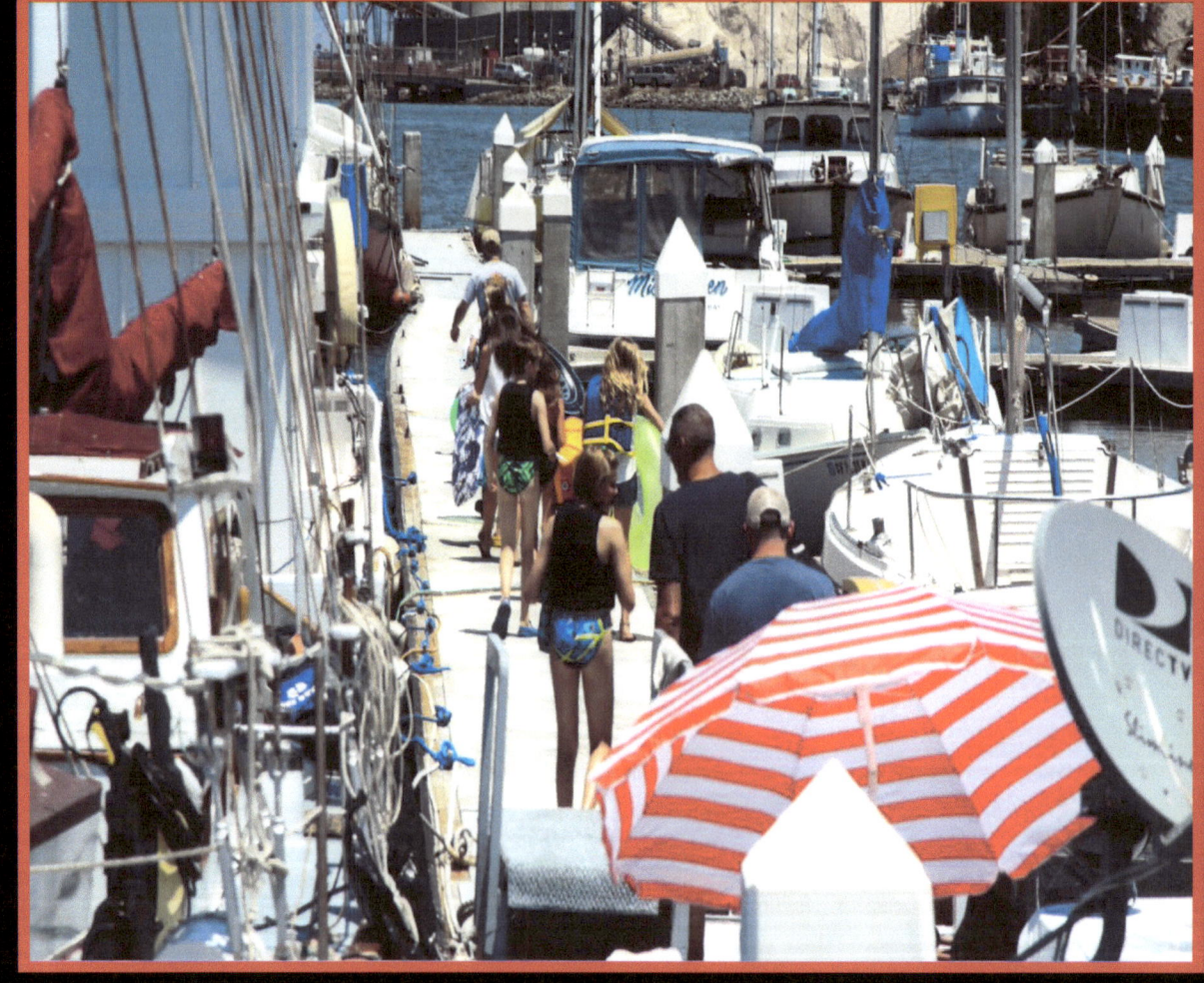

Sail me Away   Port of Redwood City, California

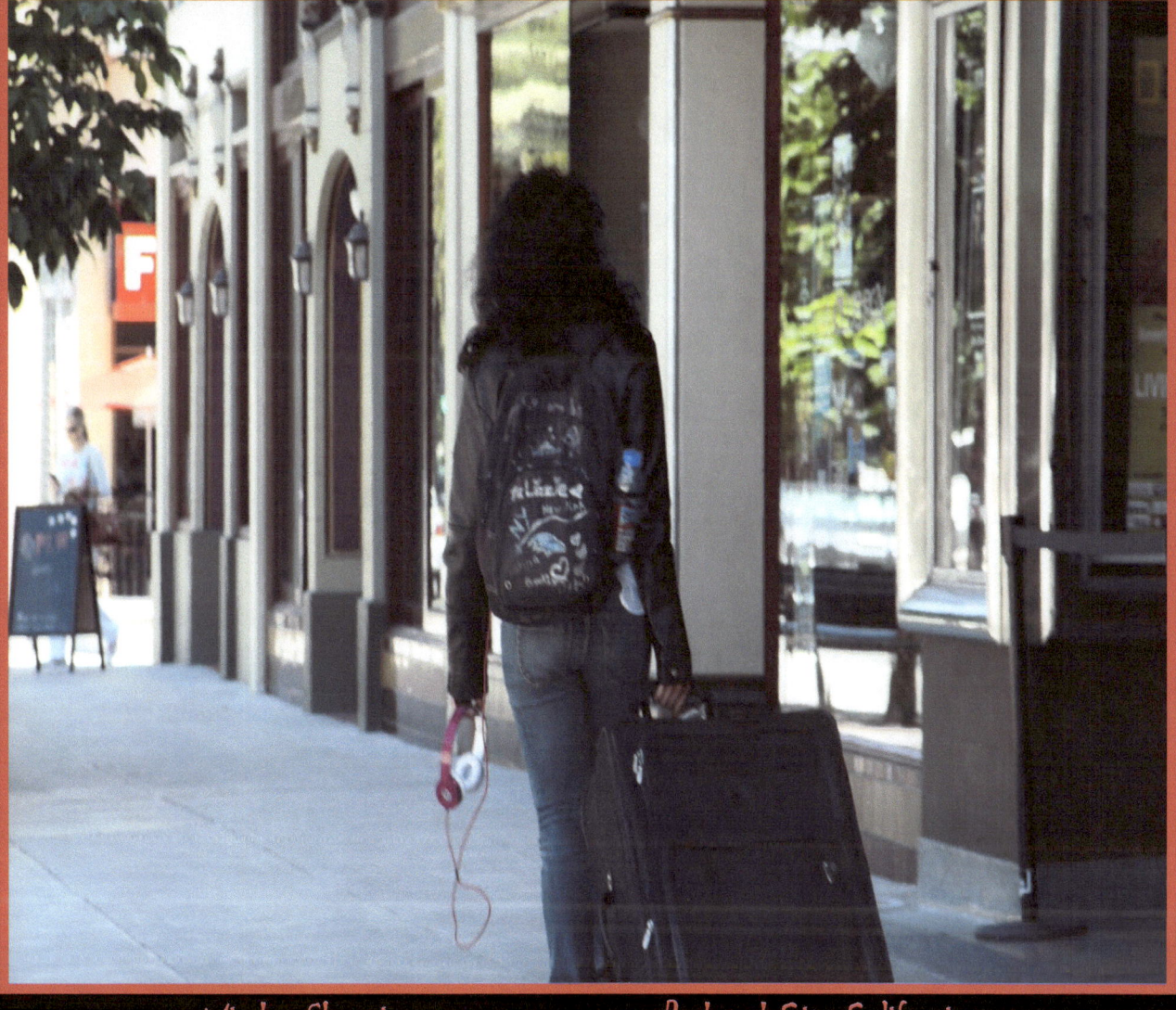

Window Shopping   Redwood City, California

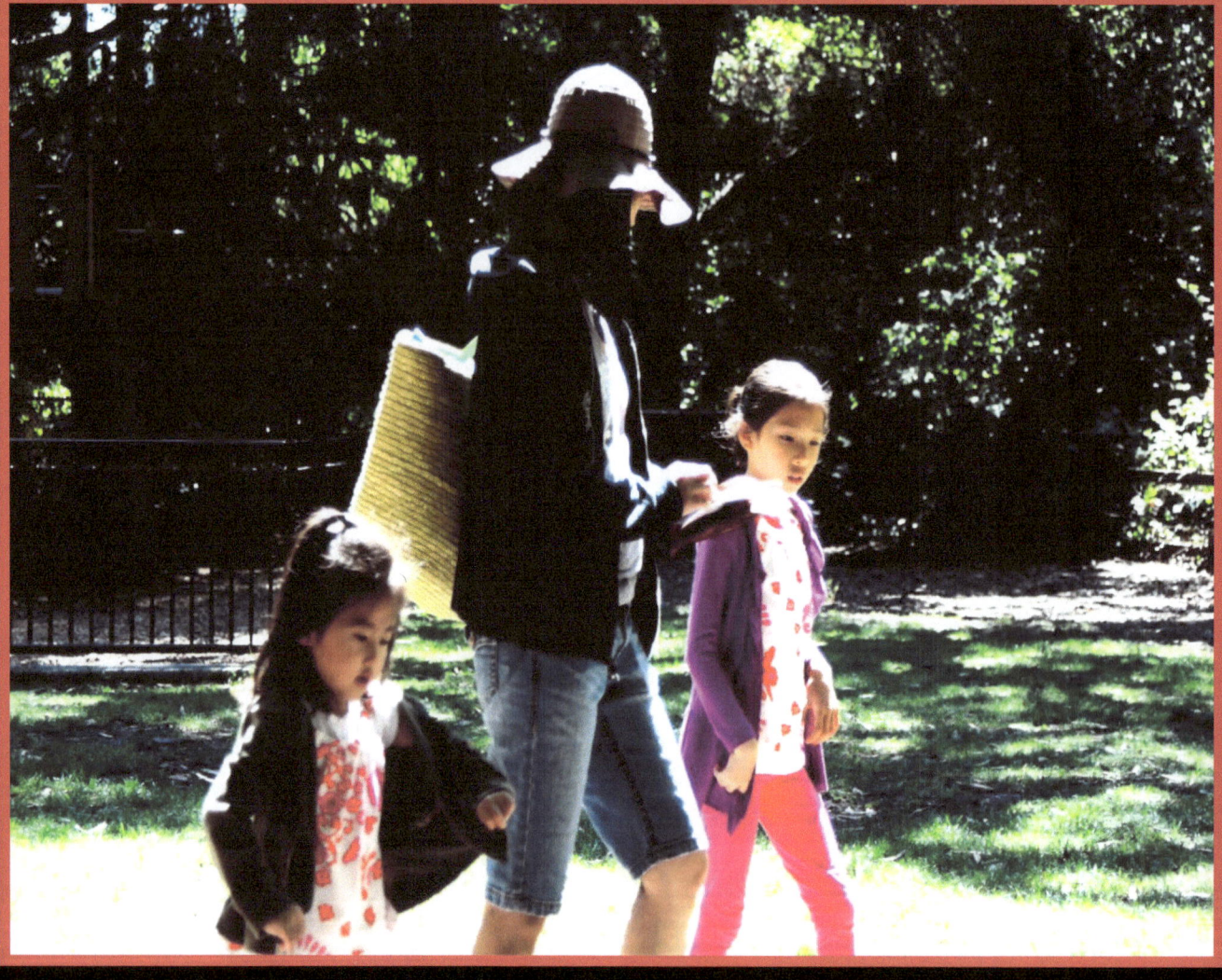

Where to Mom ?   Belmont, California

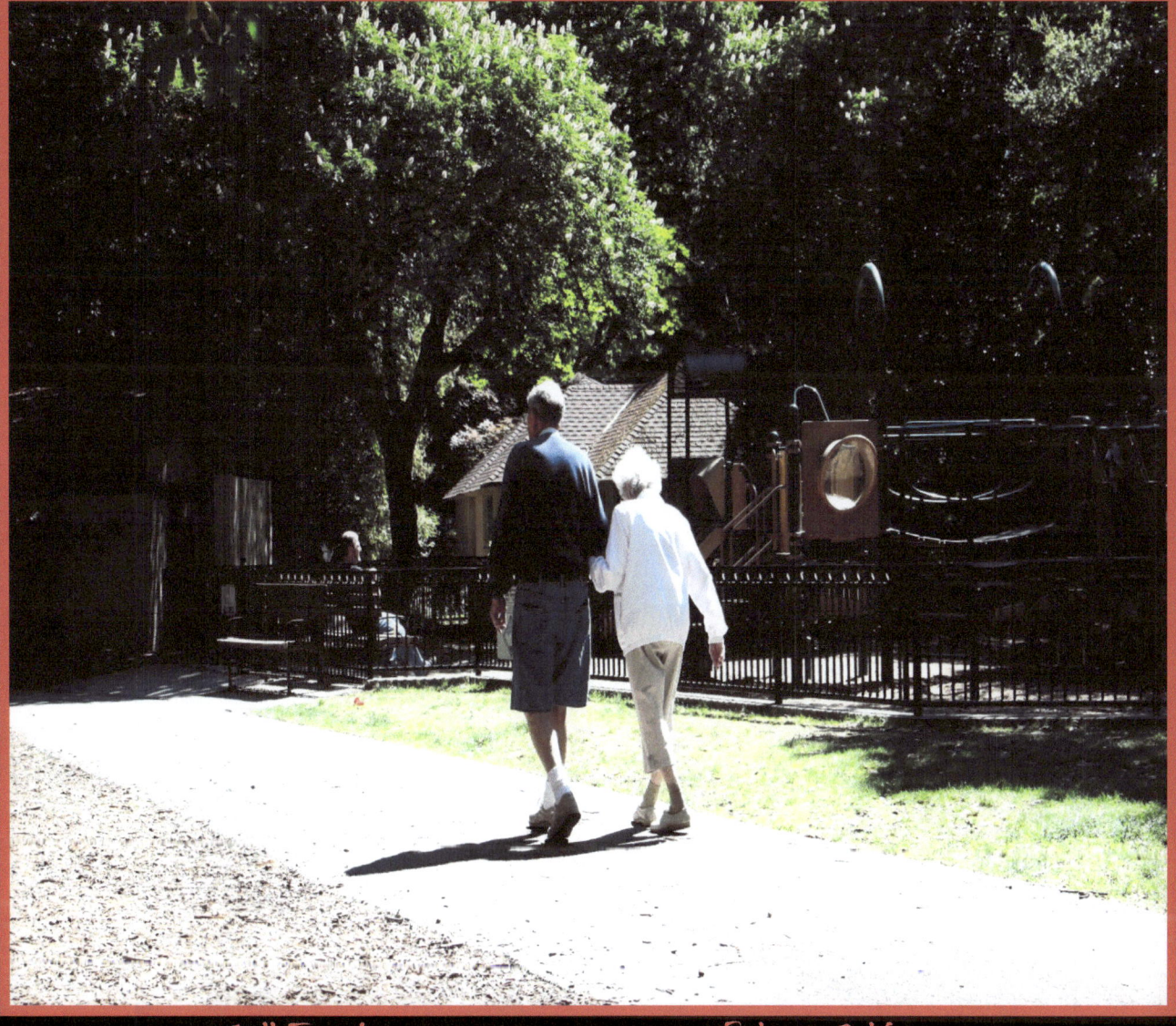

Still Together   Belmont, California

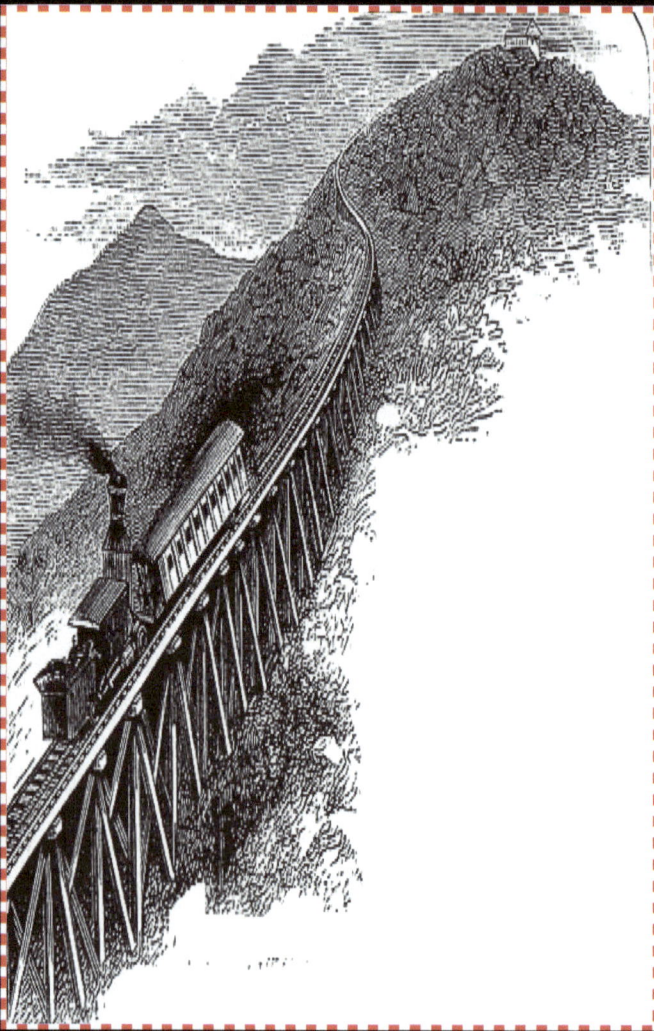

TRAINMOTION.....
shortfilm>>>>>

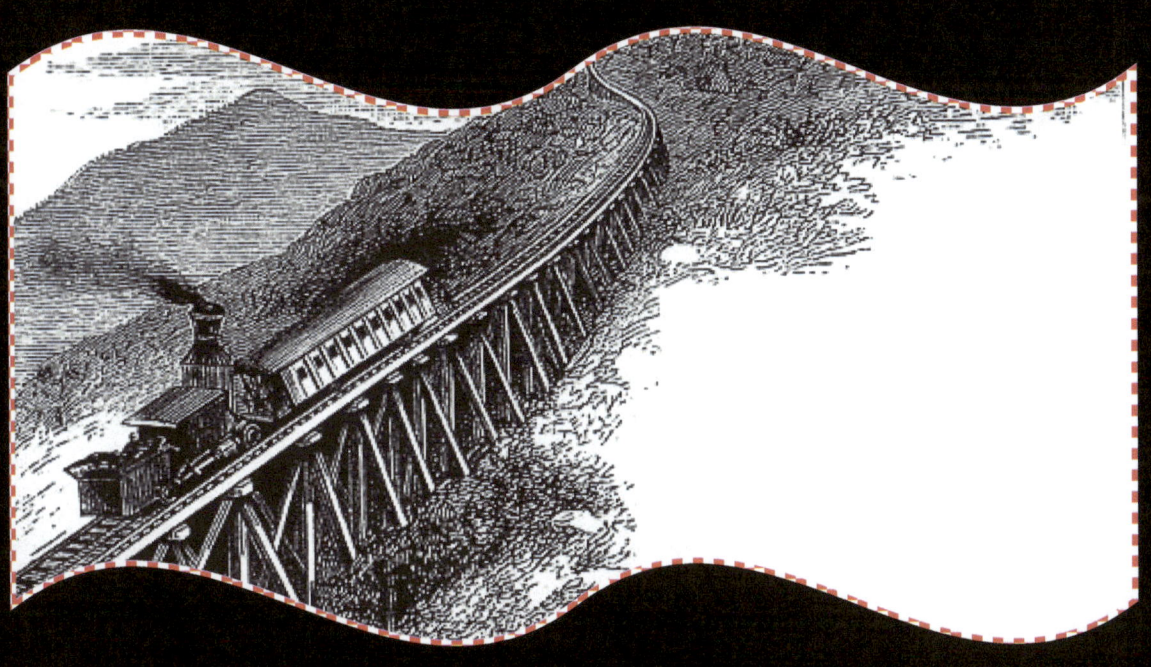

Take 1...
Just Flip the Pages
>>>>>

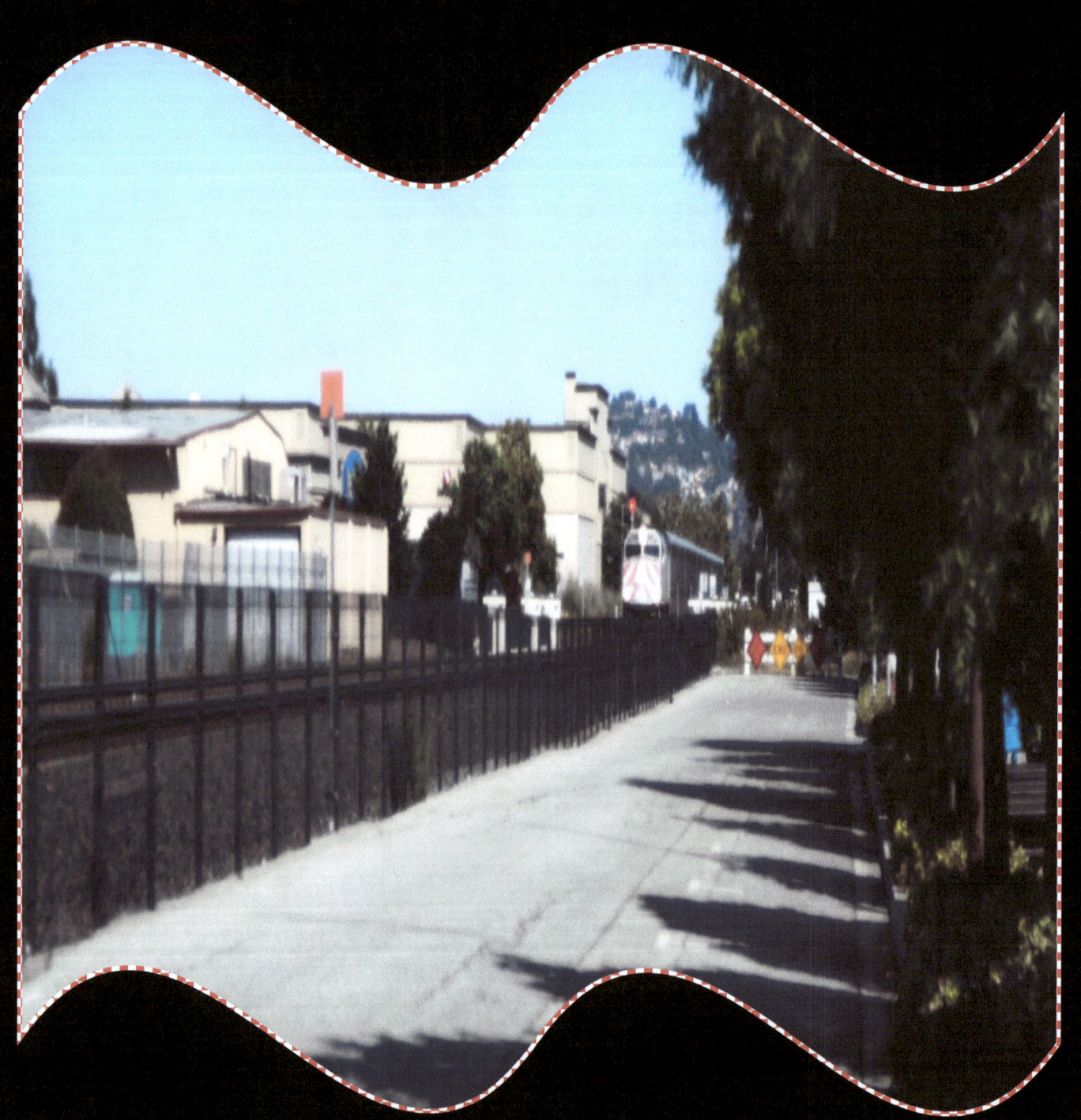

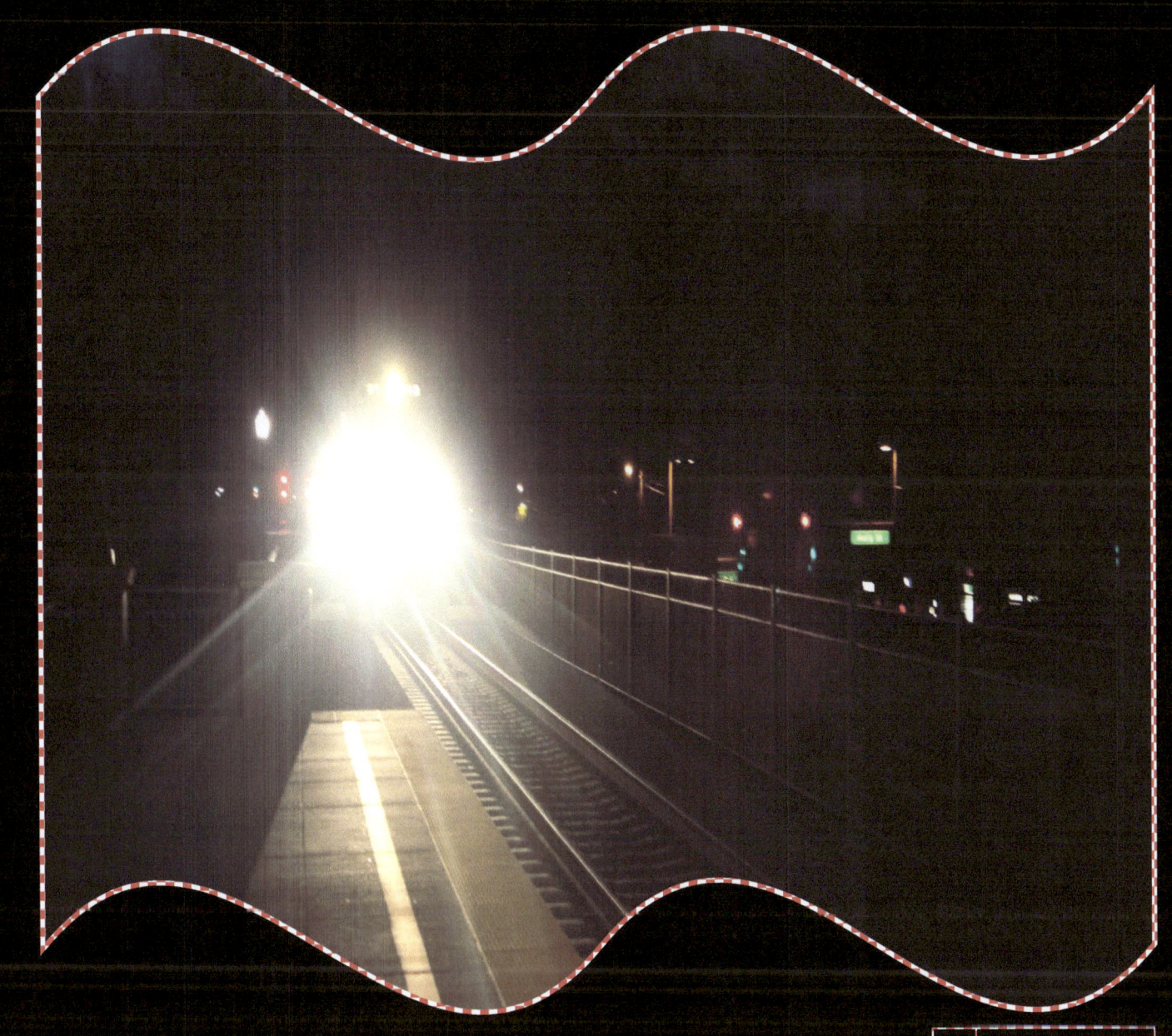

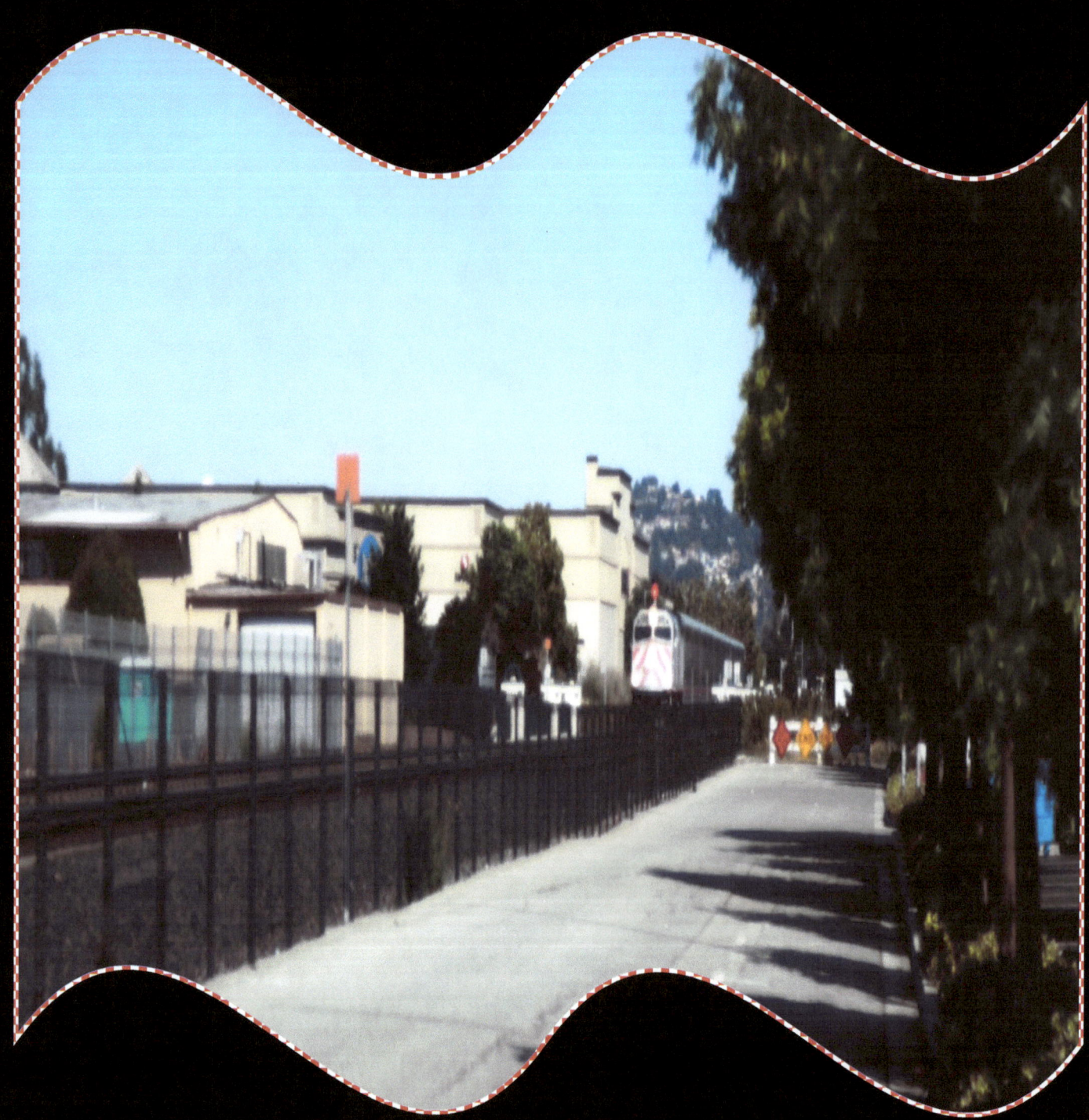

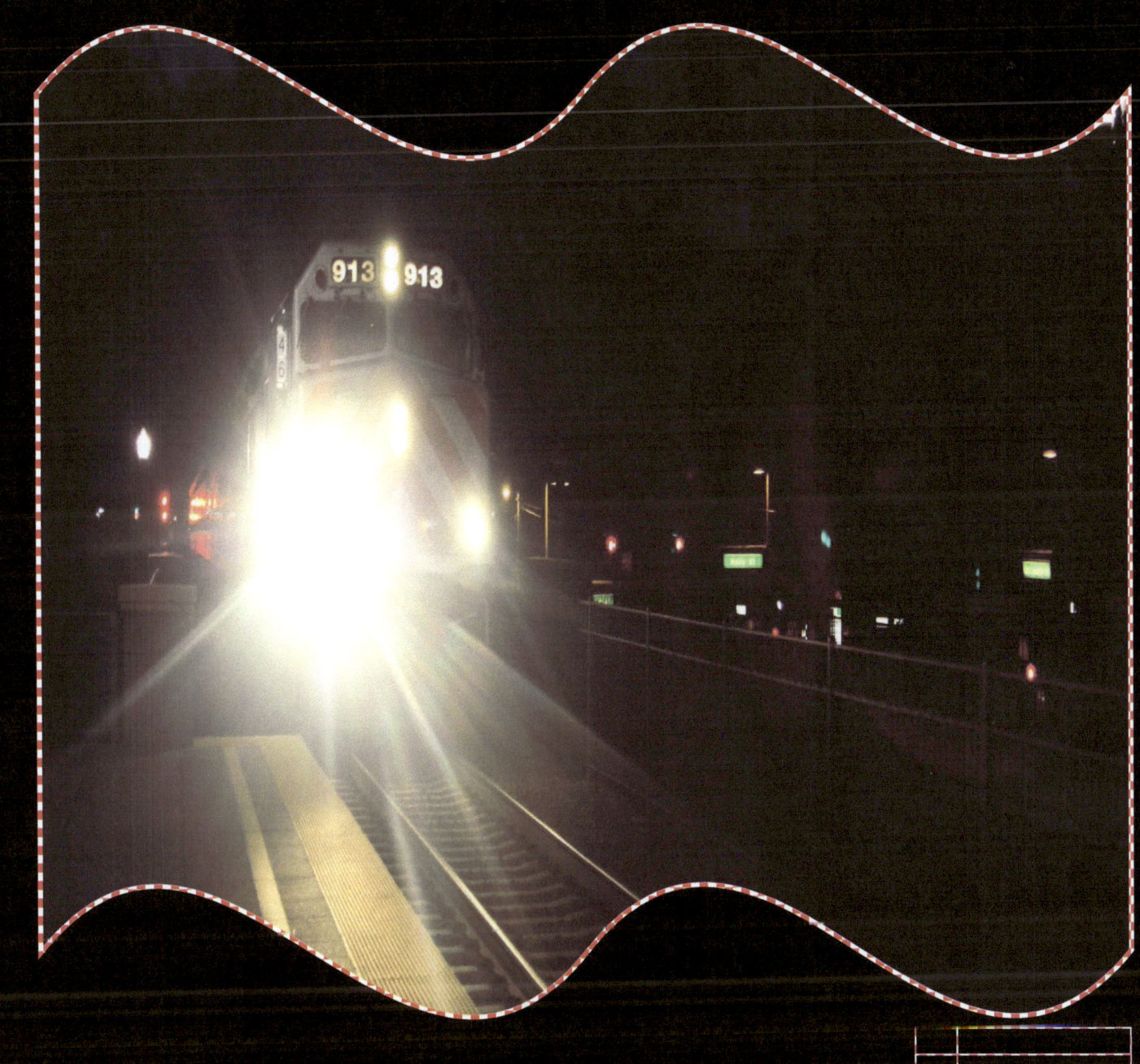

Take 3........
Flip>>>>>

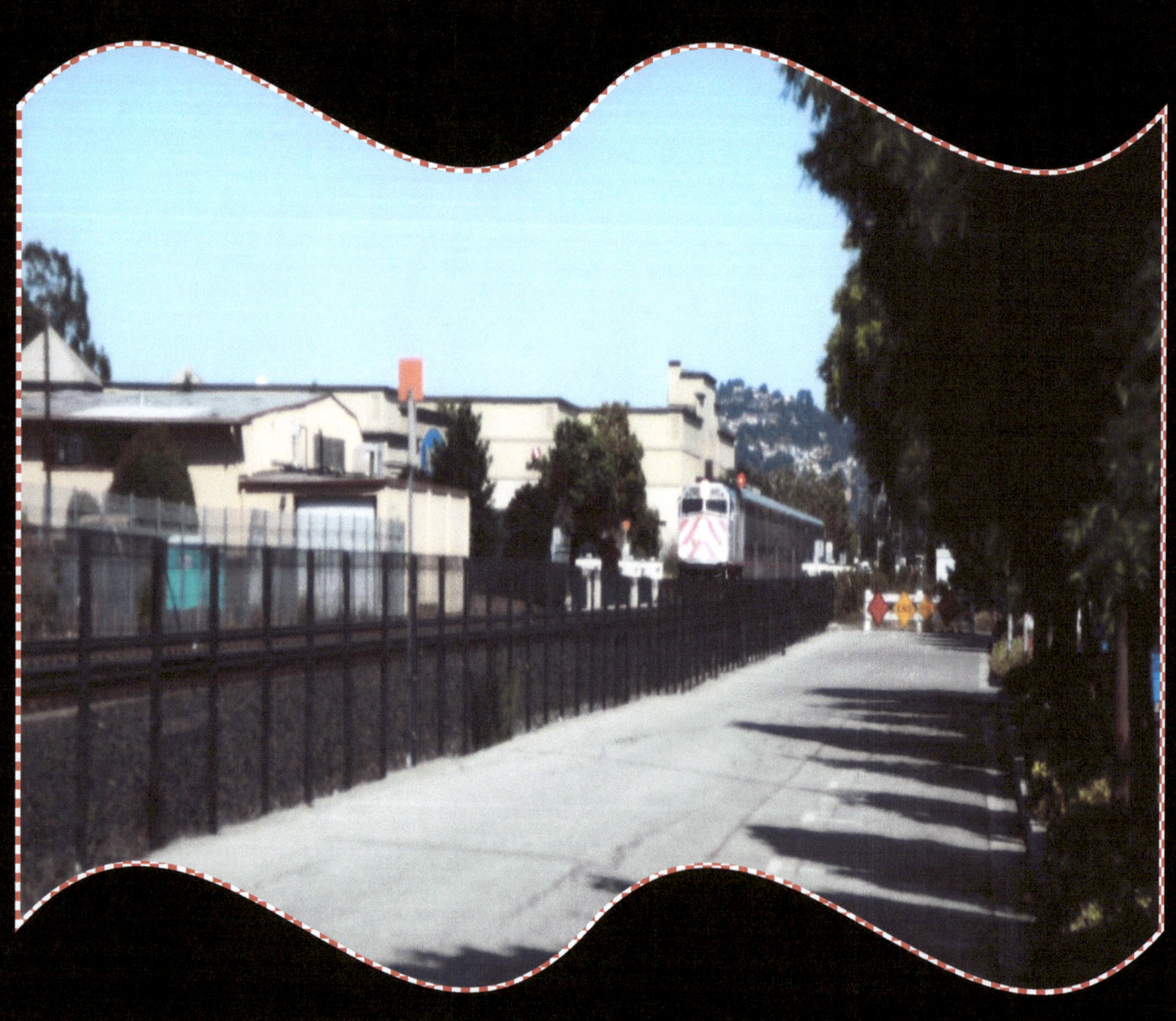

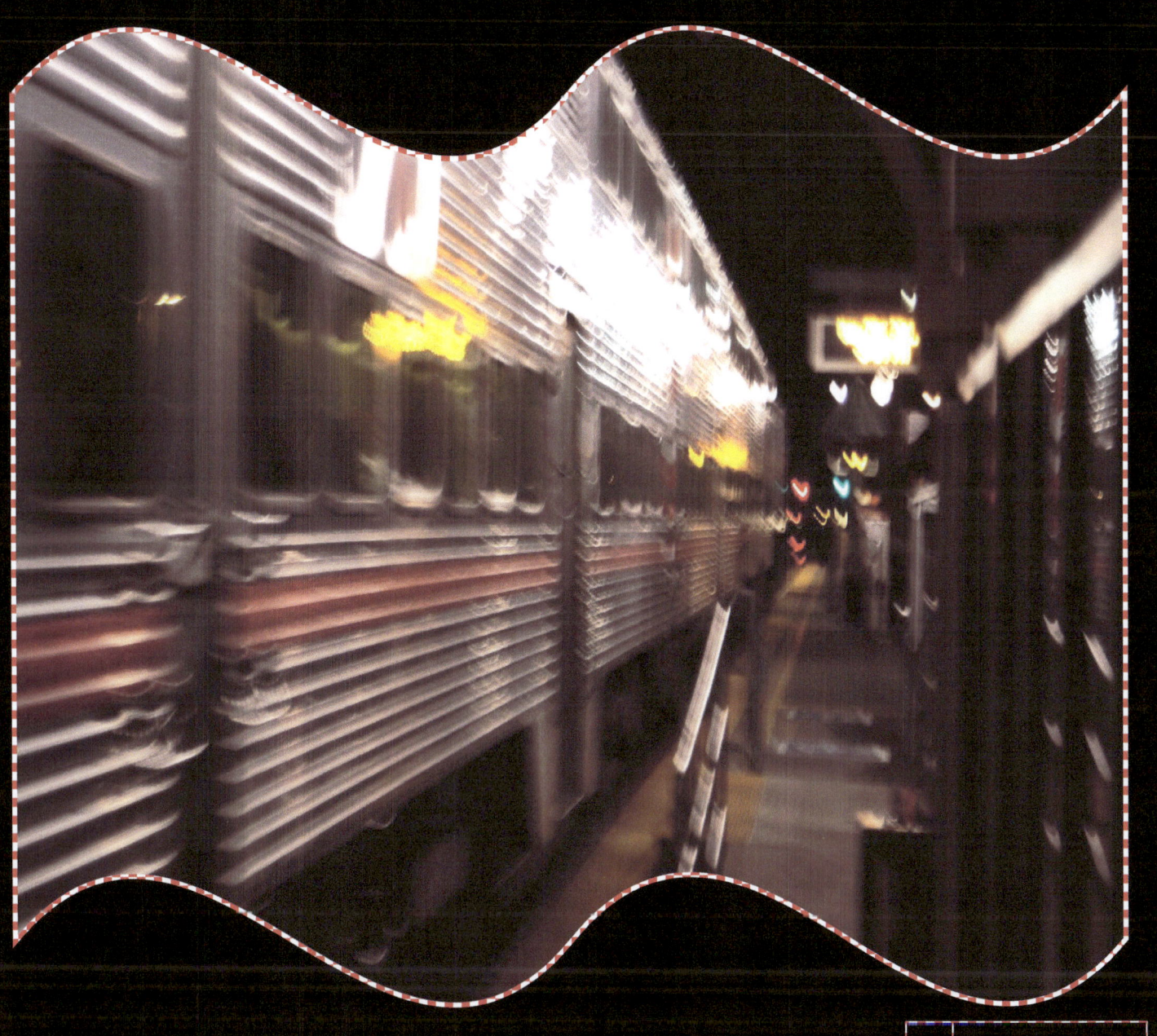

Take 4........
Flip>>>>>

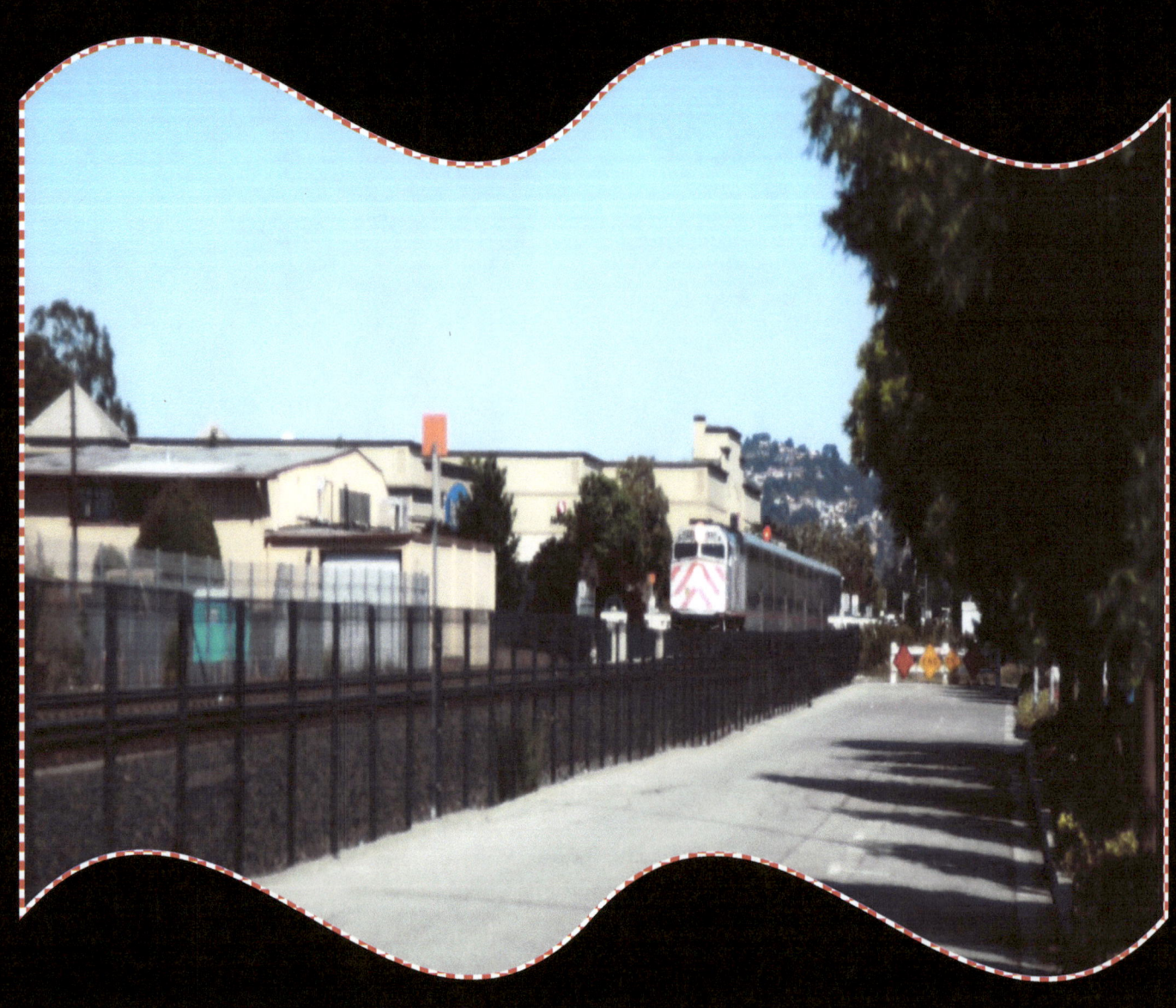

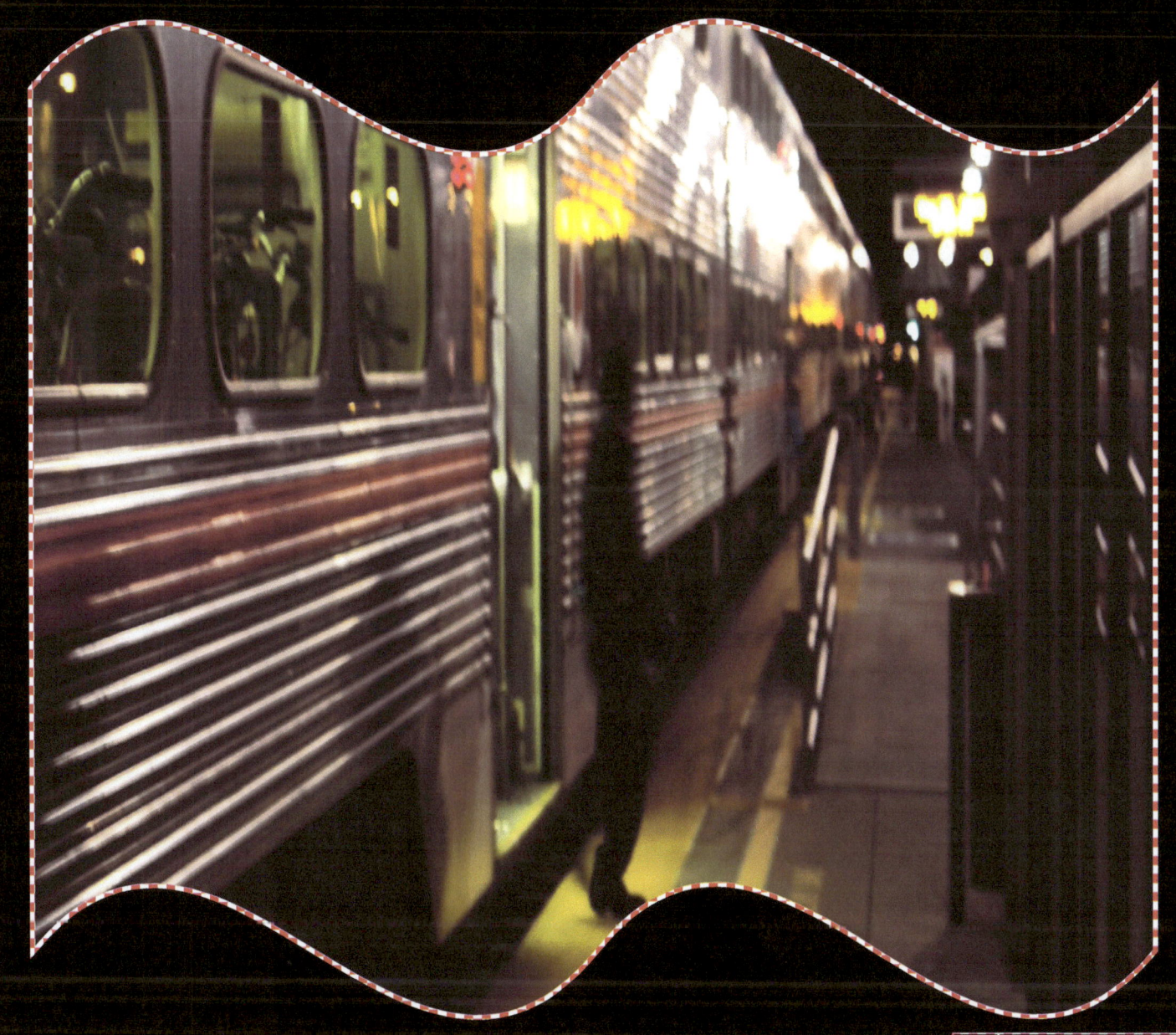

Take 5........
Flip>>>>>

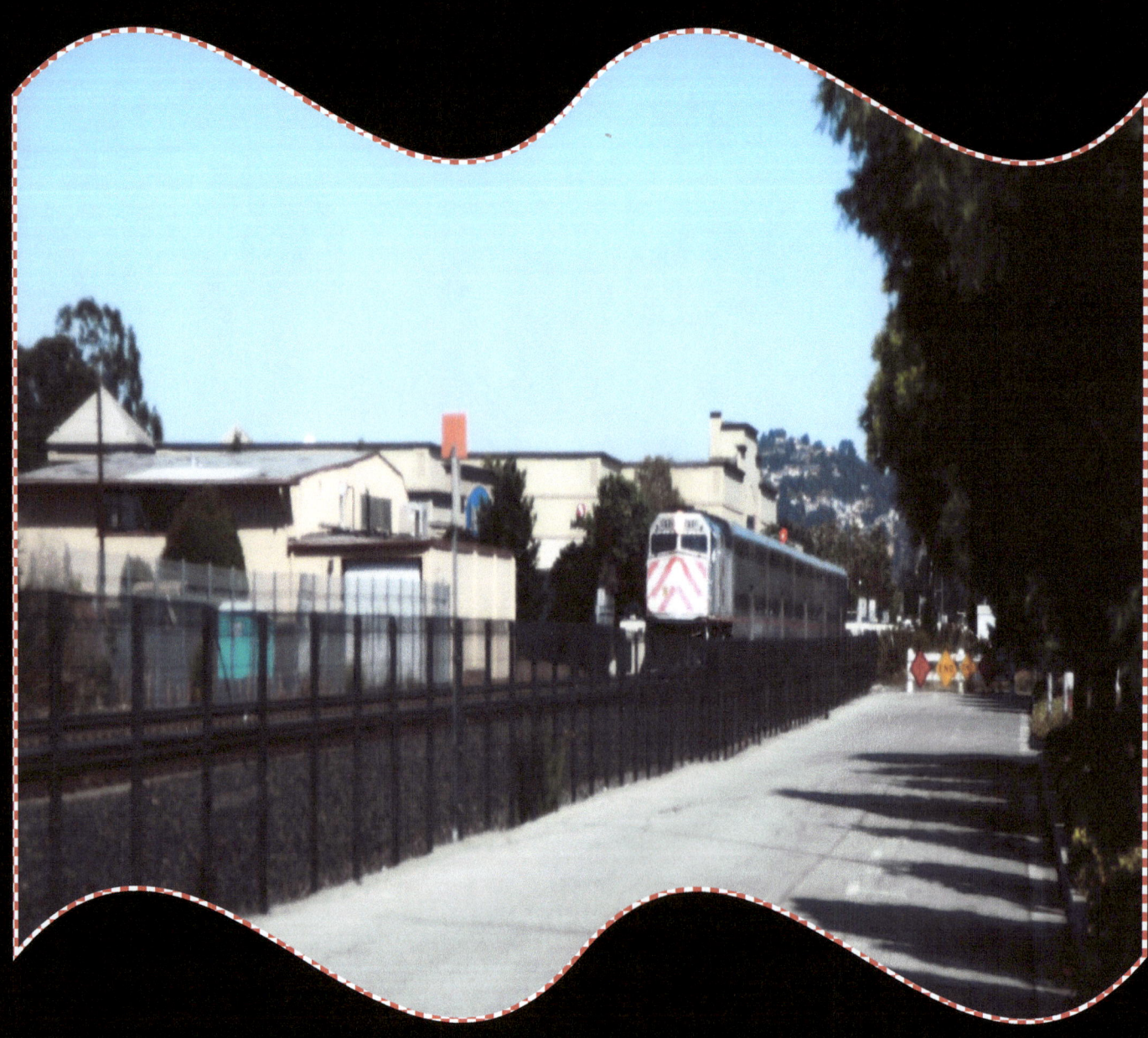

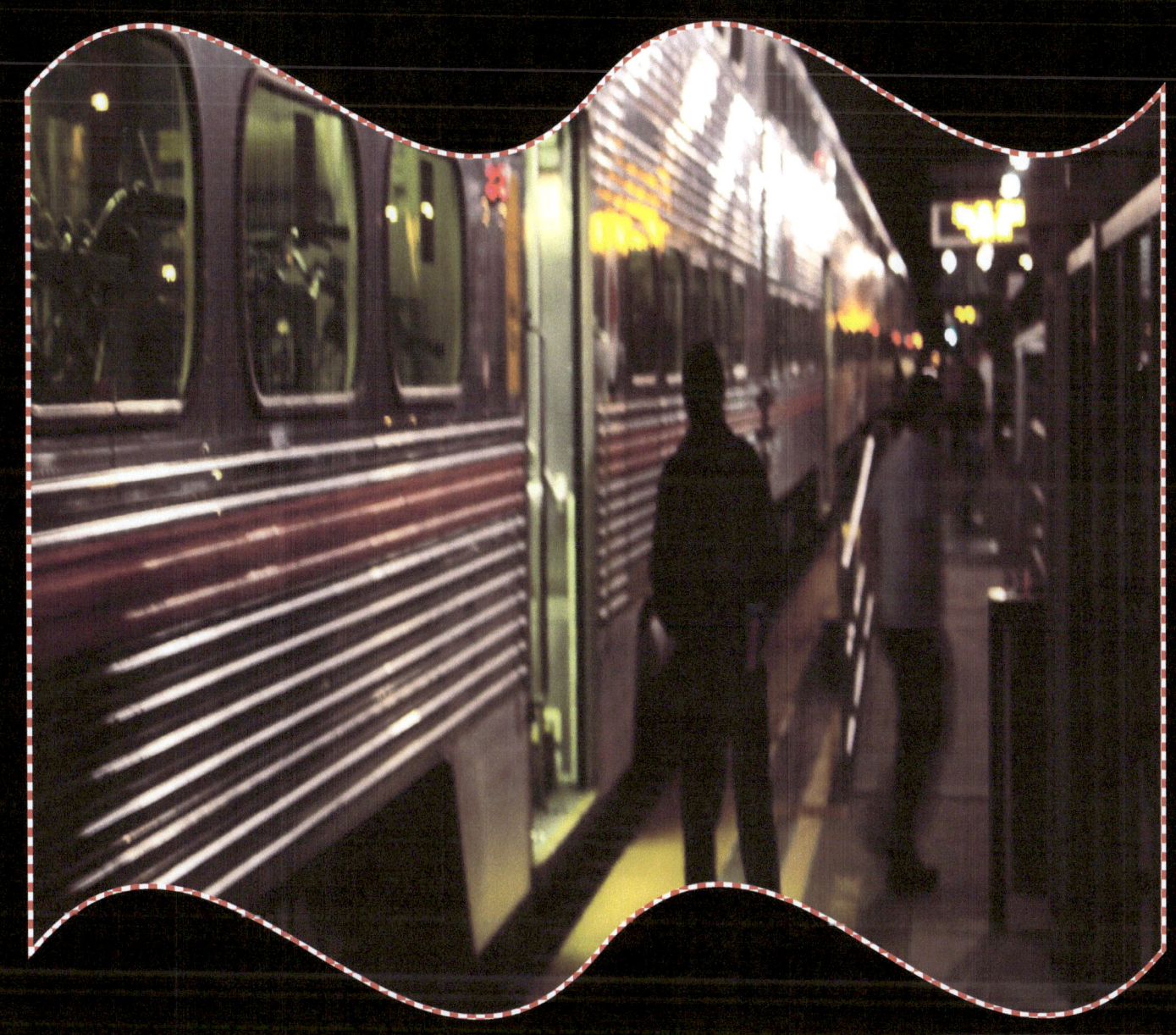

Take 6........
Flip>>>>>

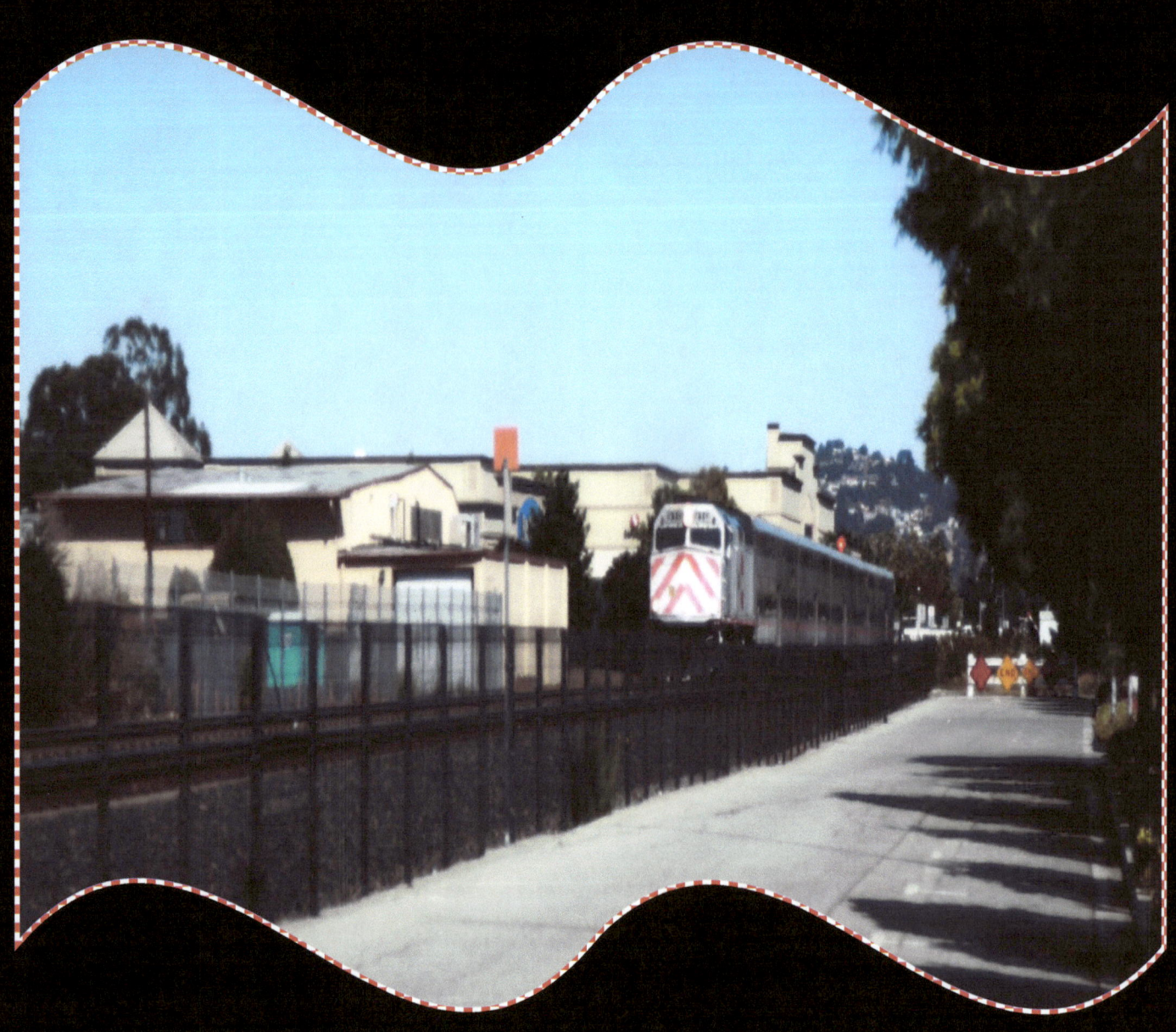

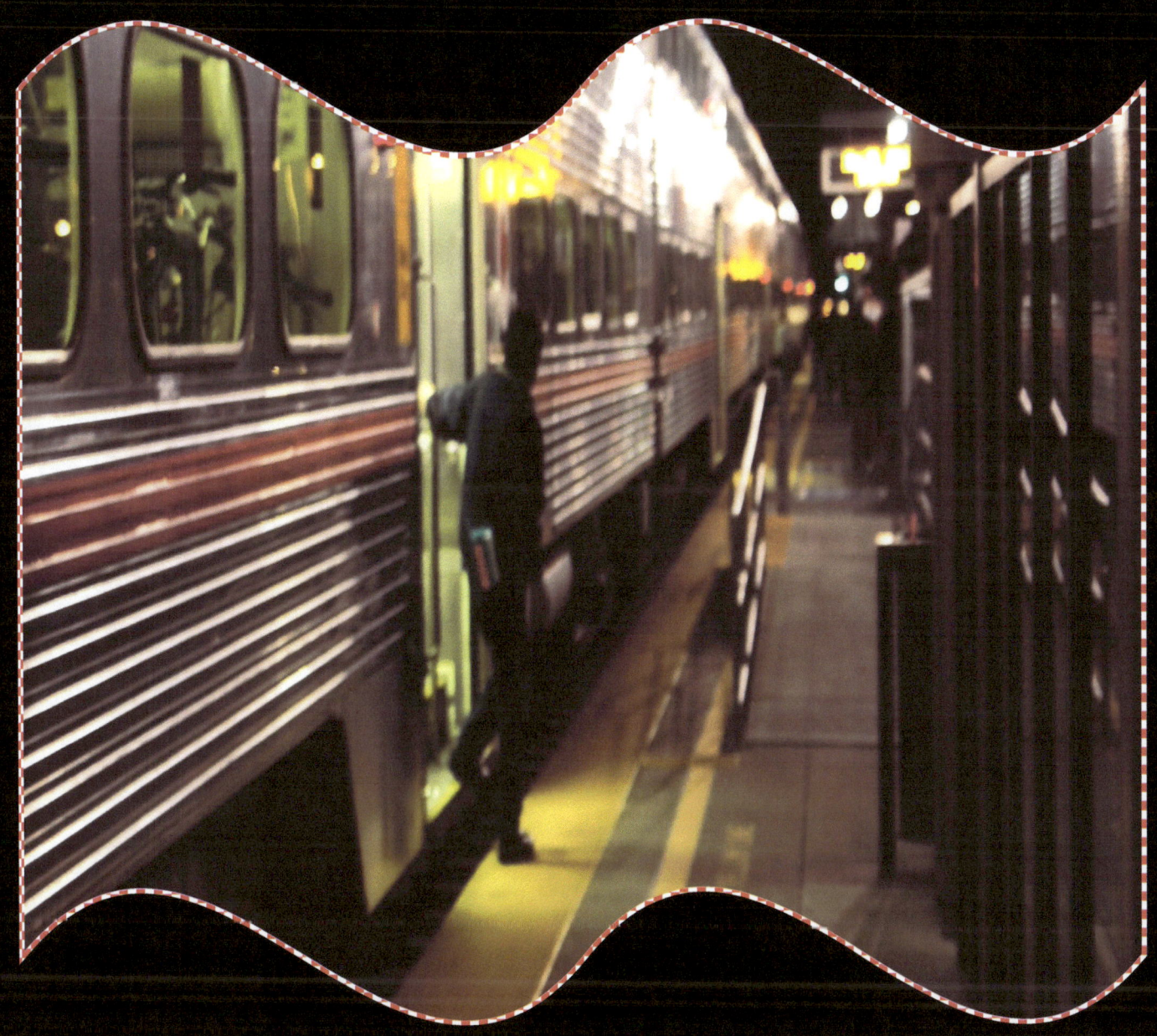

Take 7........
Flip>>>>>

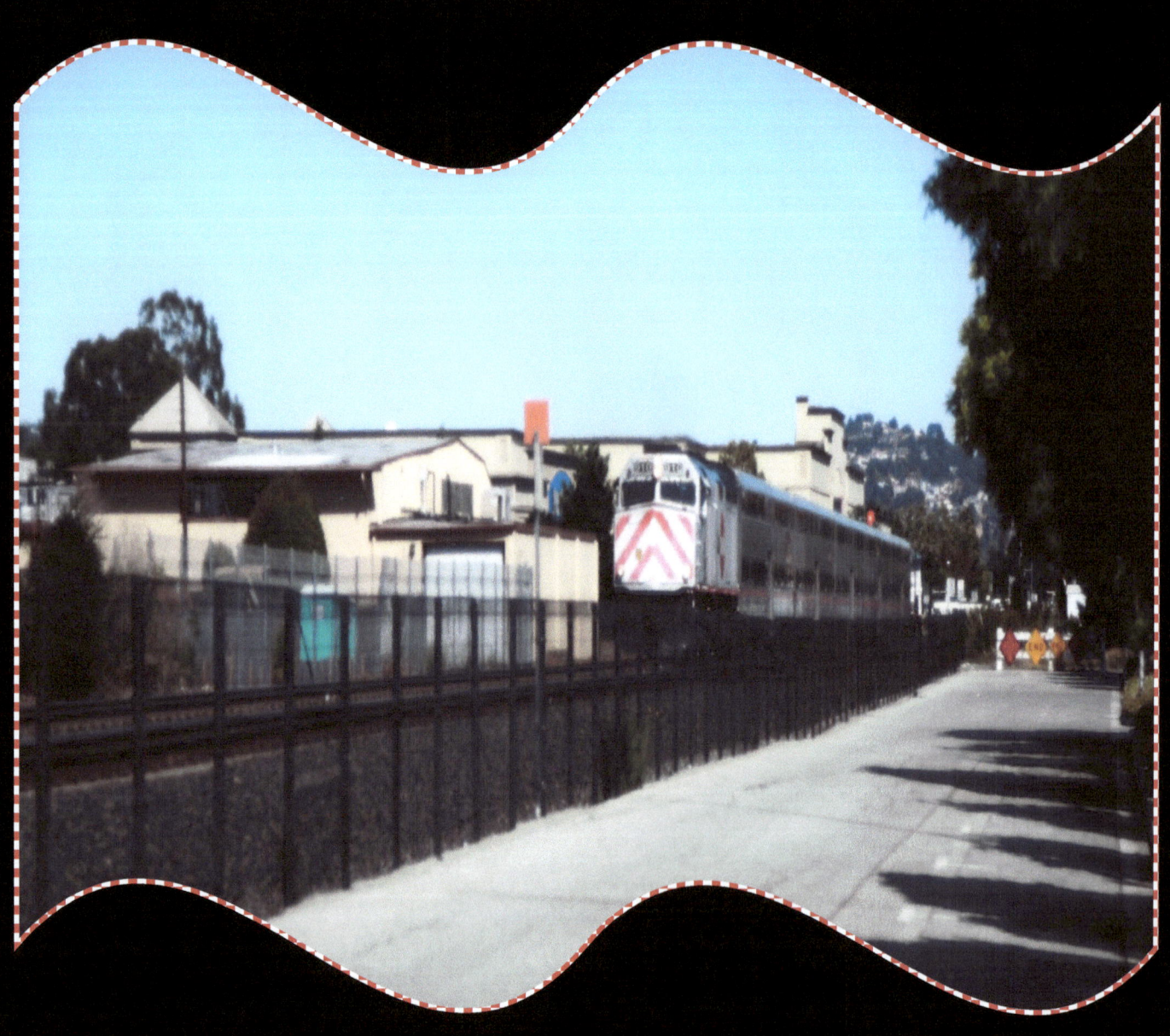

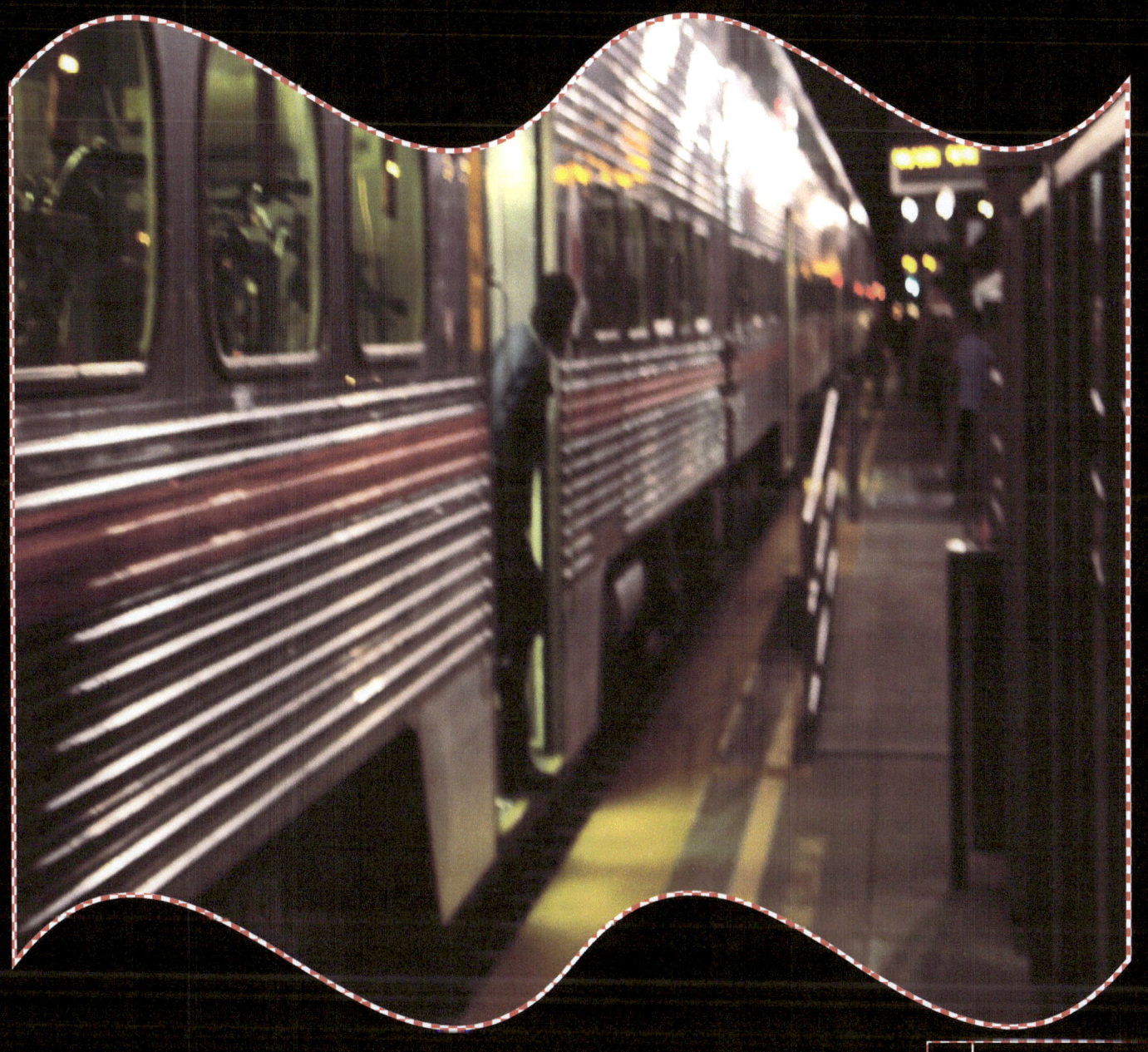

Take 8........
Flip>>>>>

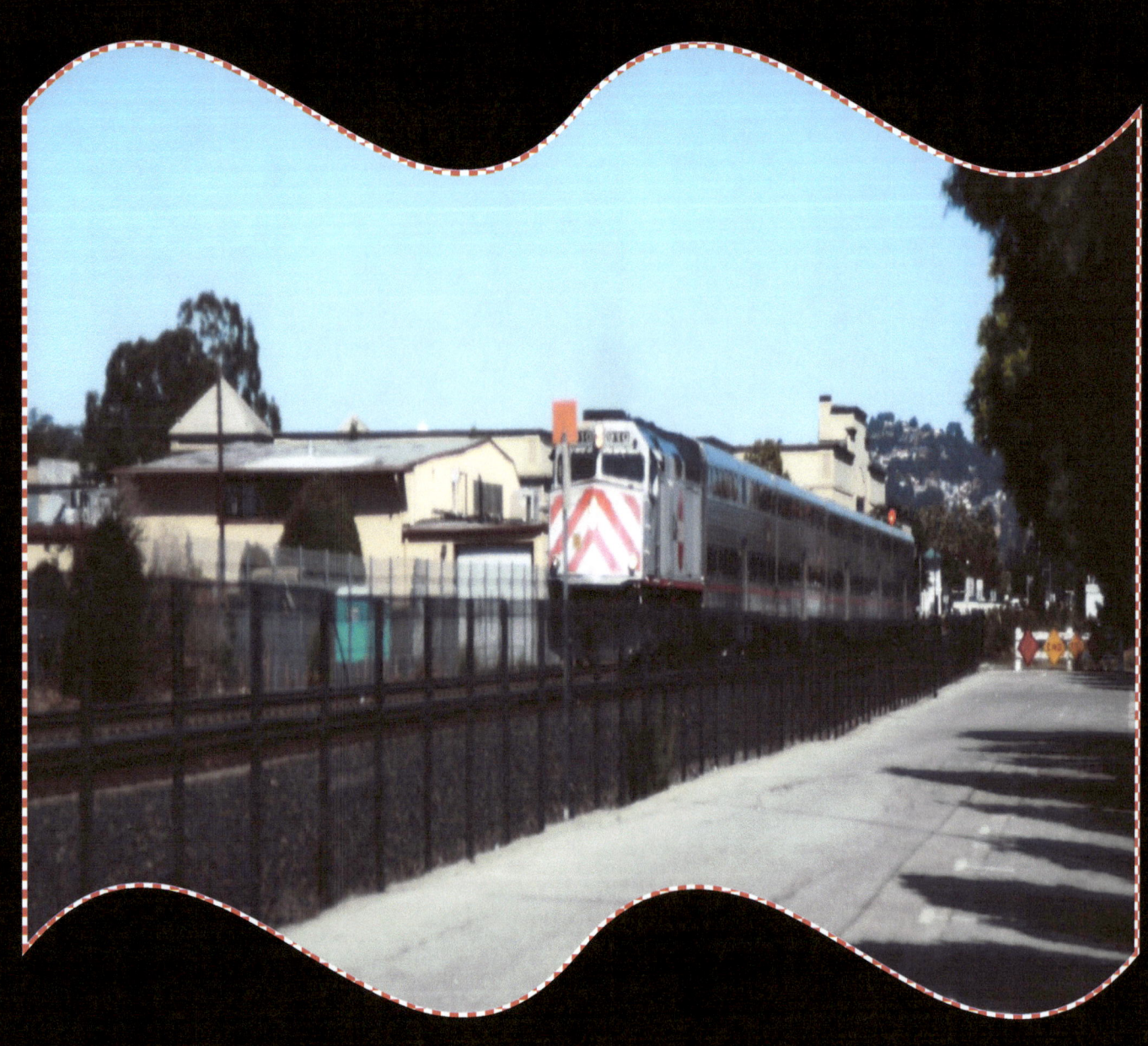

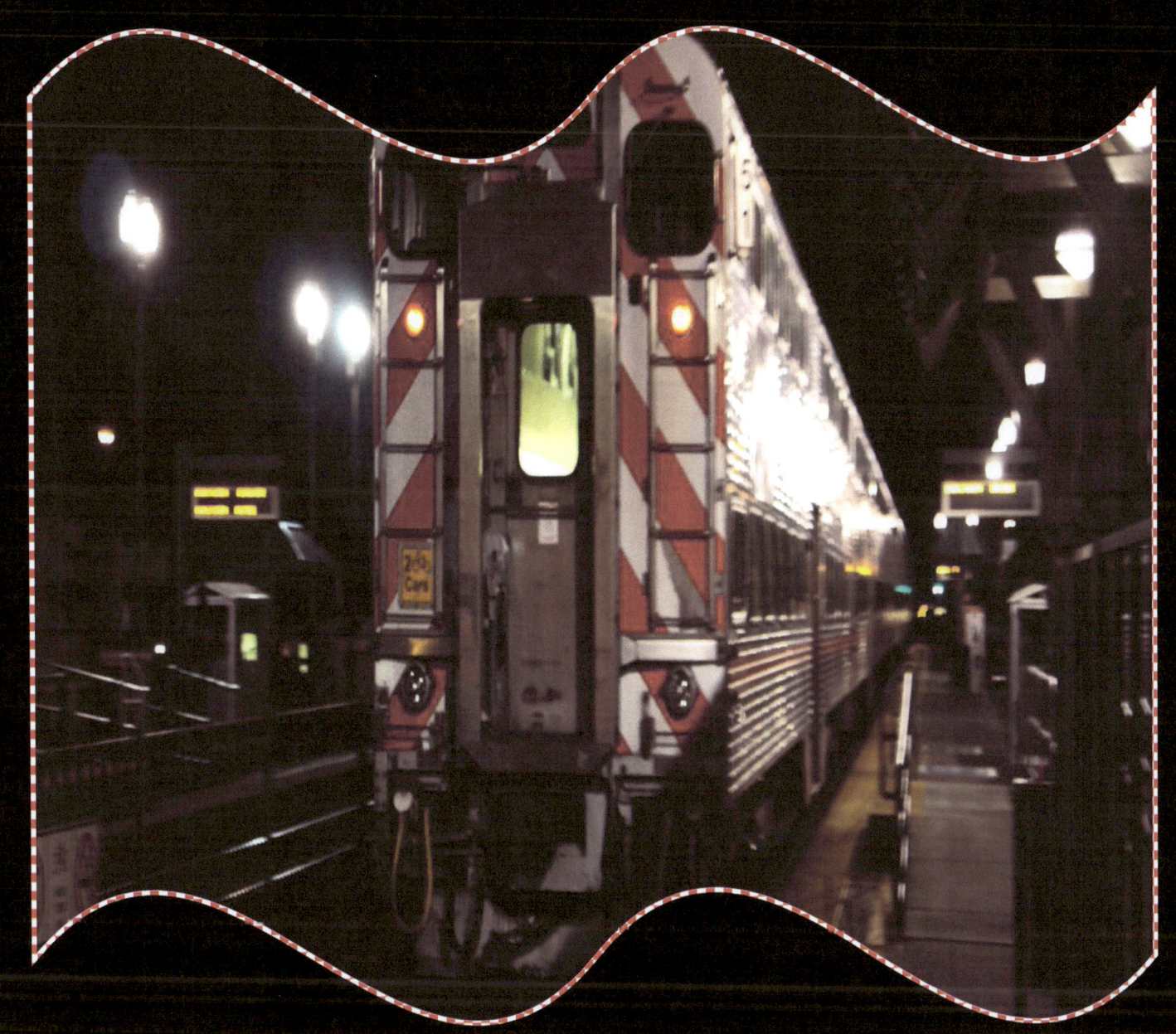

Take 9........
Flip>>>>>

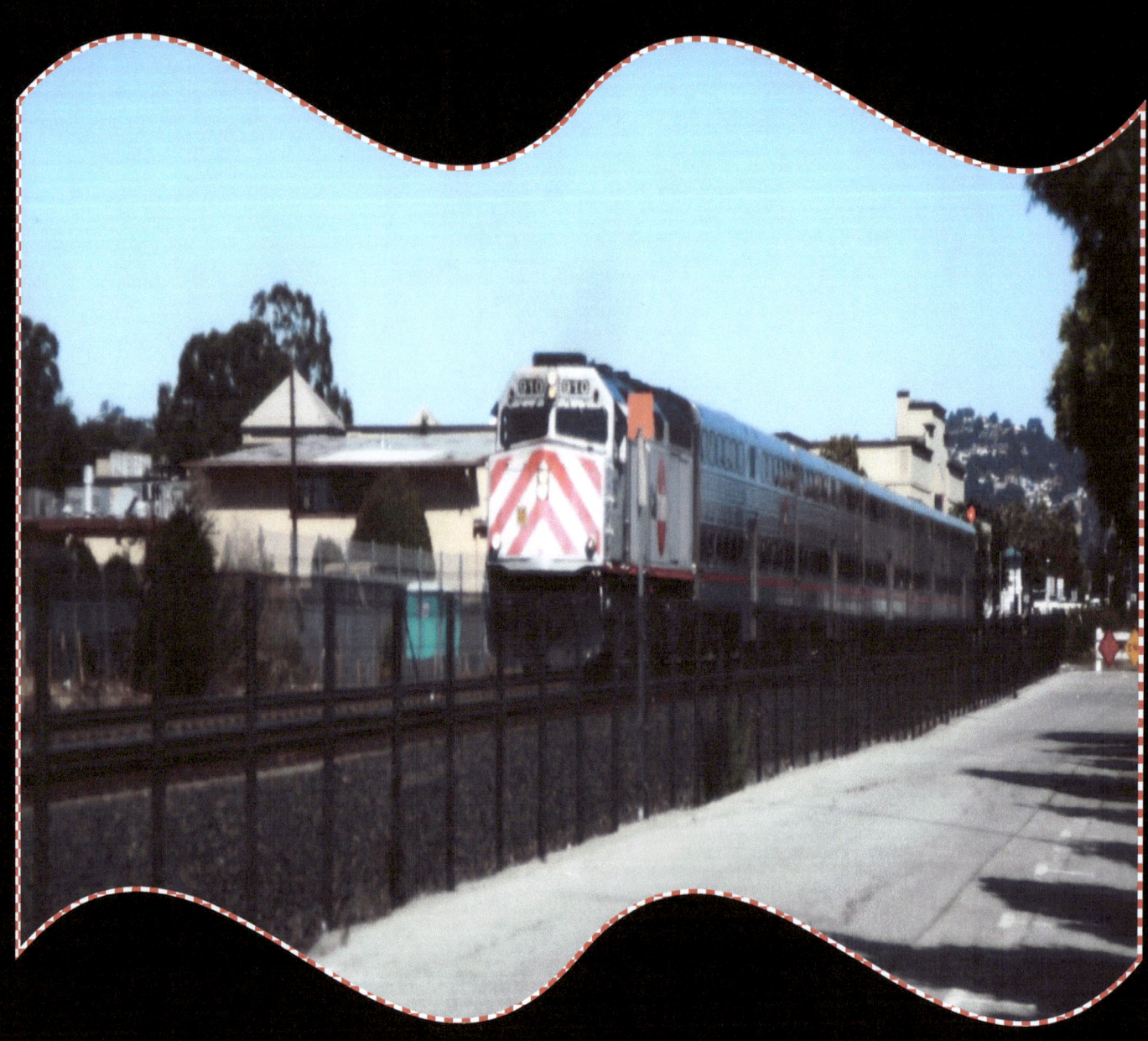

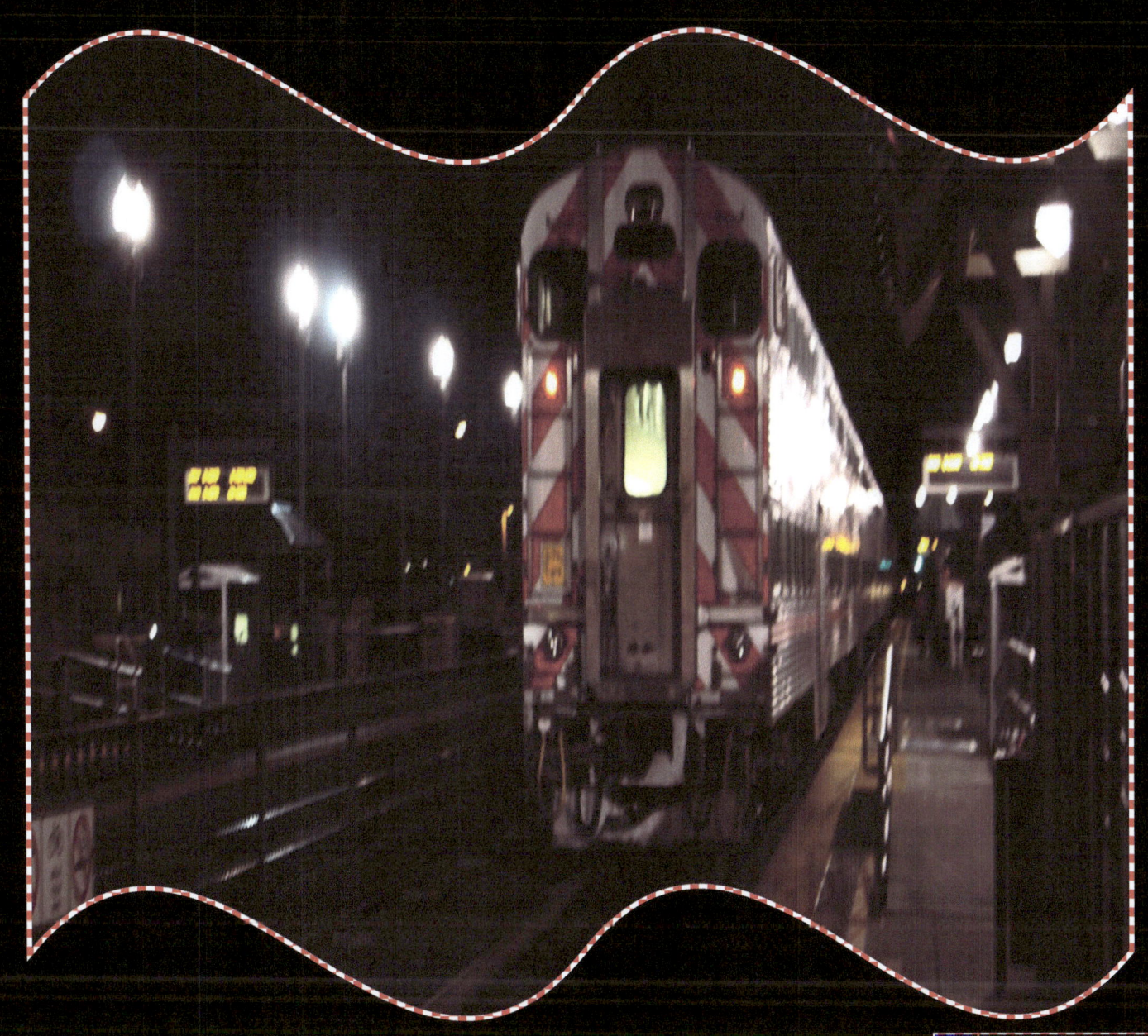

Take 10.......
Flip>>>>>

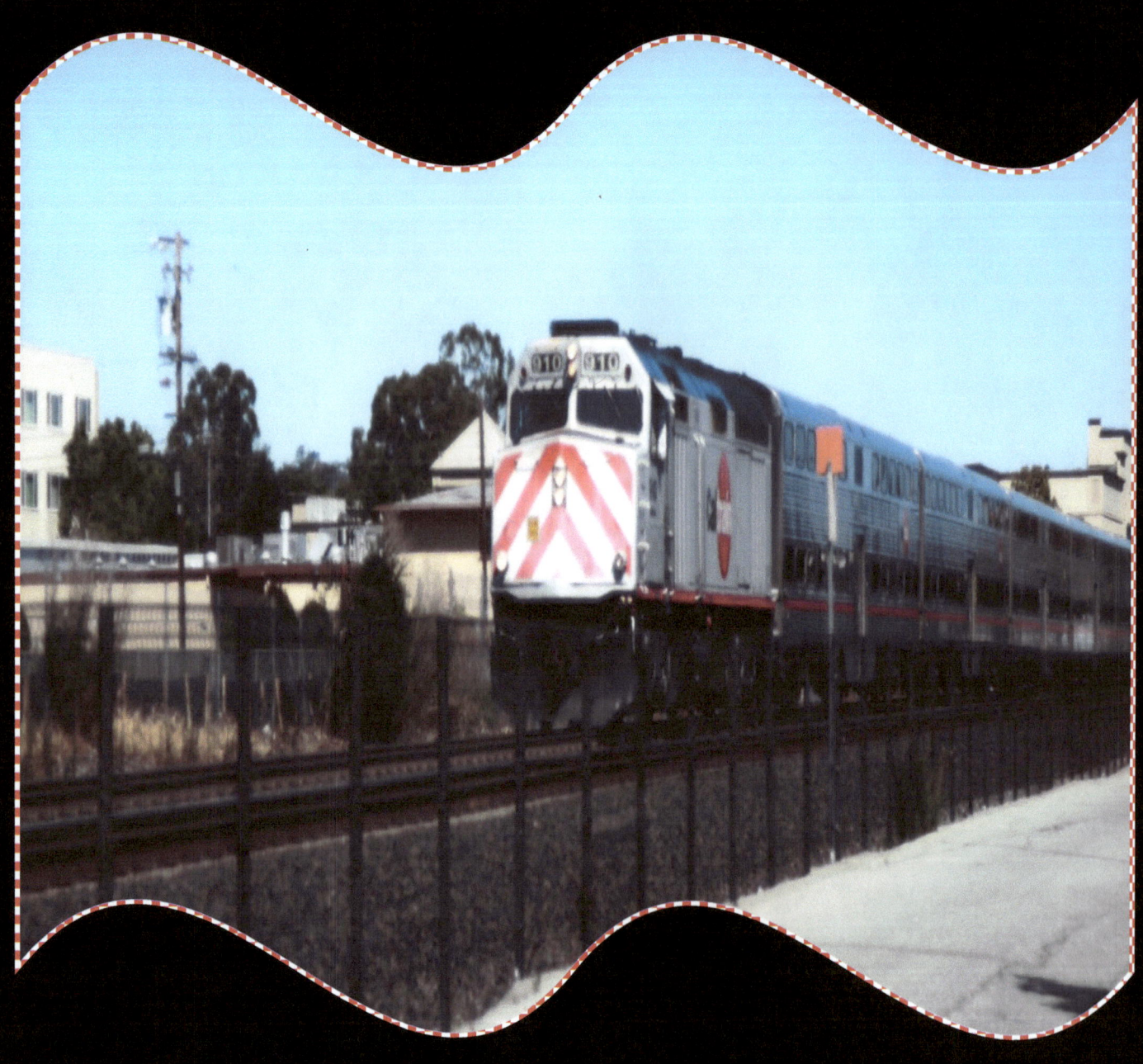

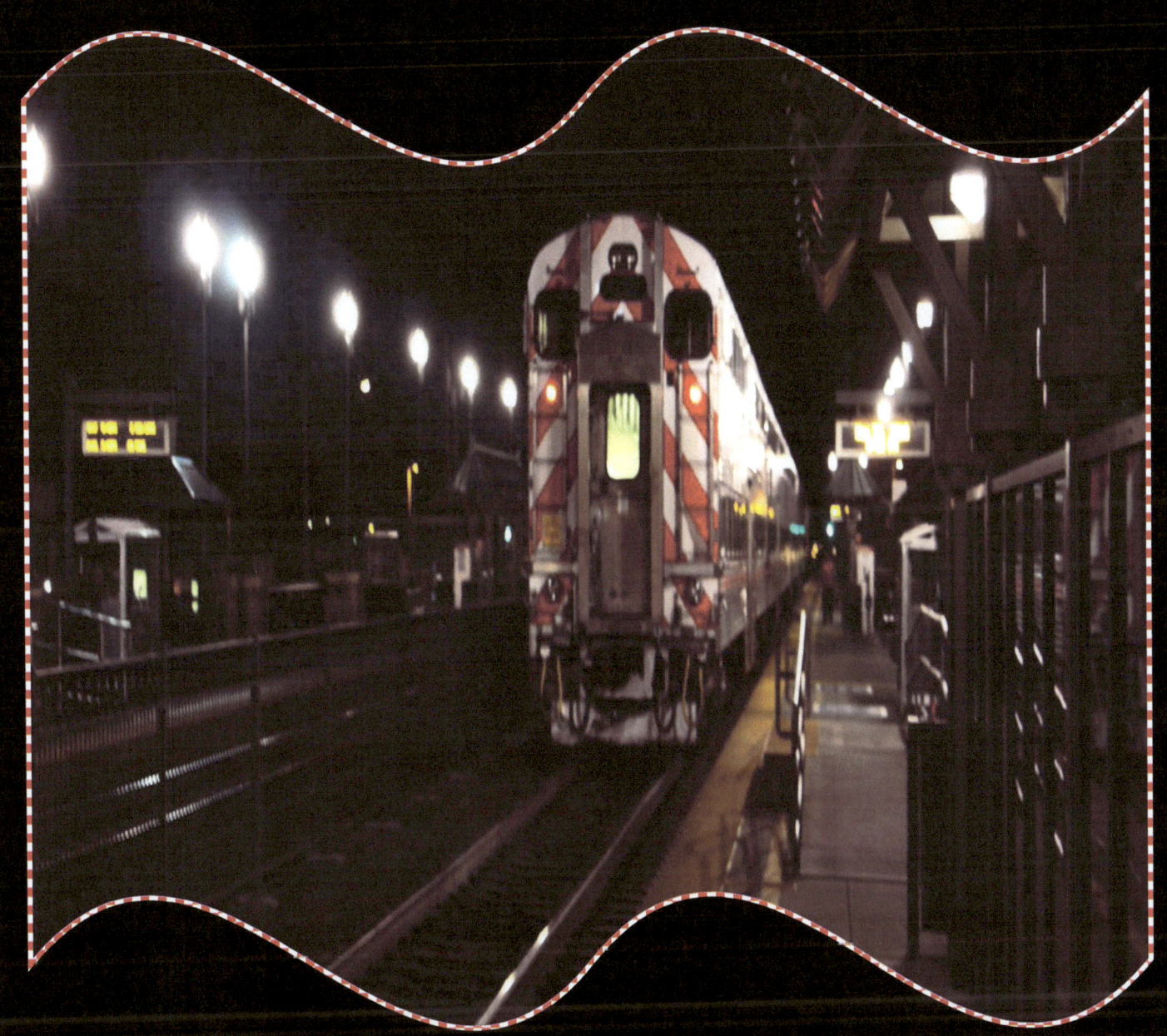

Take 11......
Flip>>>>>

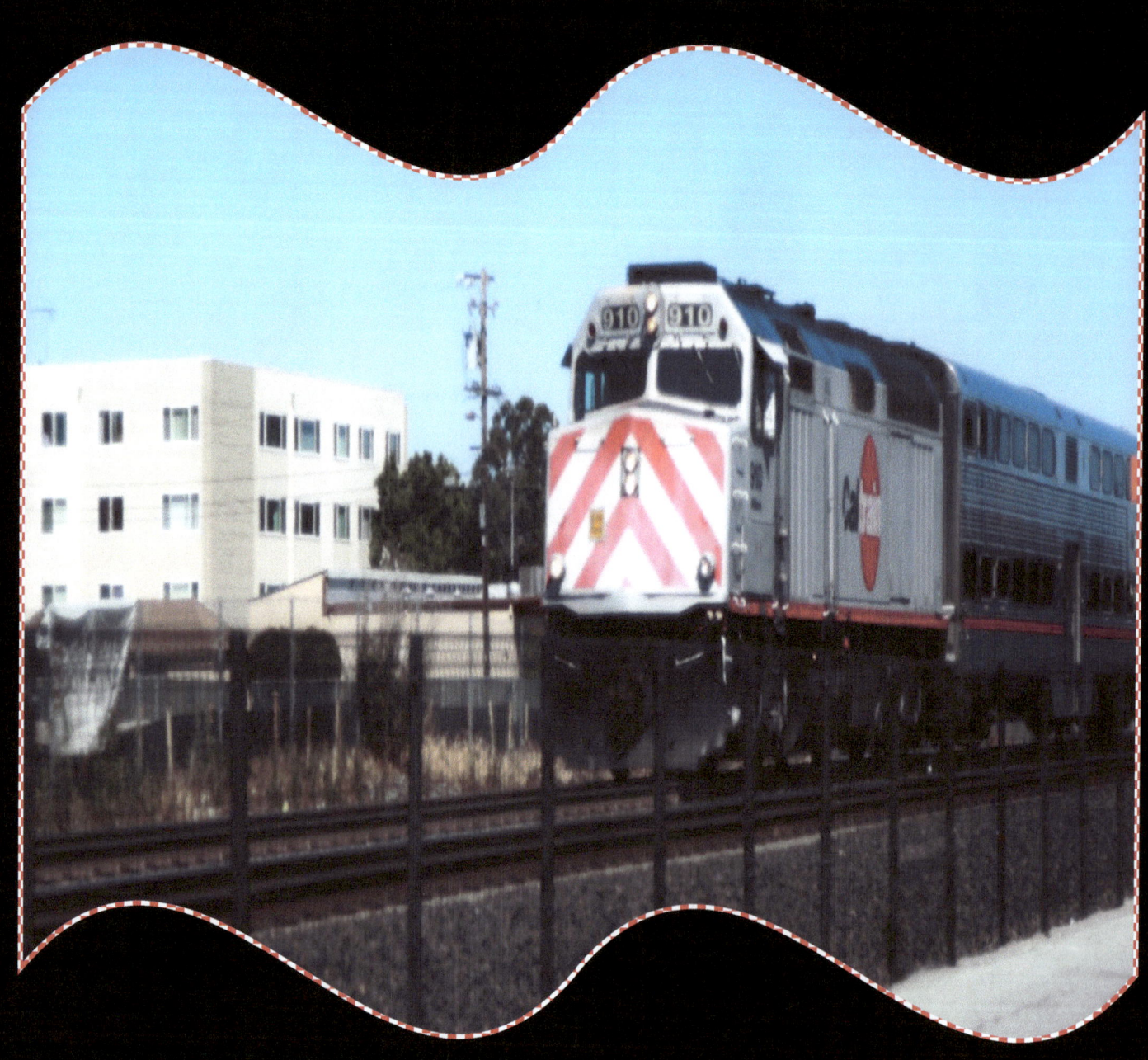

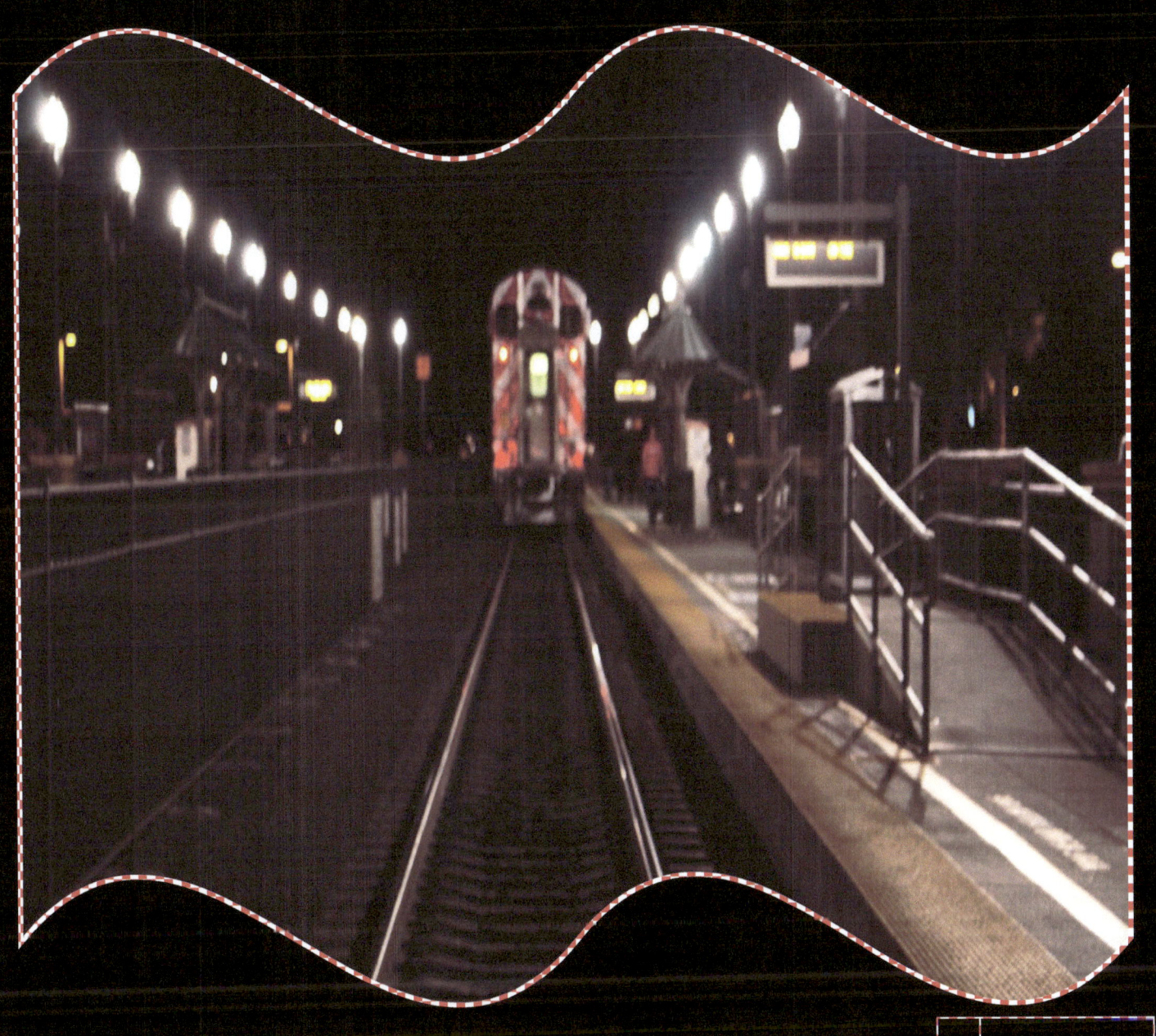

Cut ! That's a Rap.

Angles, Curves and Shadows

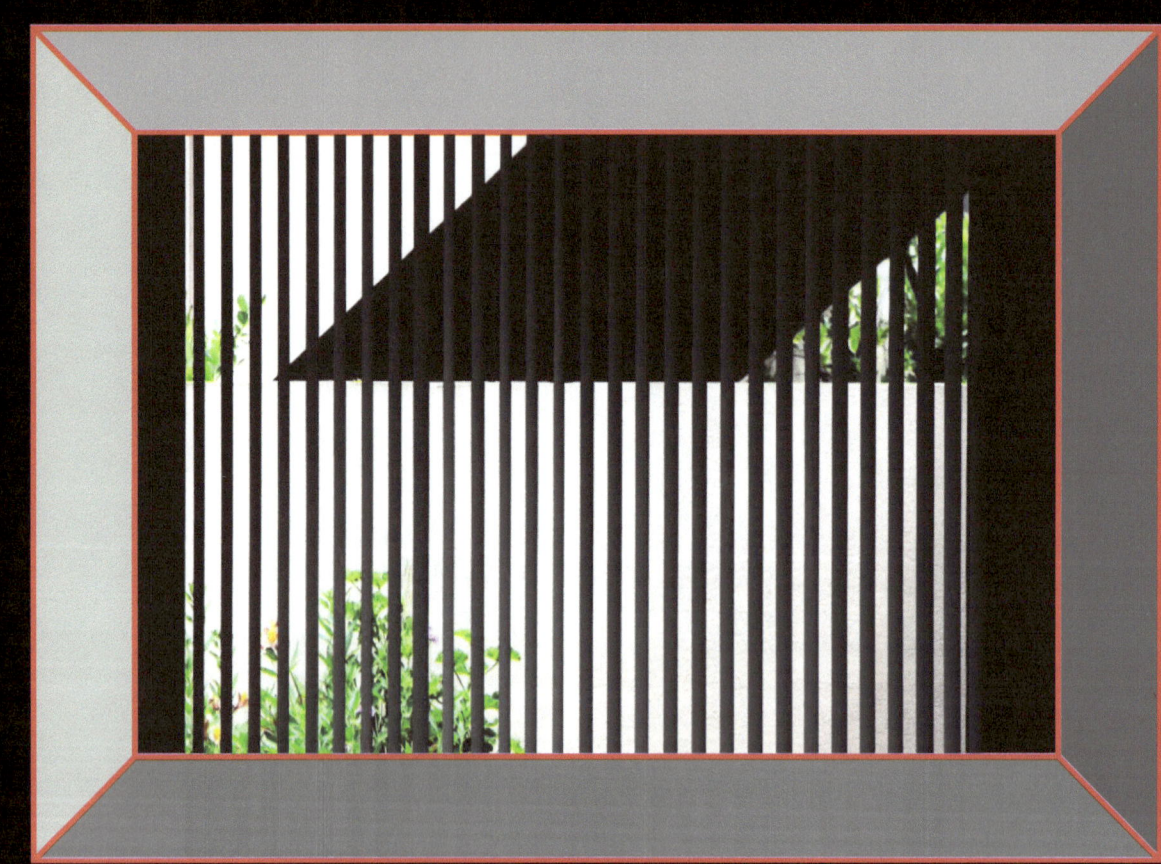

Plate I

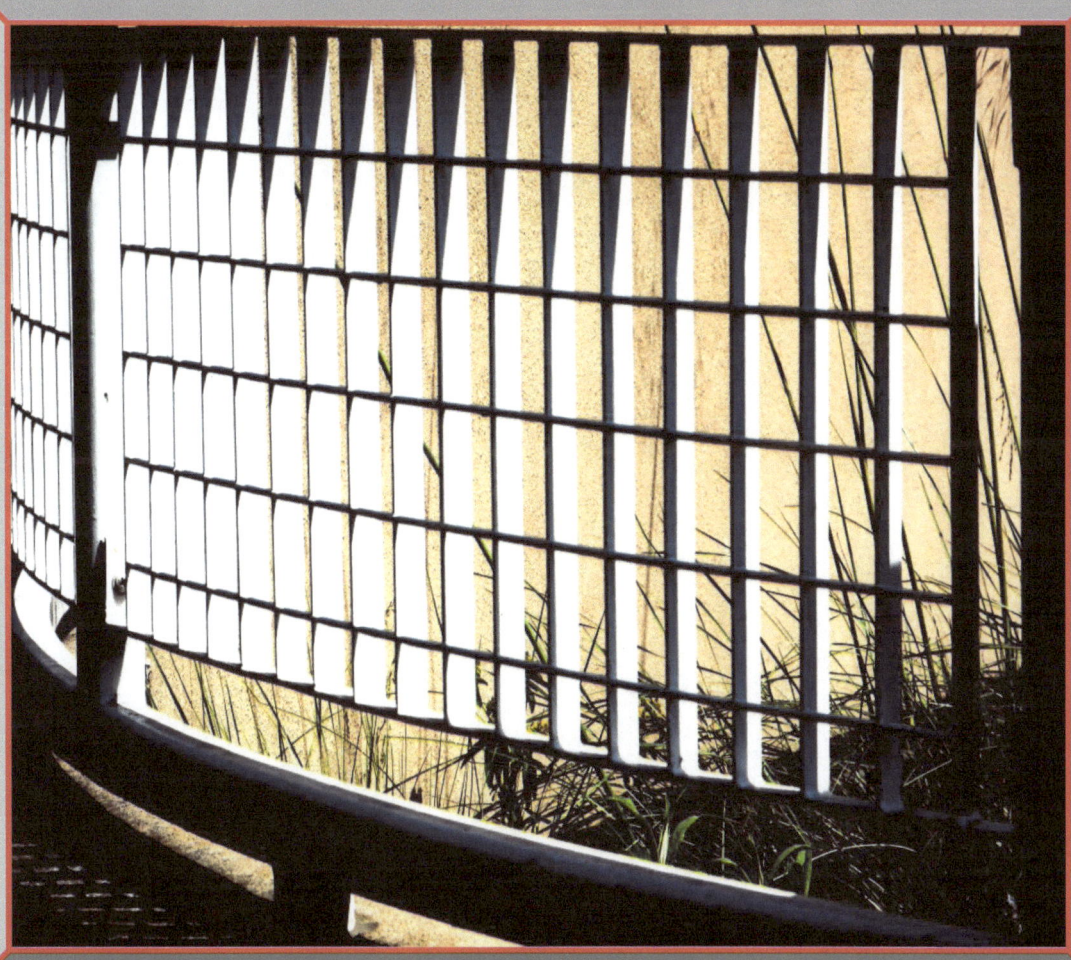

Plate 2

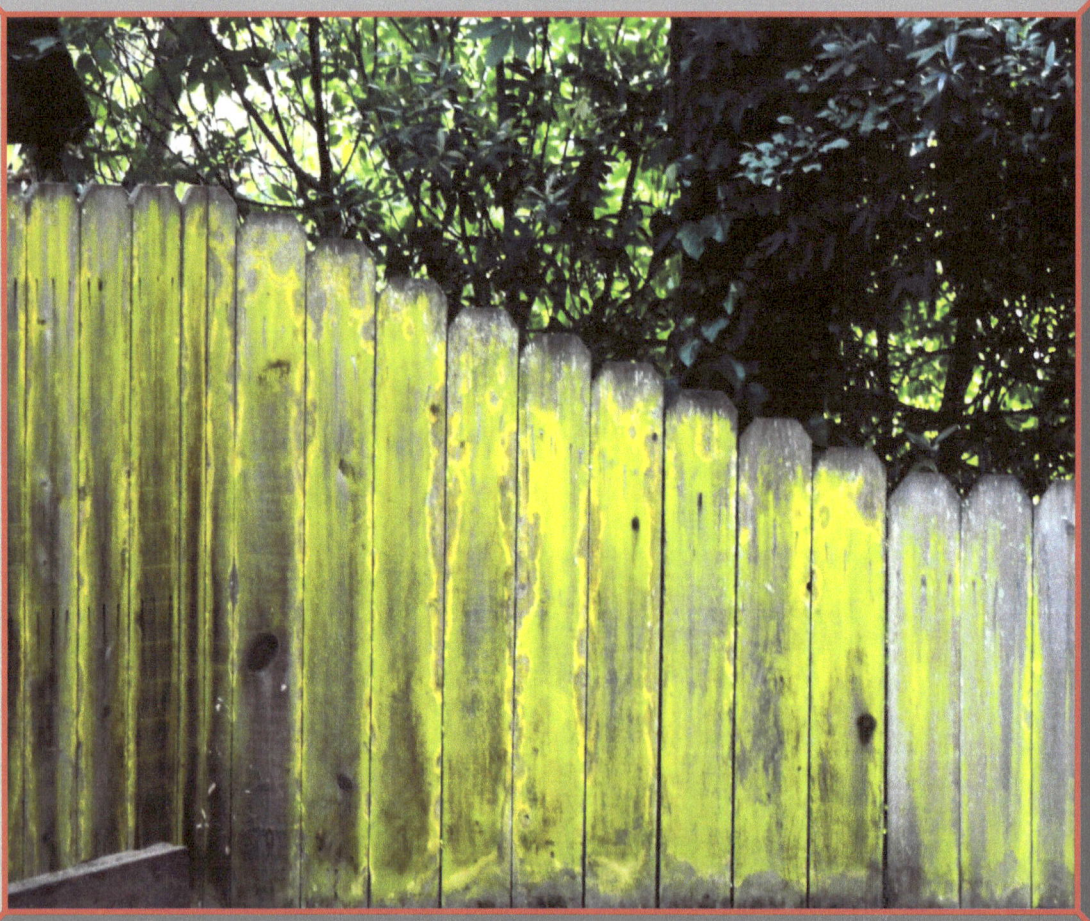

Plate 3

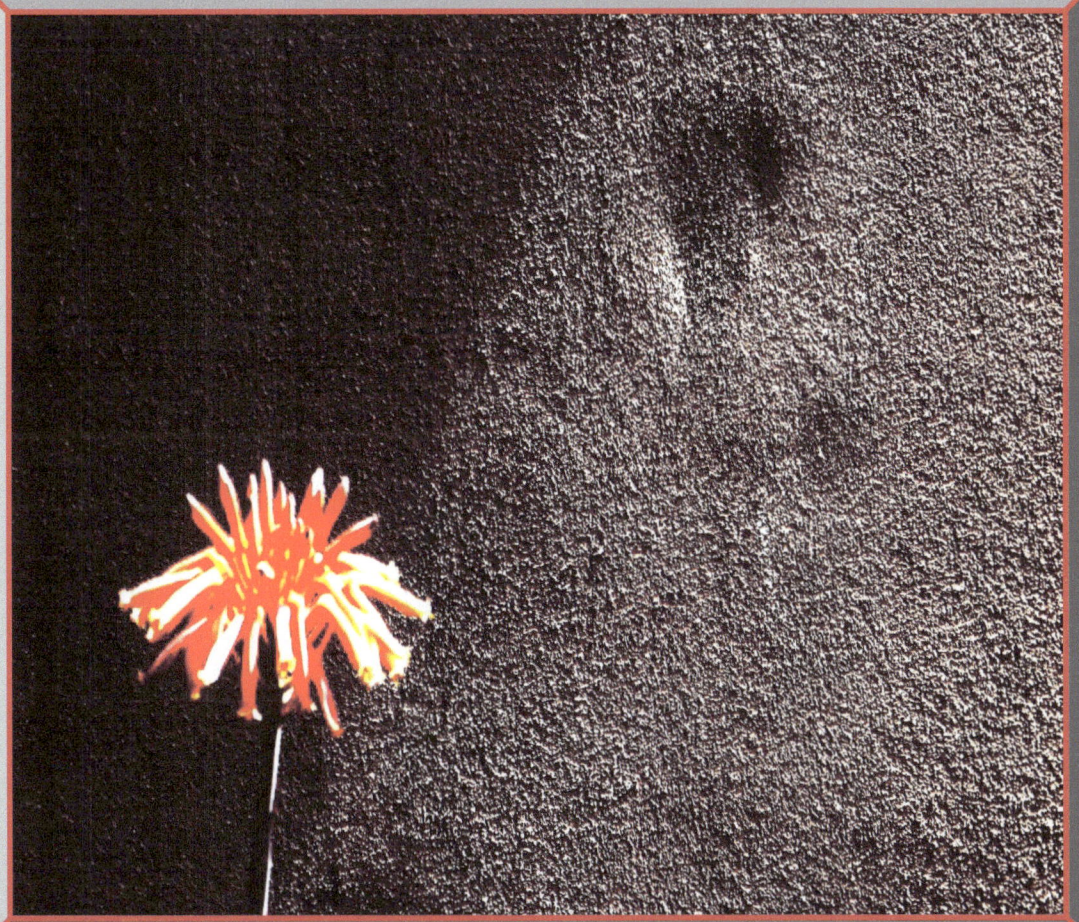

Plate 4

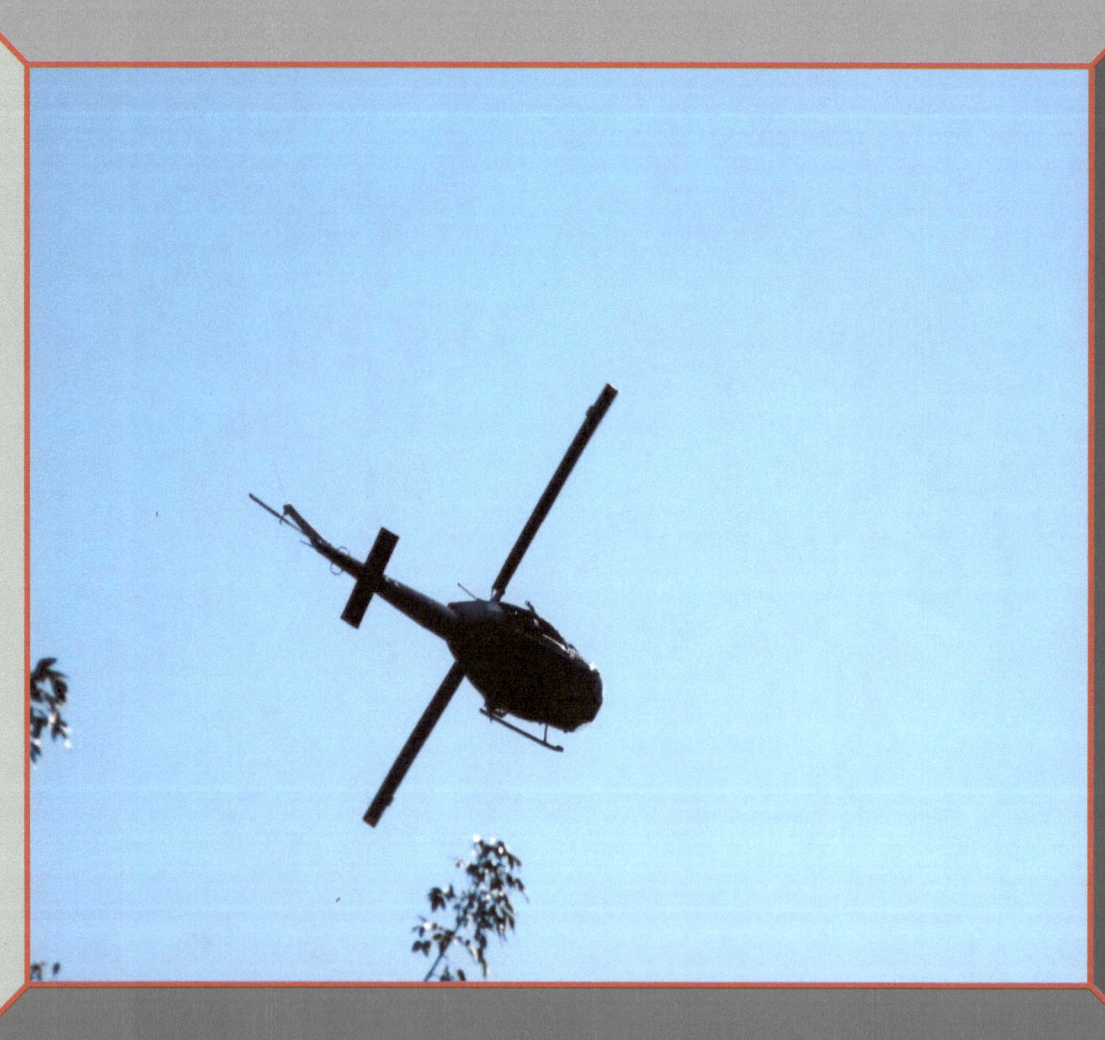

Plate 5

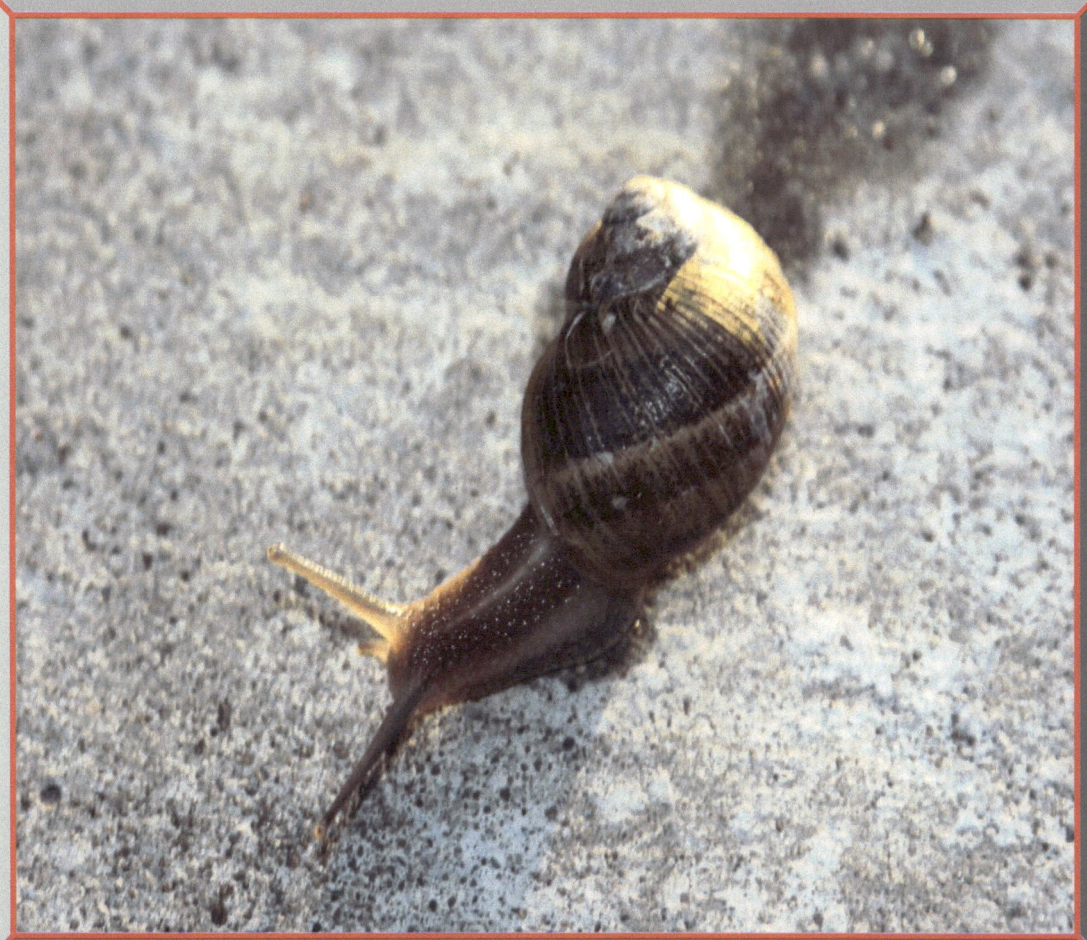

Plate 6

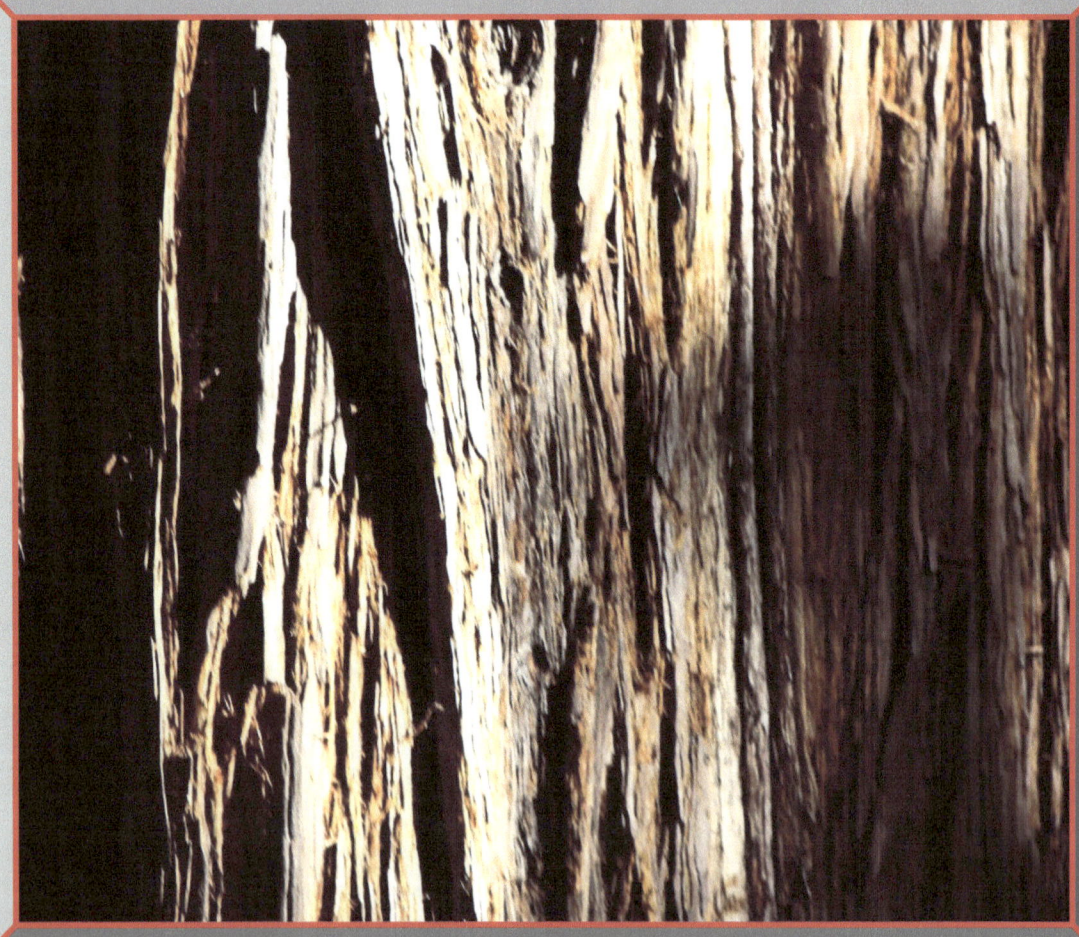

Plate 7

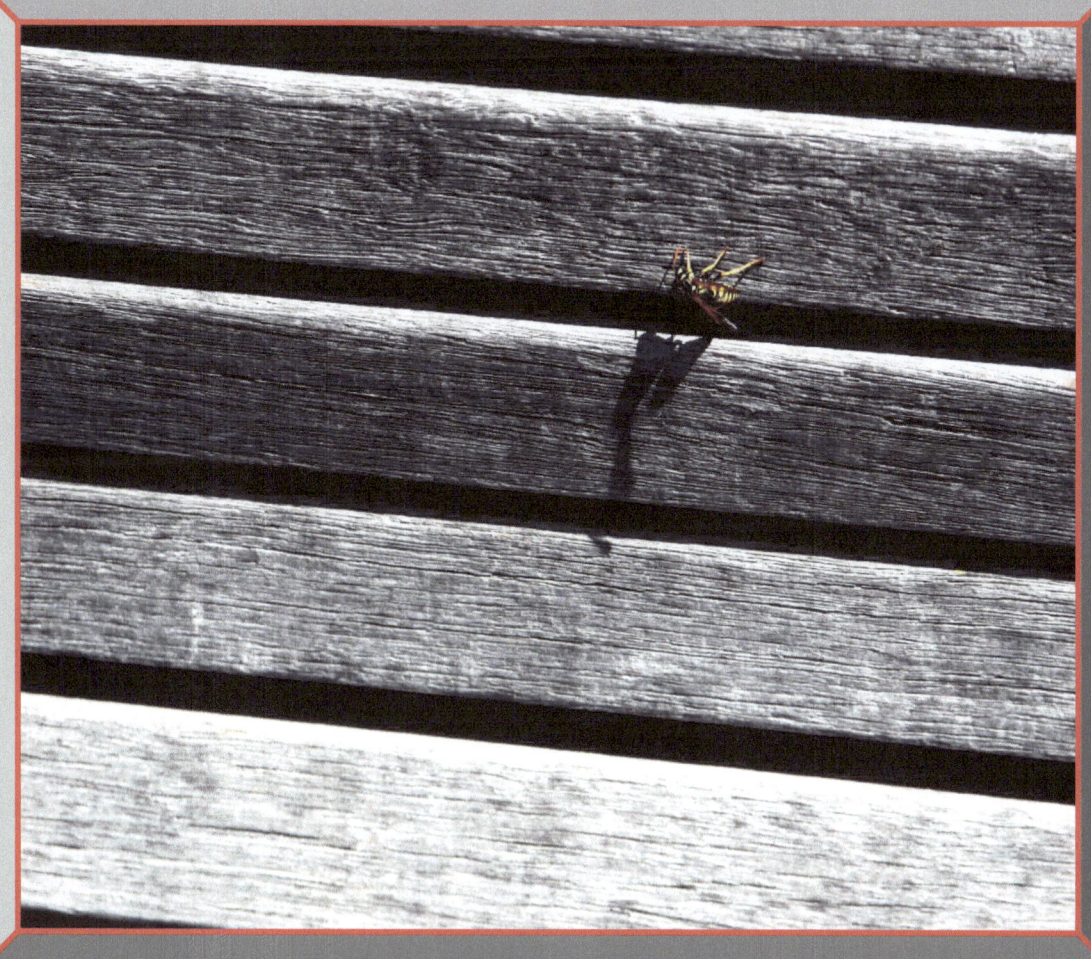

Plate 8

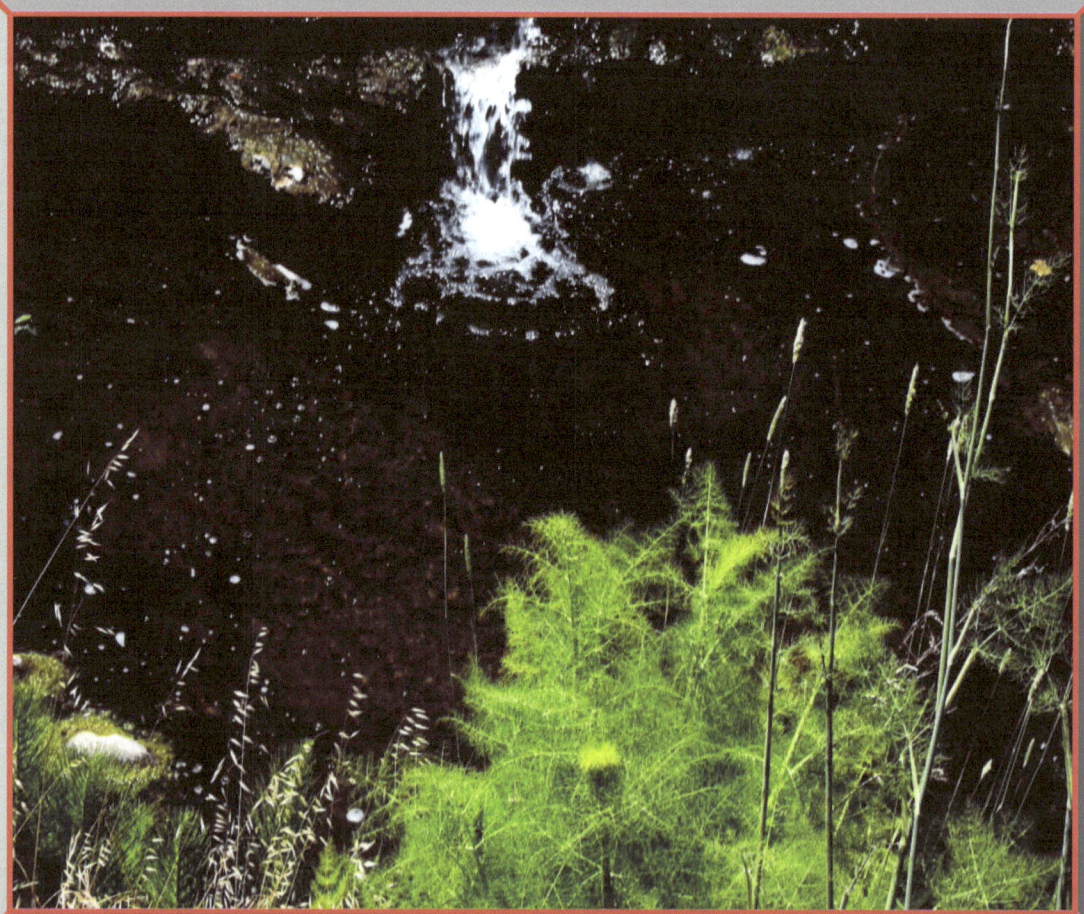

Plate 9

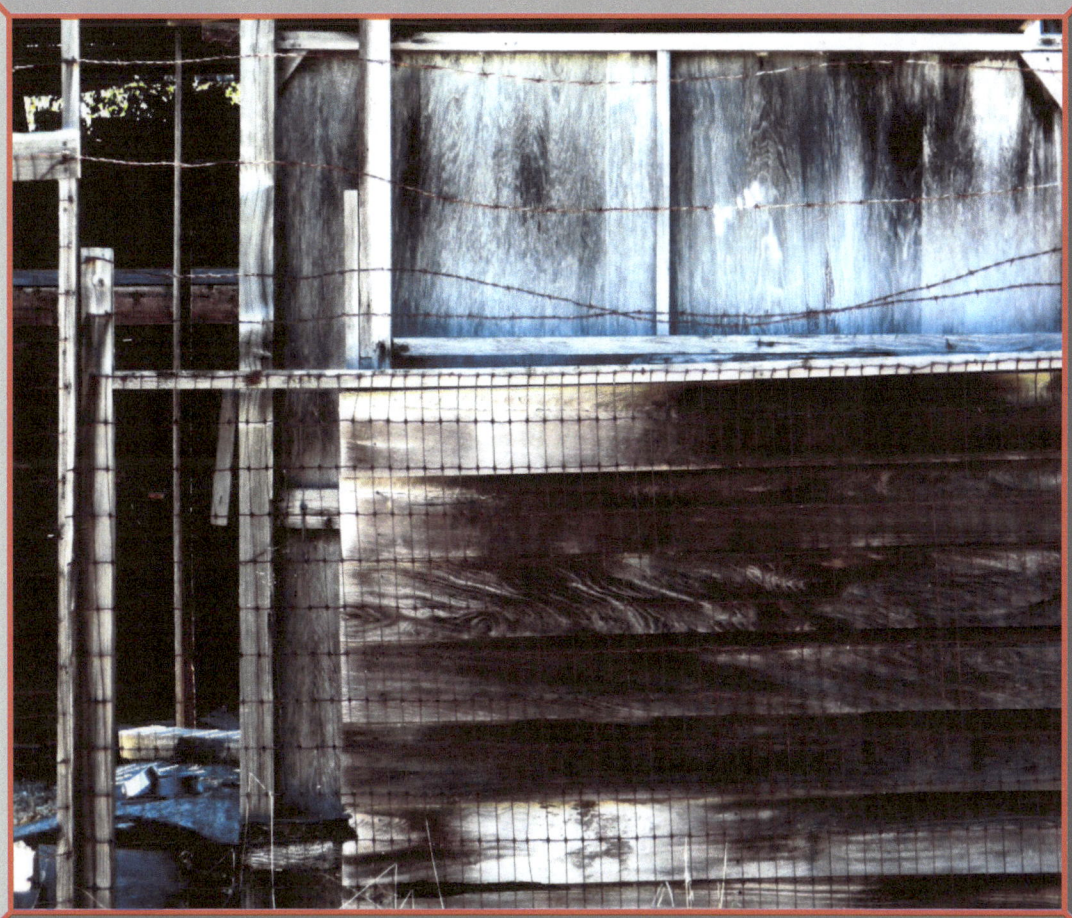

Plate 10

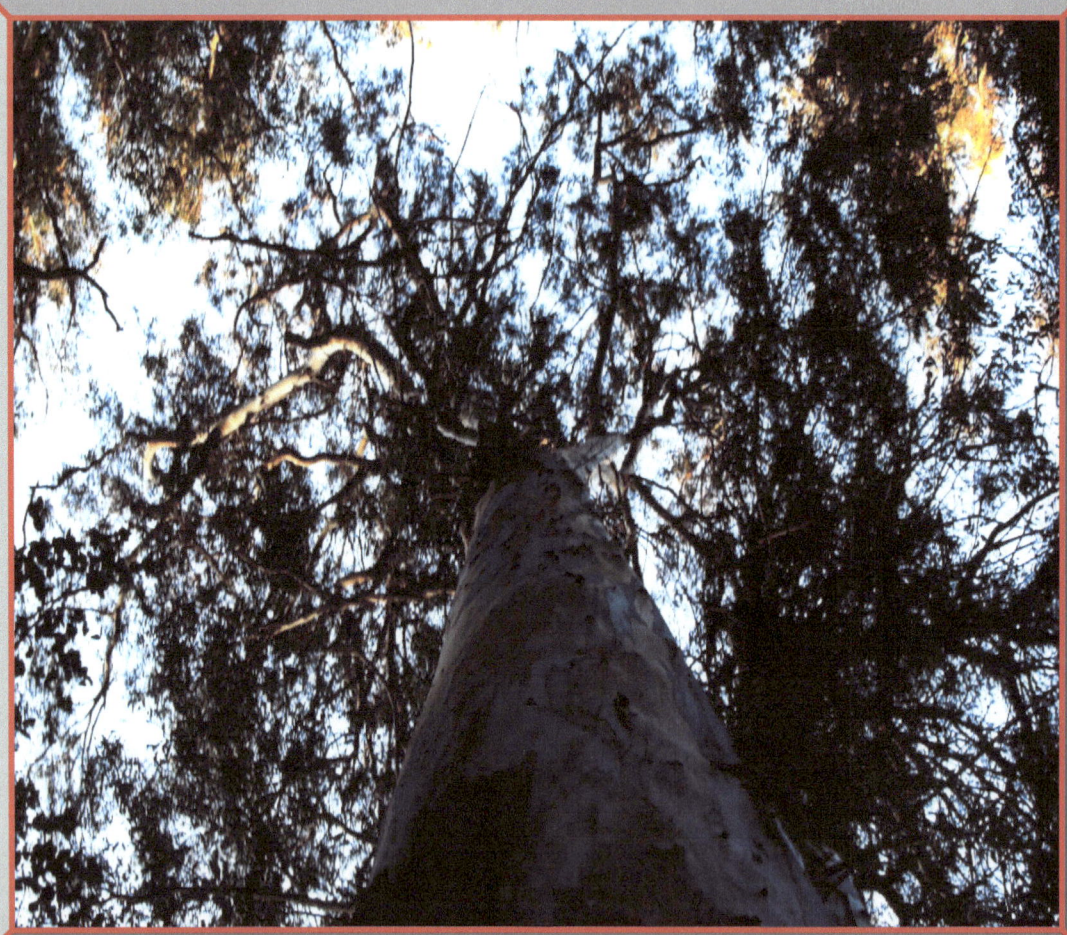

Plate 11

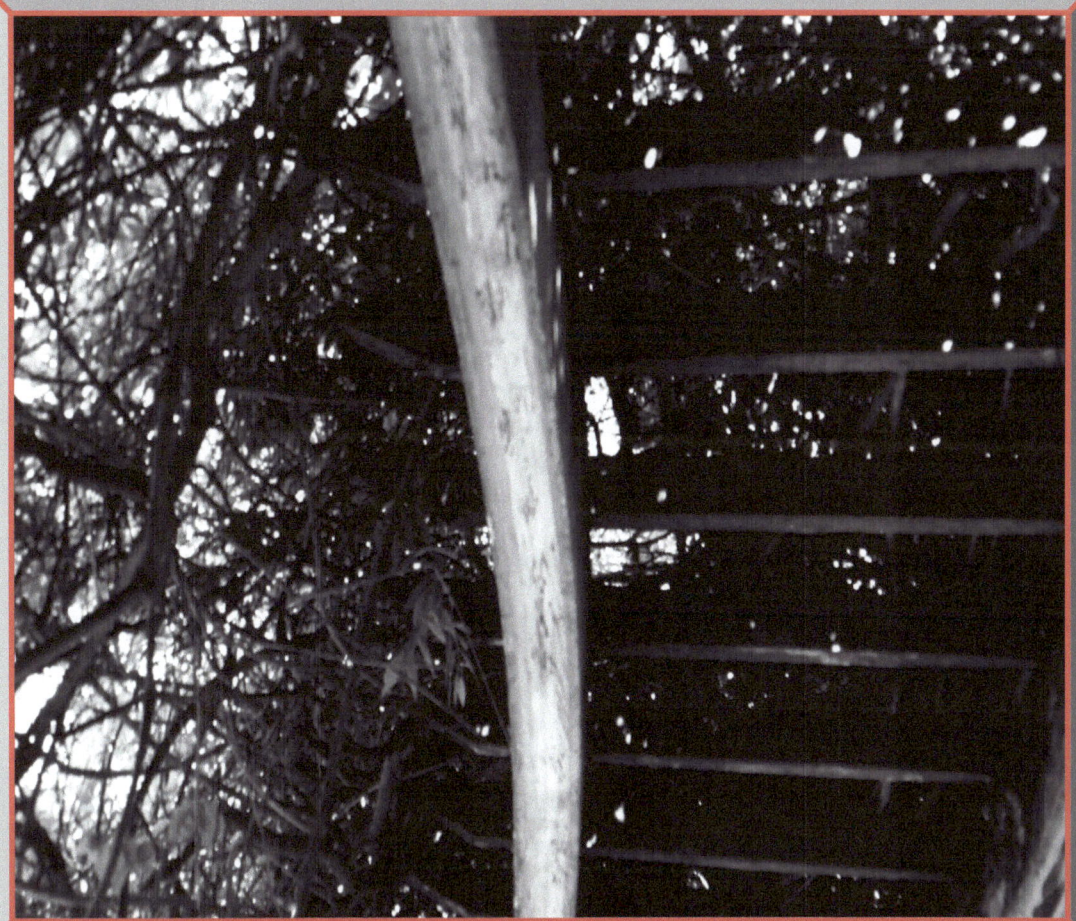

Plate 12

Plate 13

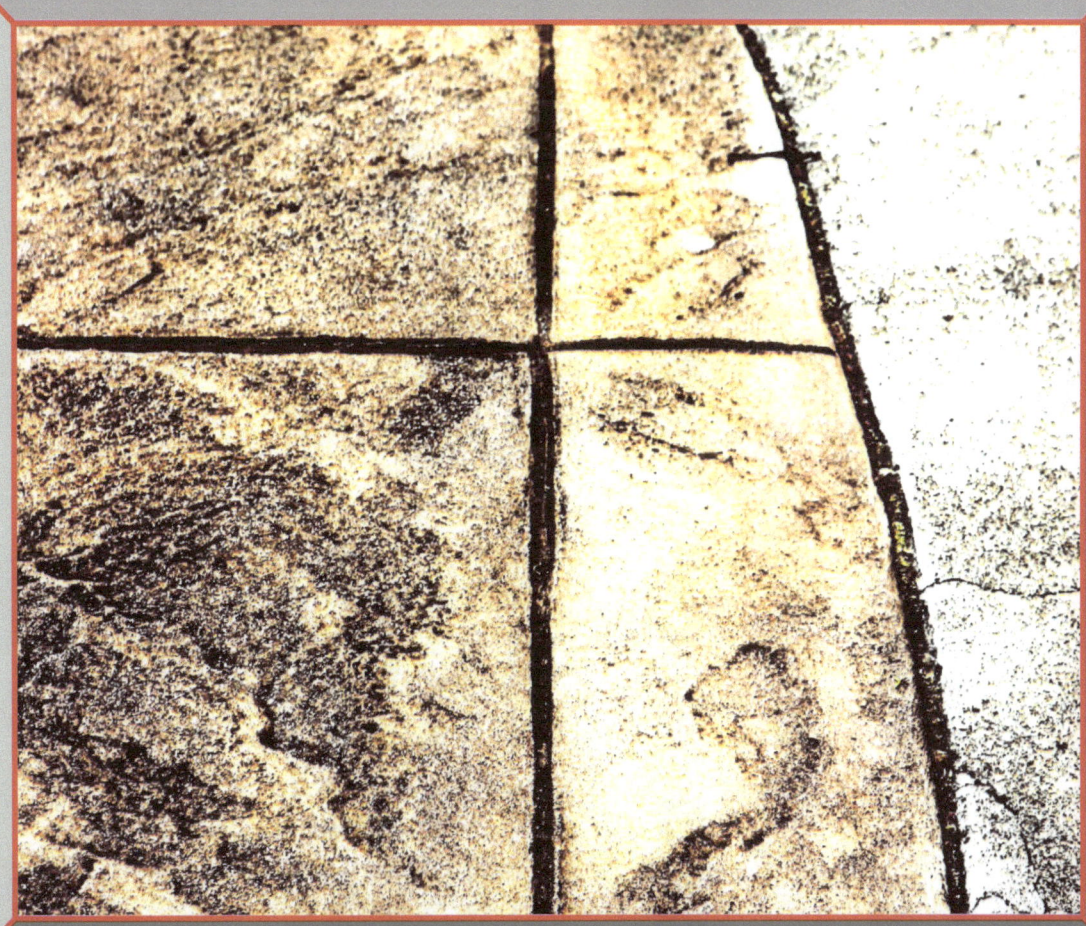

Plate 14

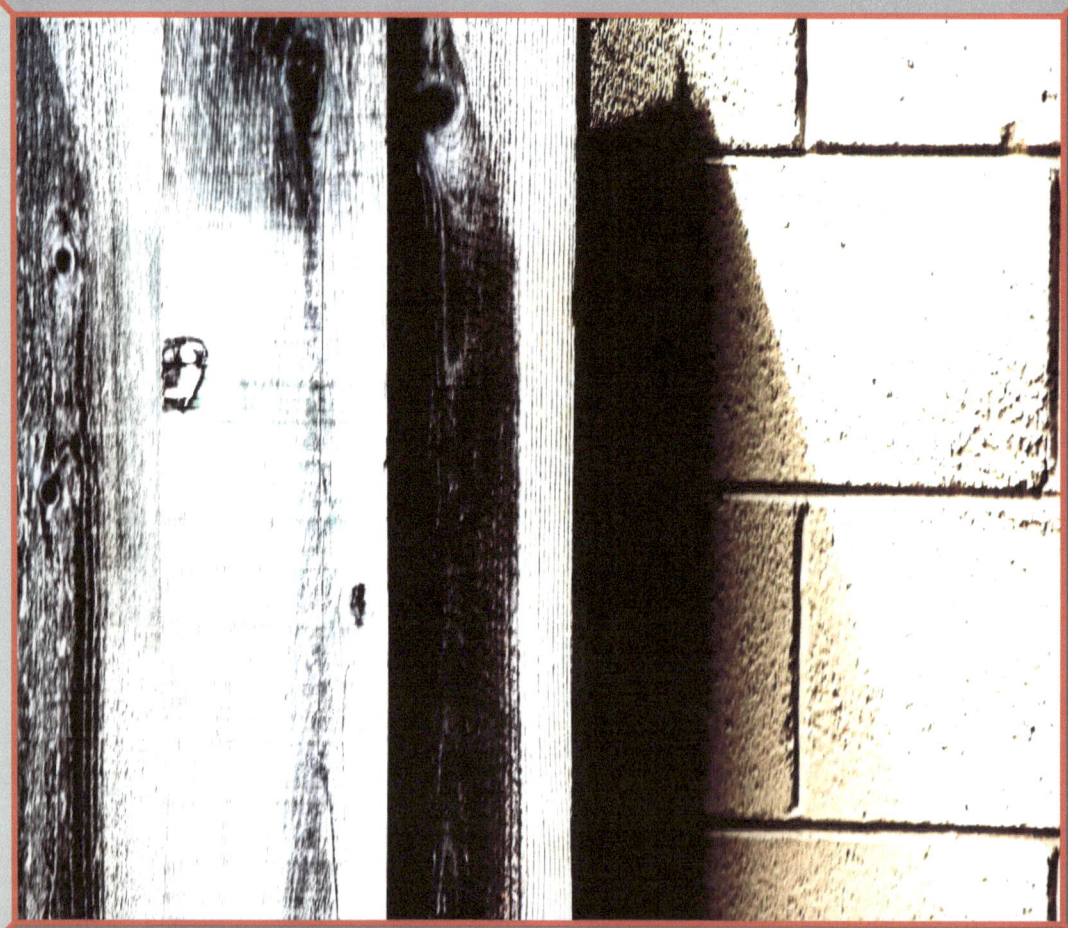

Plate 15

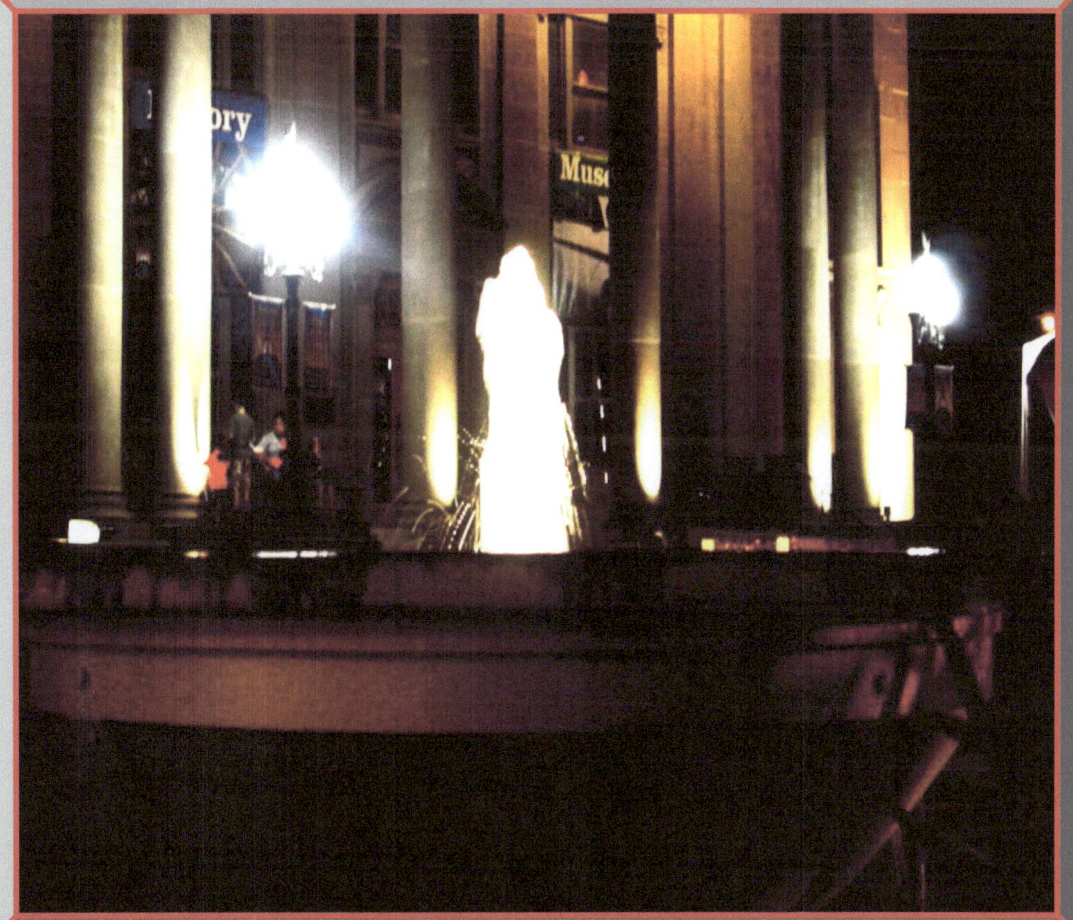

Plate 16

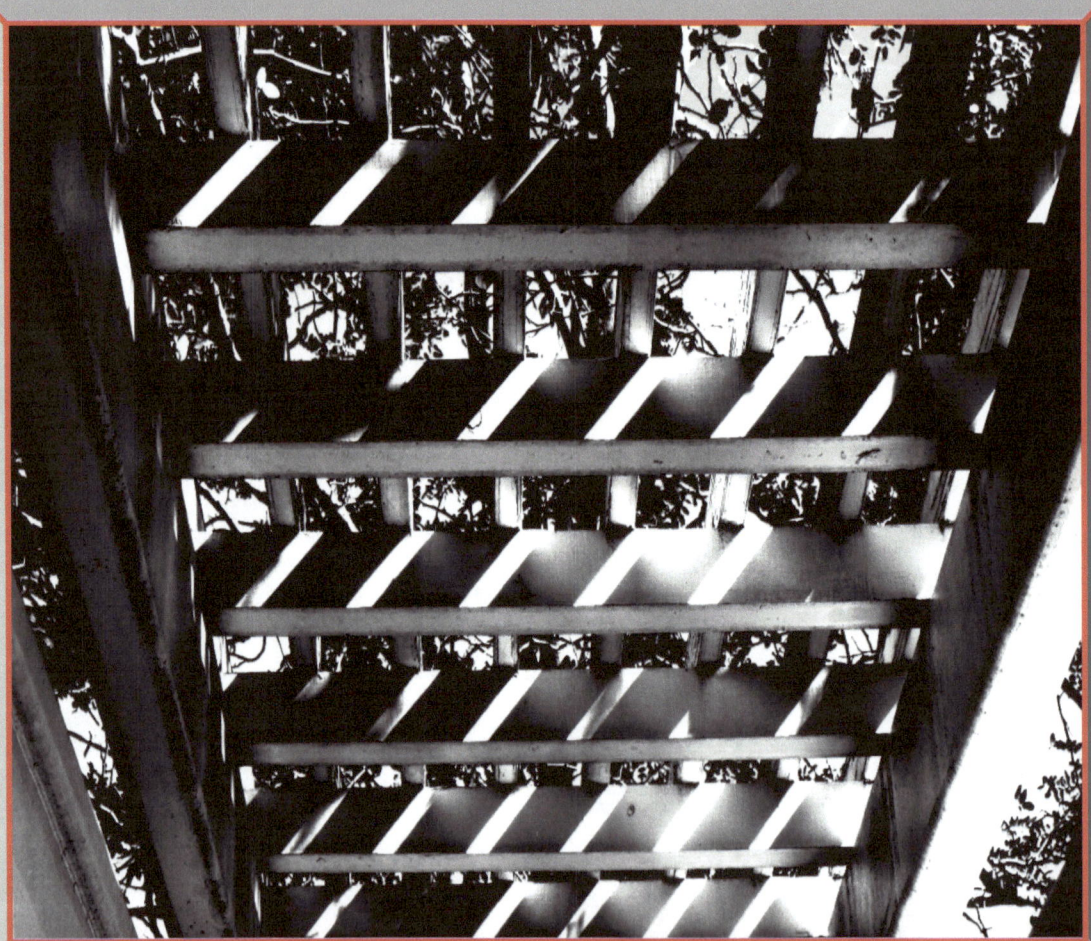

Plate 17

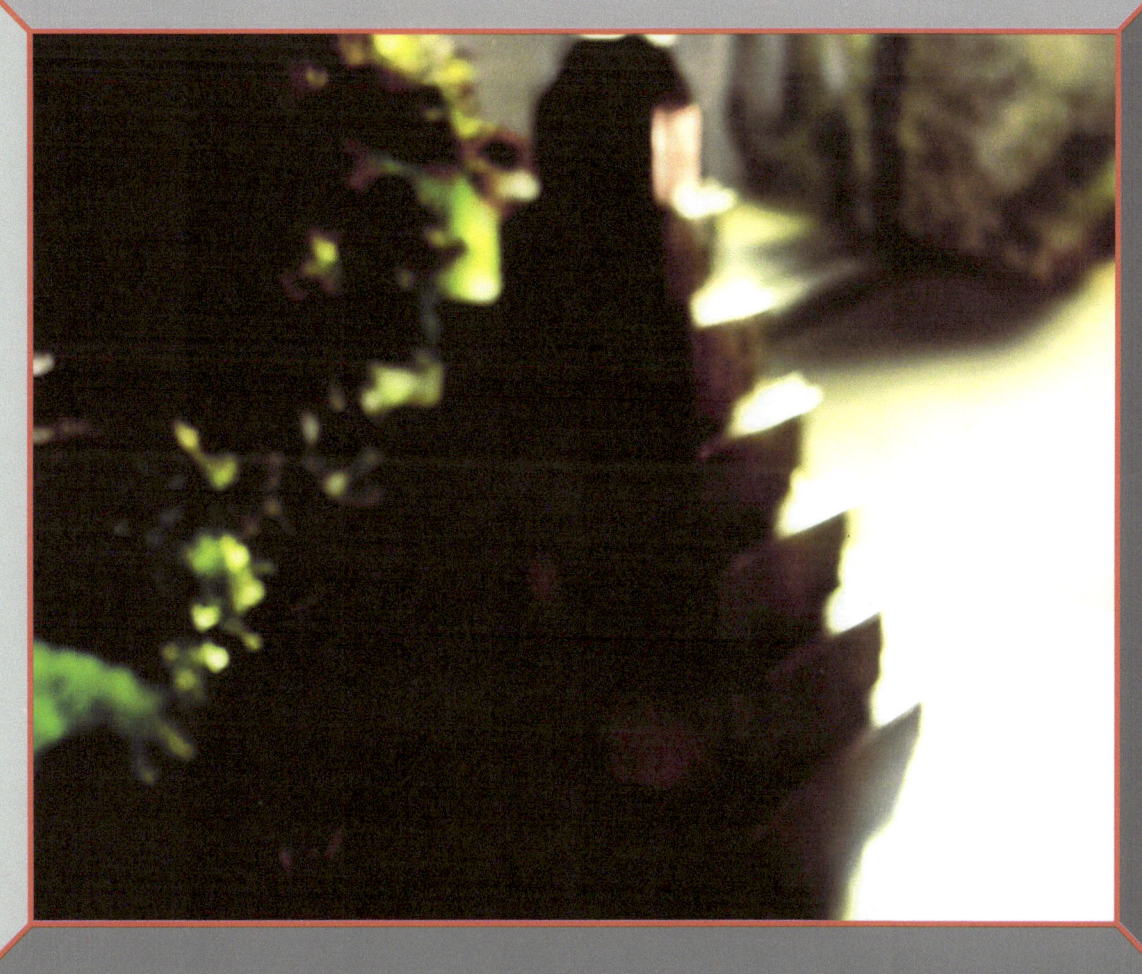

Plate 18

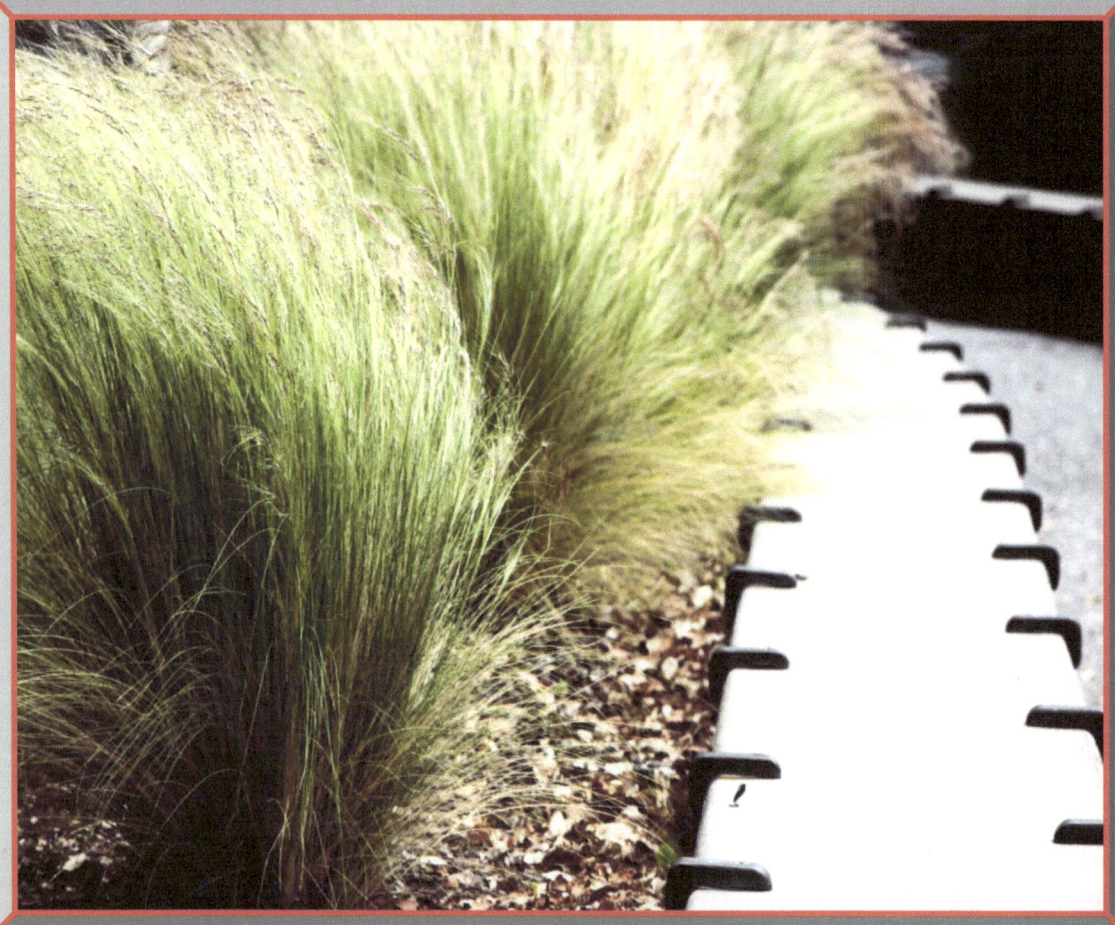

Plate 19

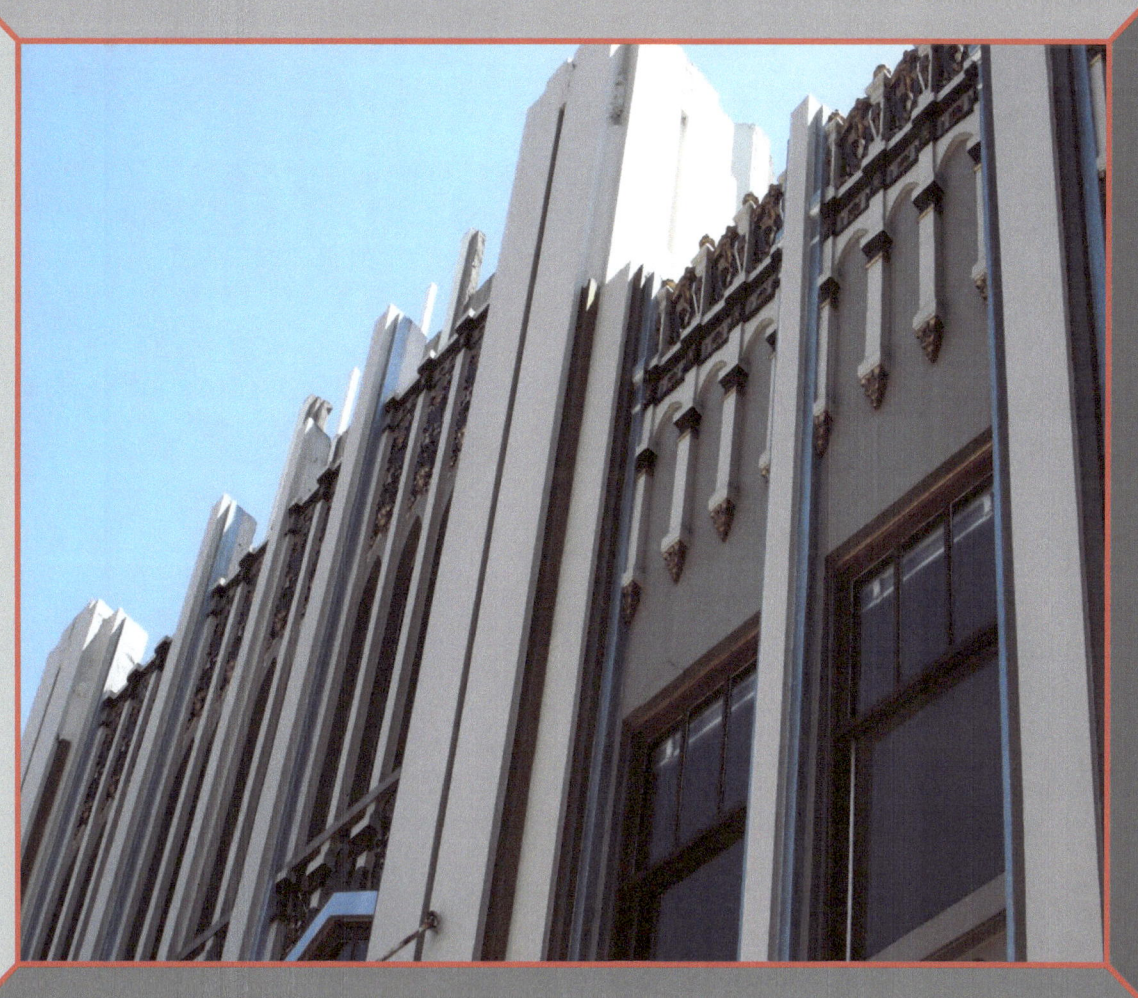

Plate 20

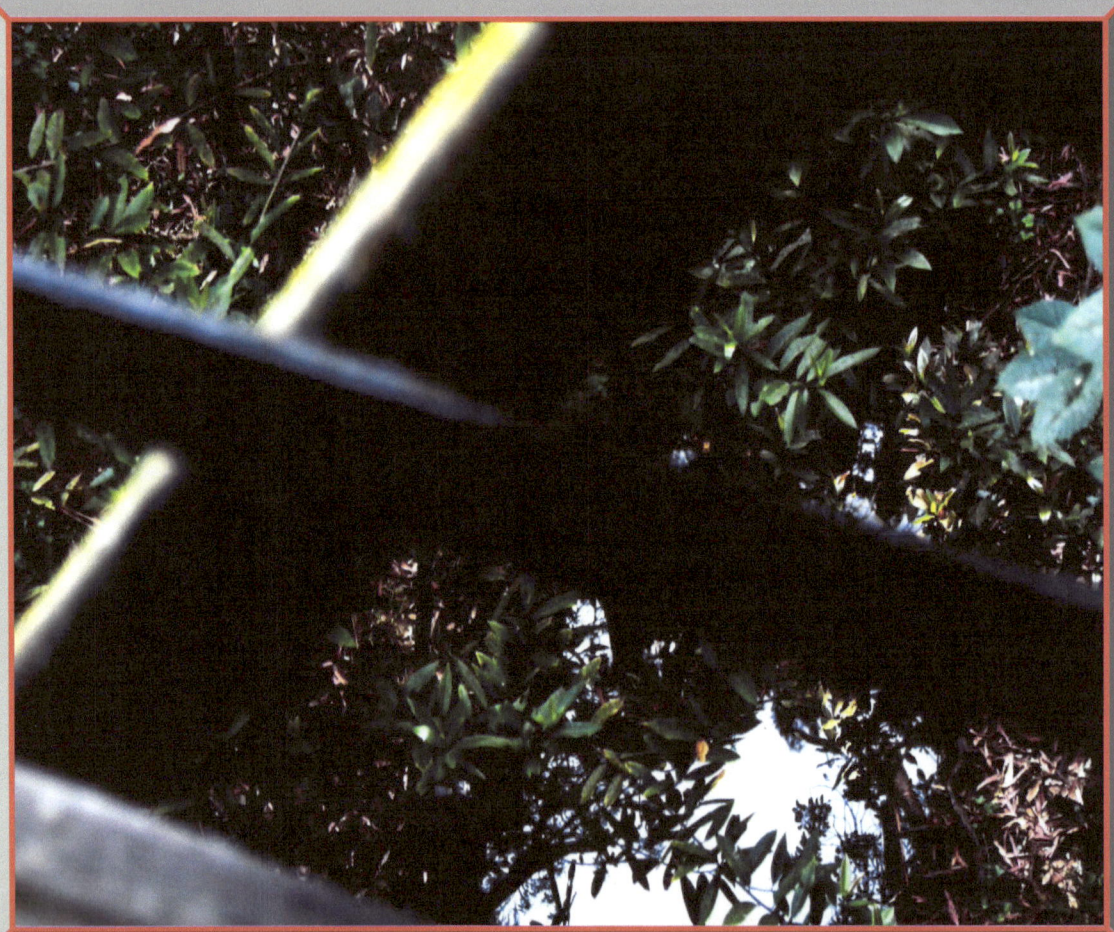

Plate 21

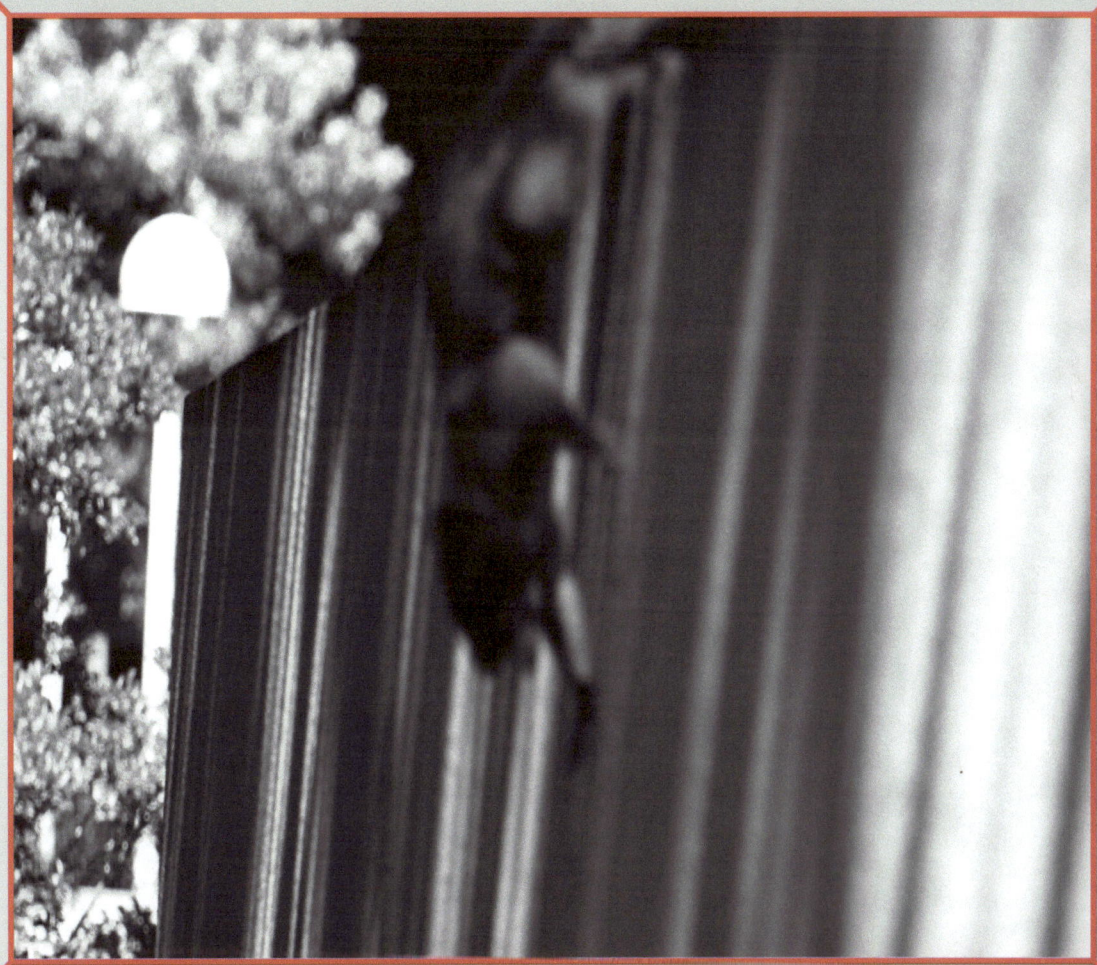

Plate 22

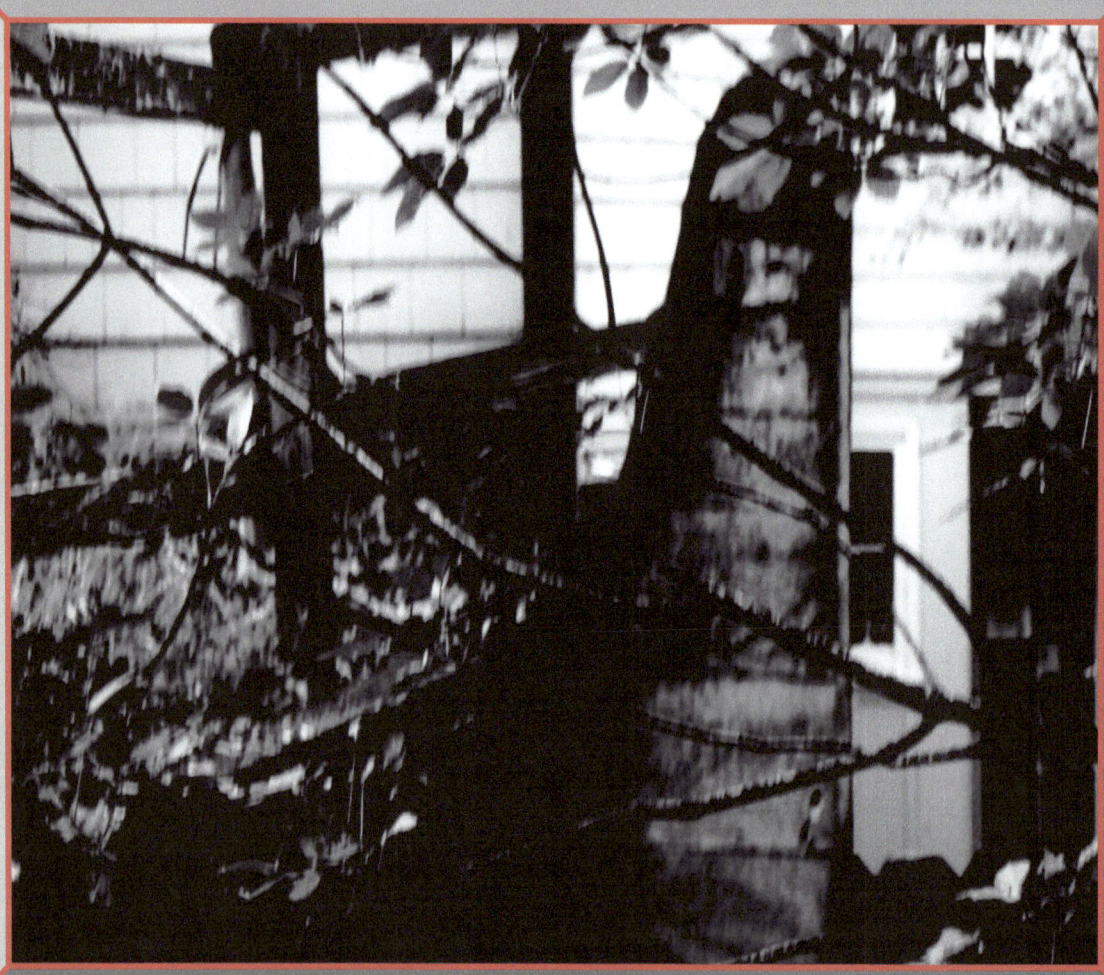

Plate 23

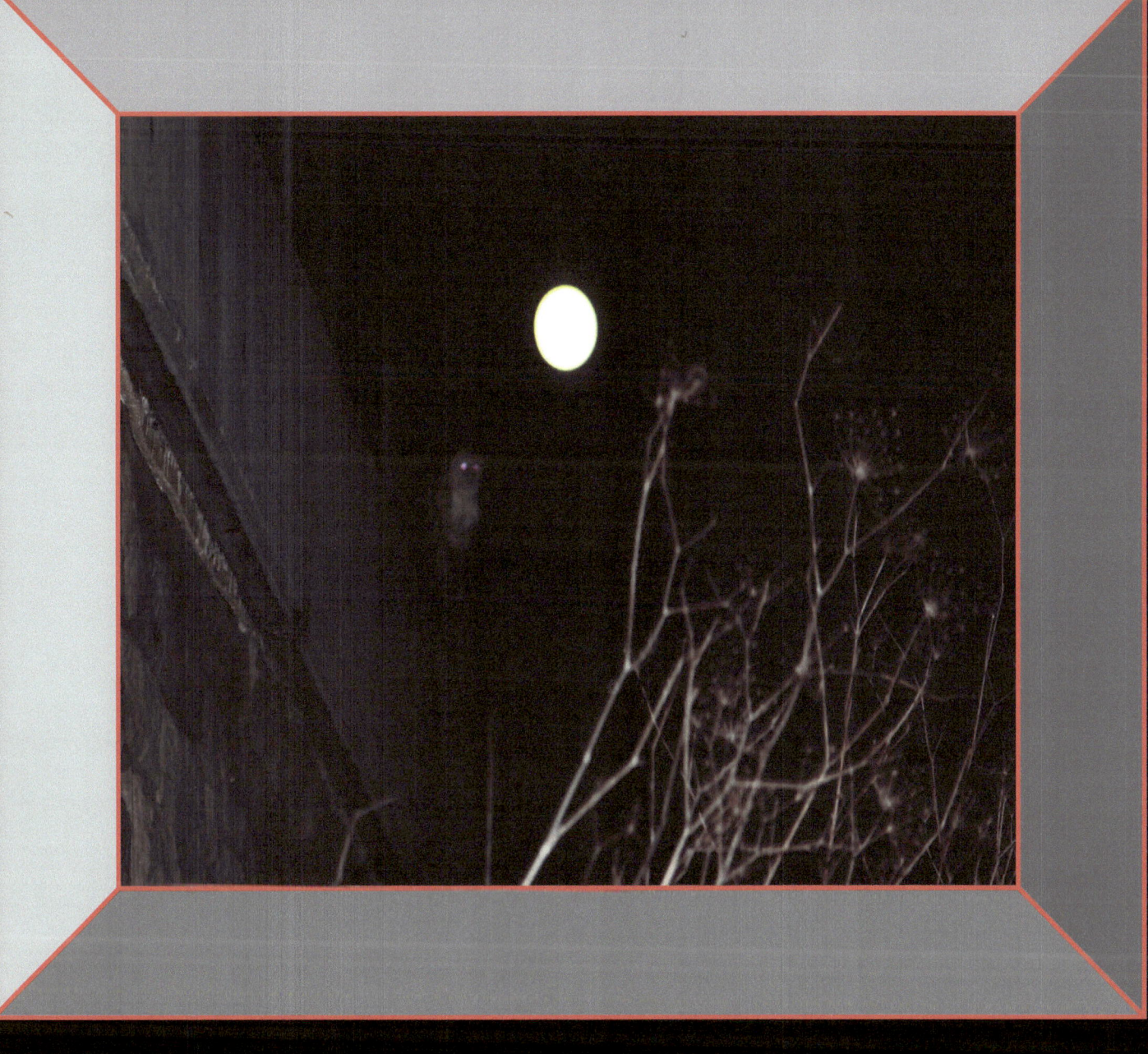

Plate 24

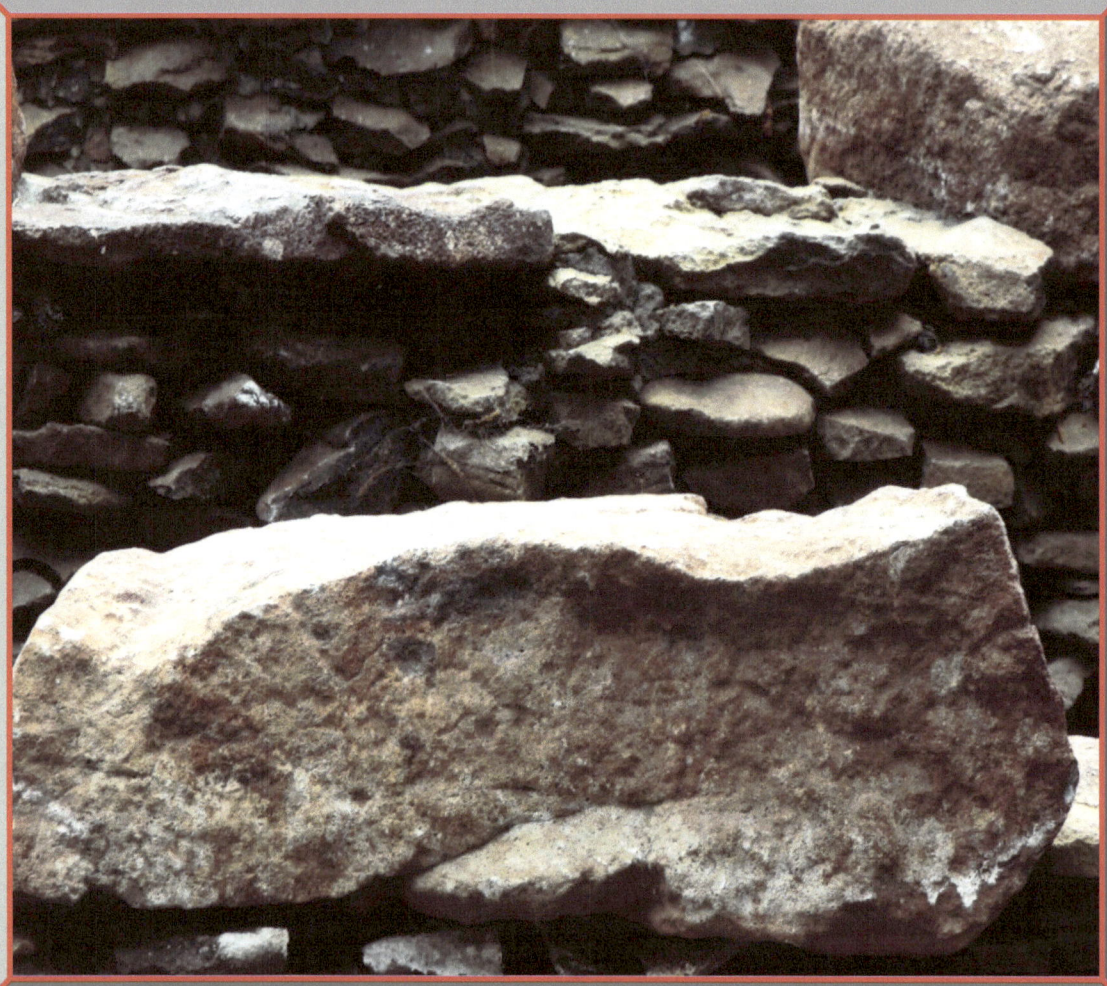

Plate 25

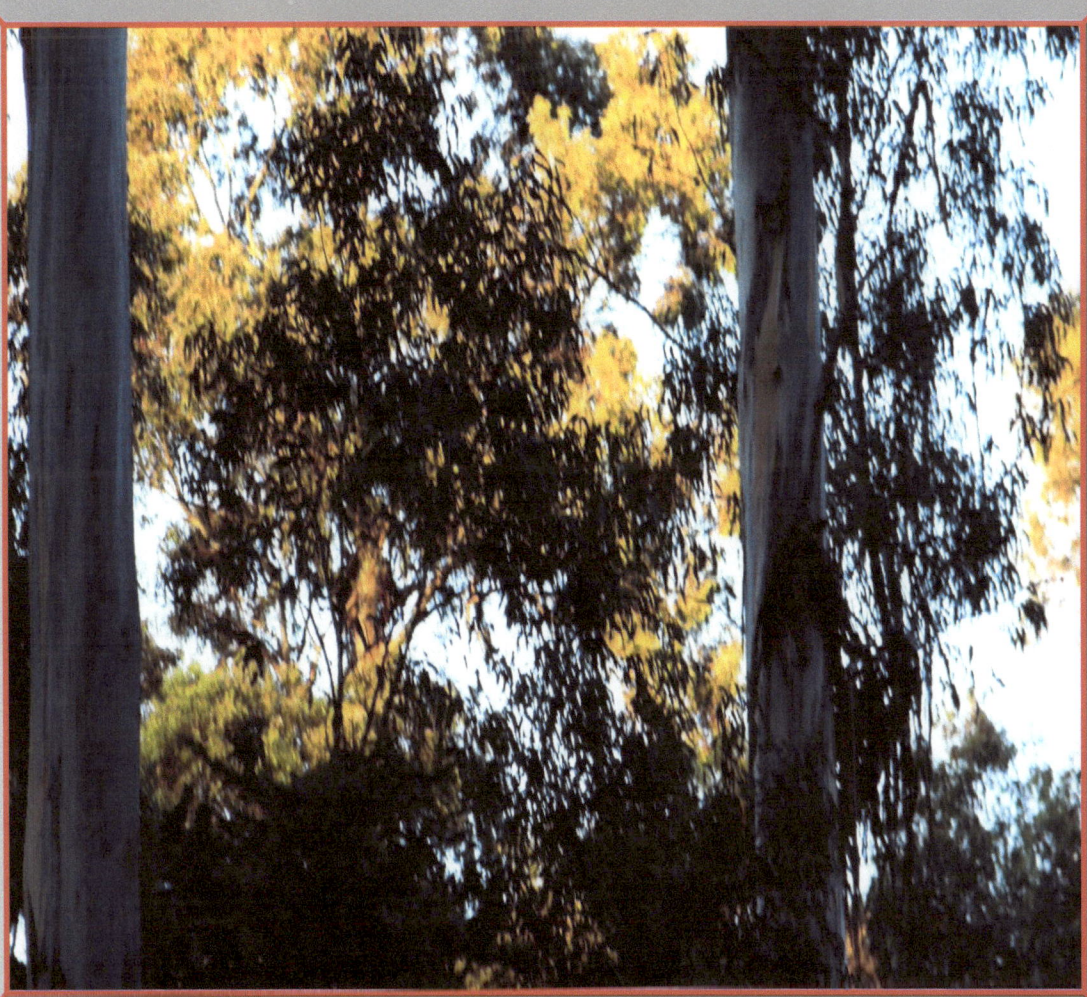

Plate 26

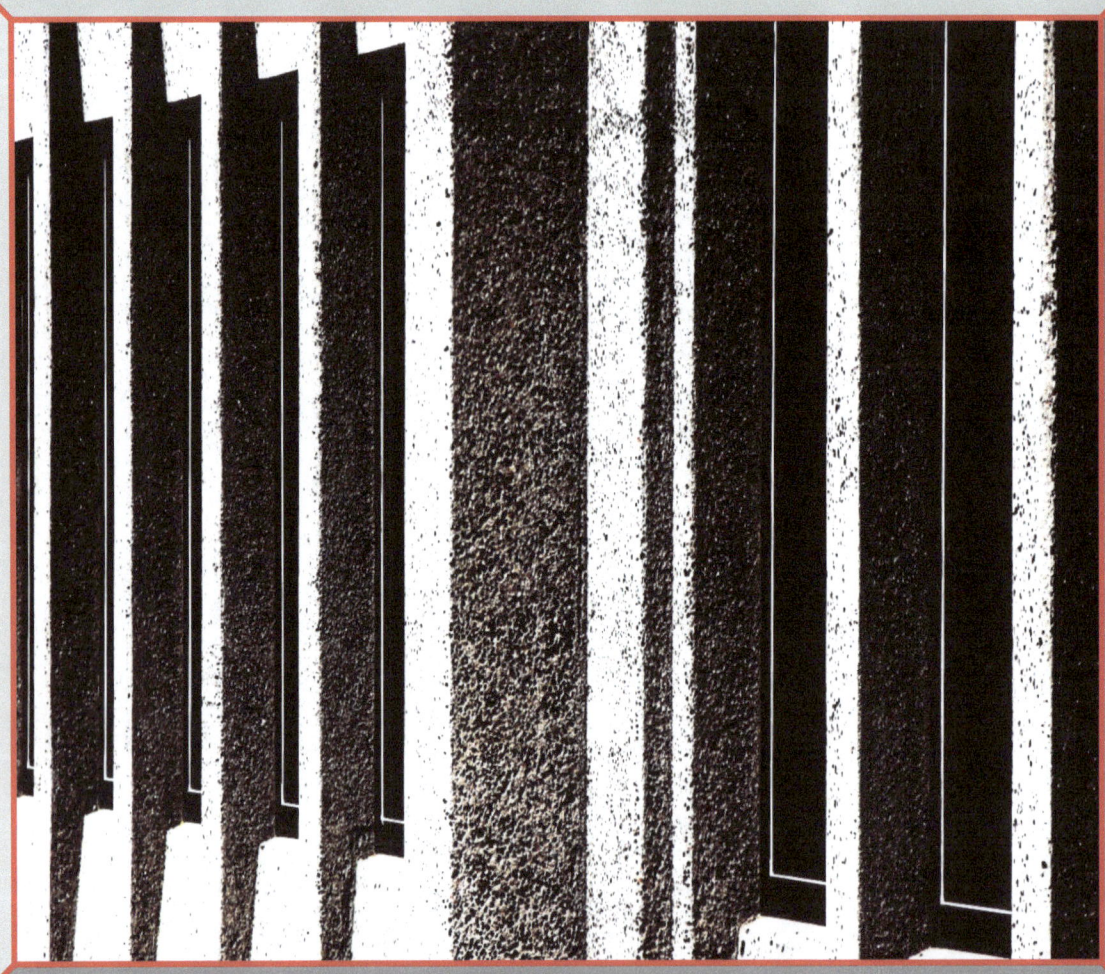

Plate 27

Dances
with
LIGHT

Dance No. 1

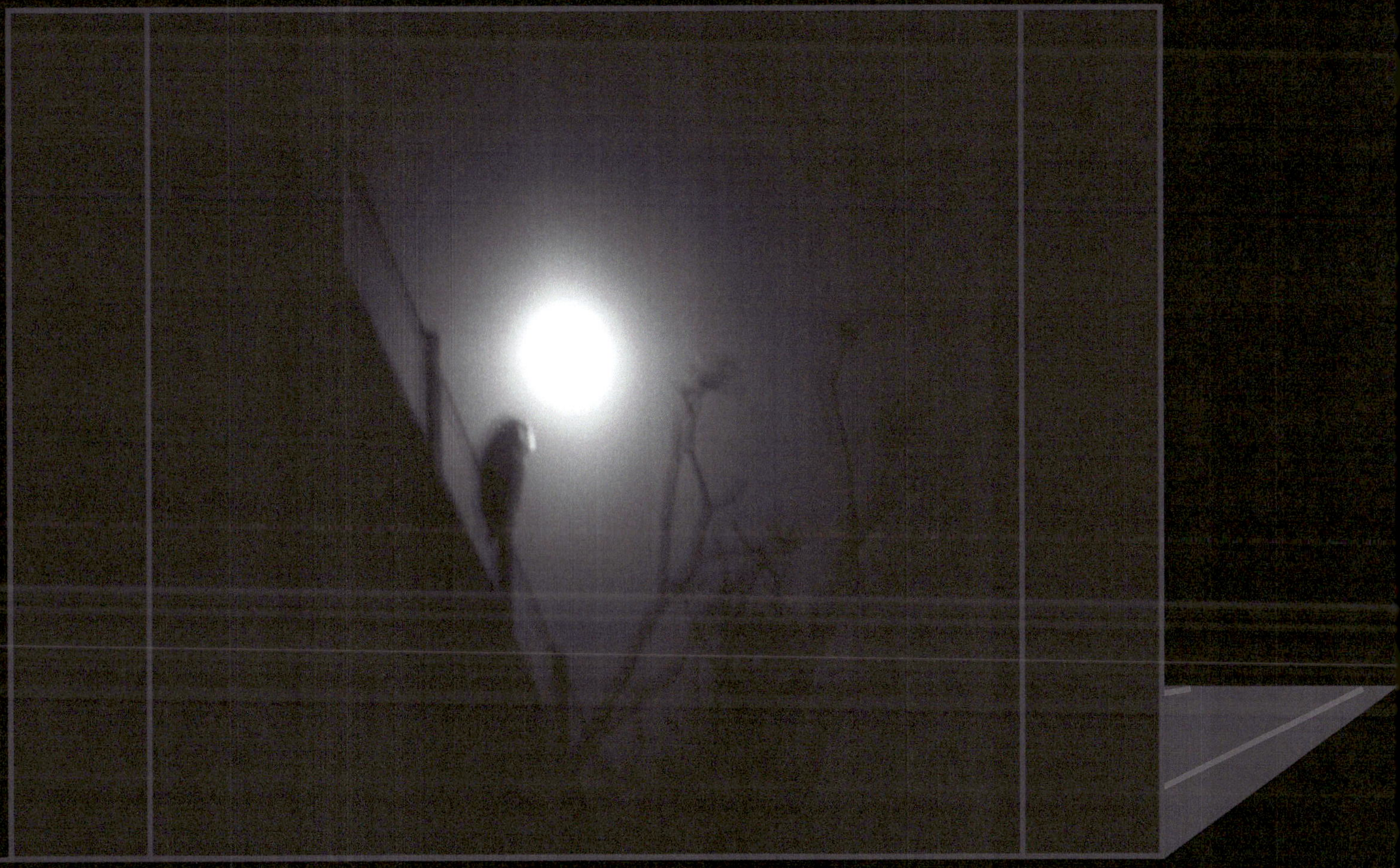

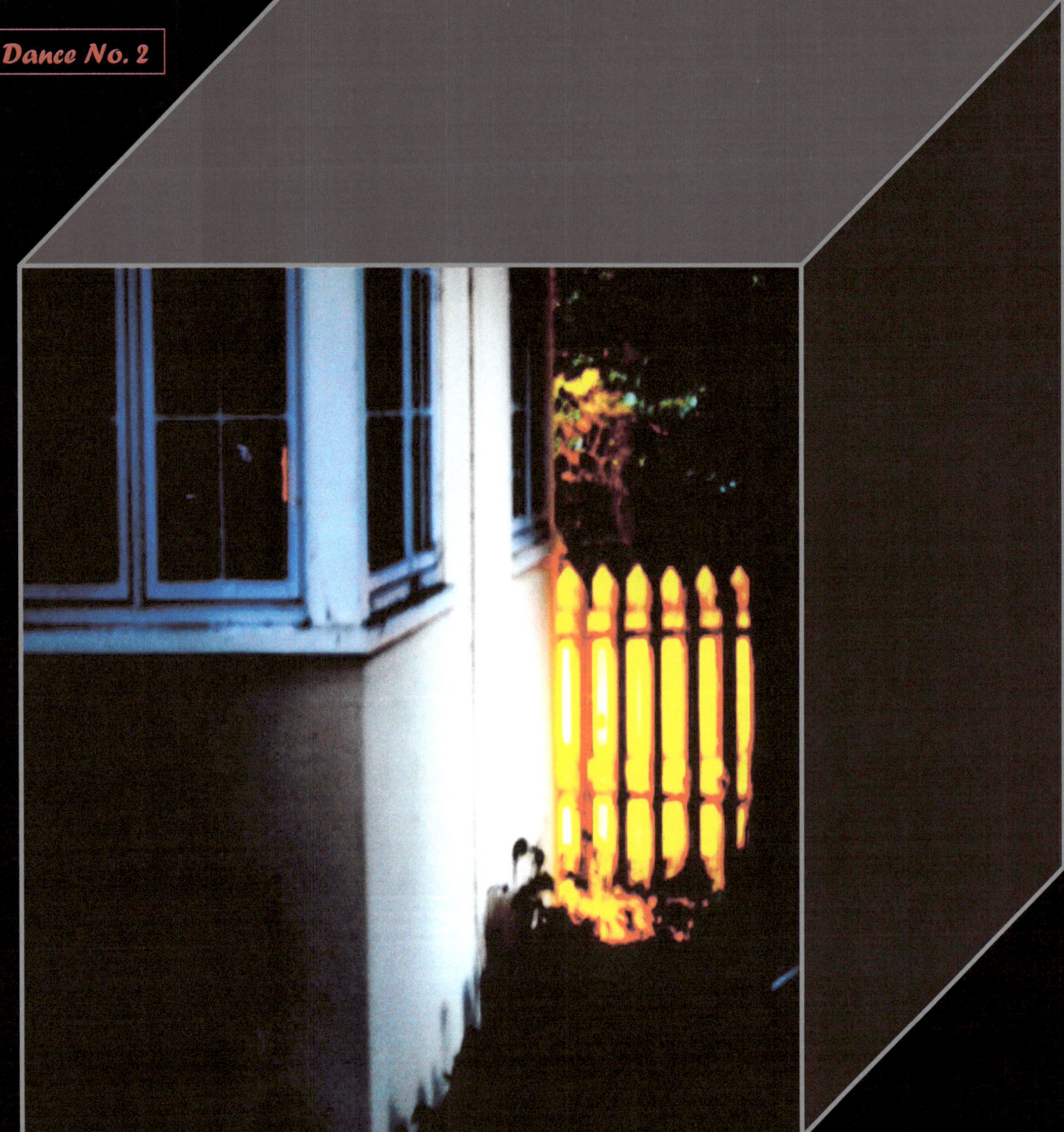

Dance No. 2

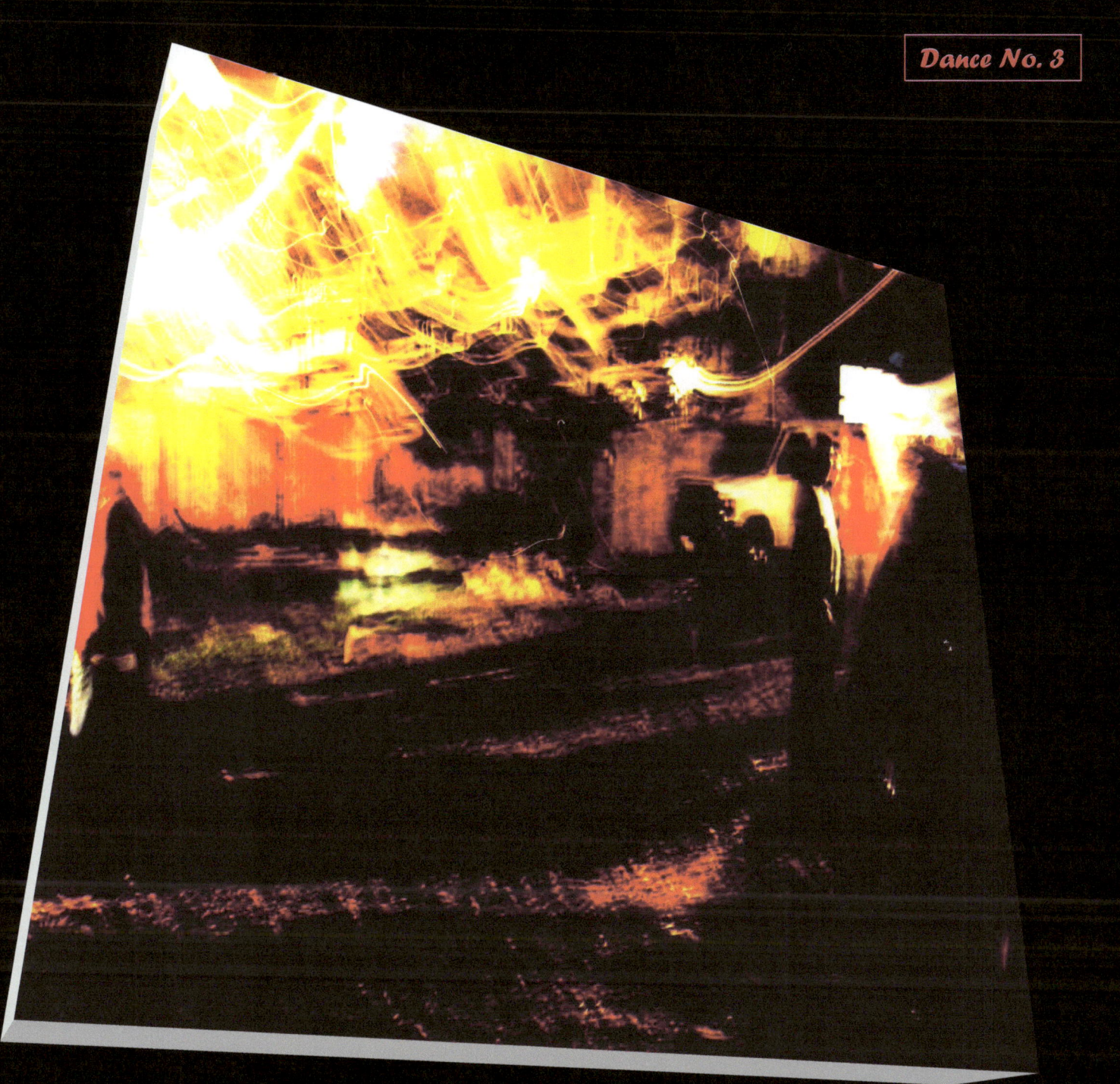

Dance No. 3

Dance No. 4

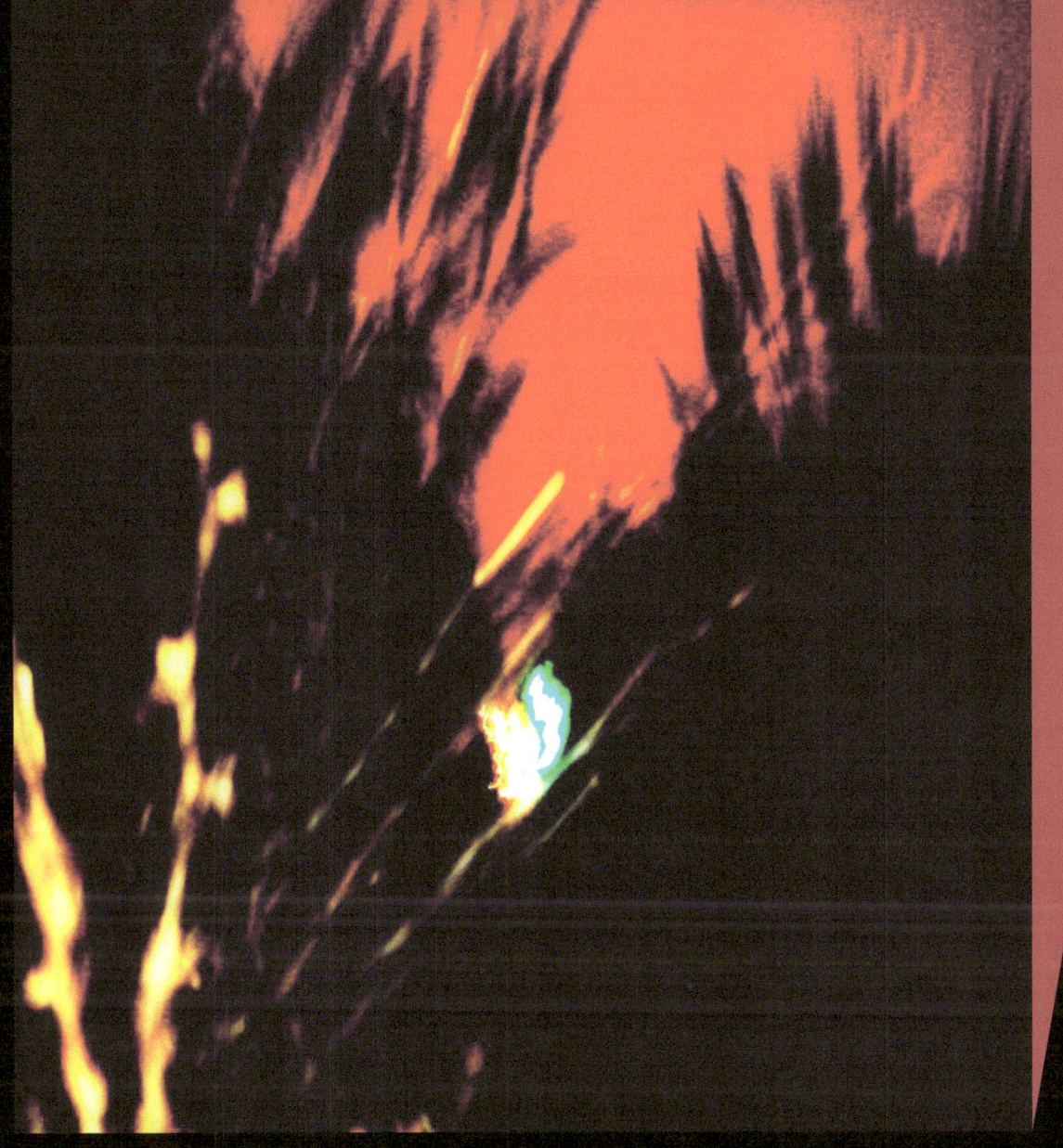

Dance No. 6

Dance No. 7

Dance No. 8

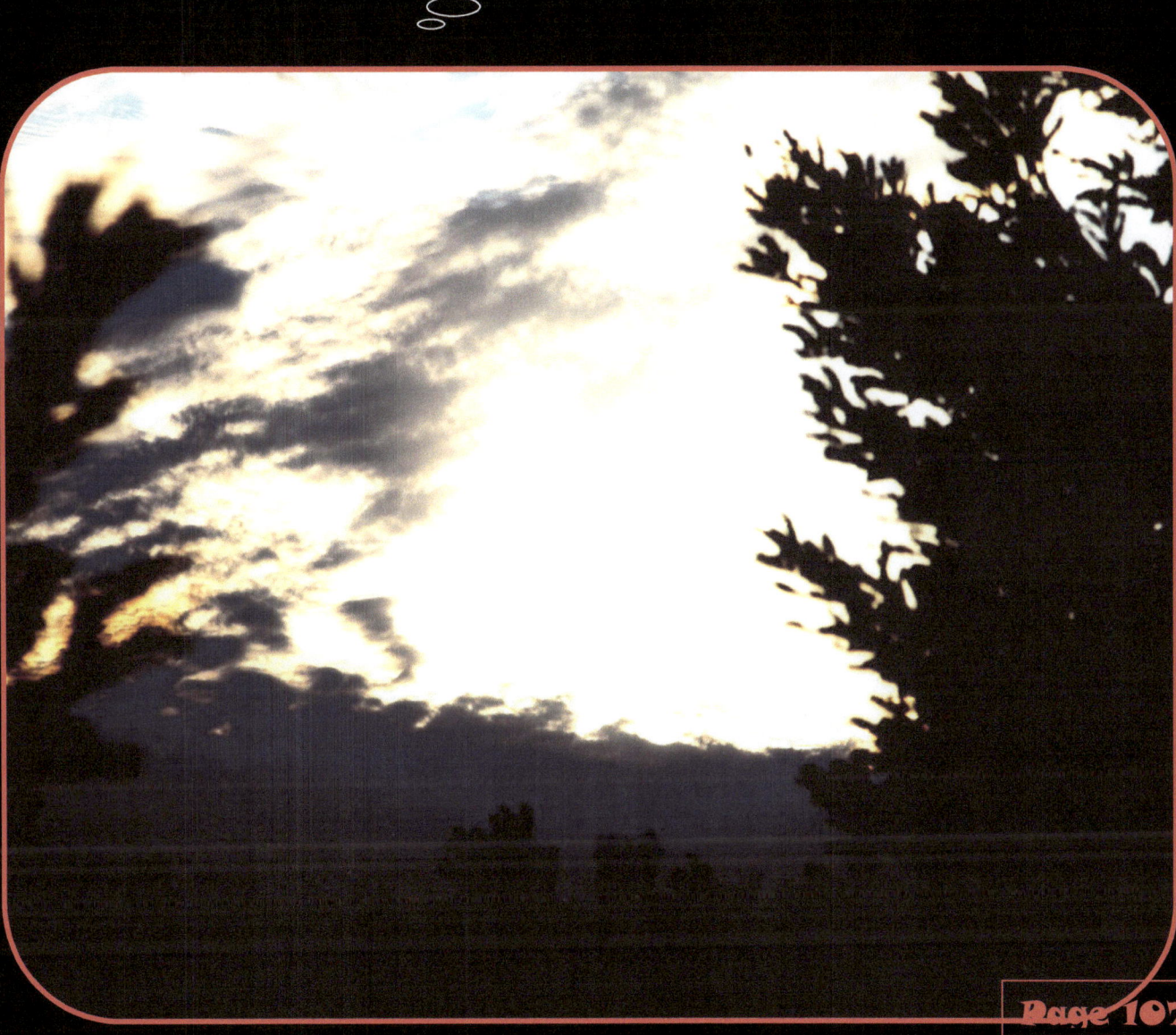

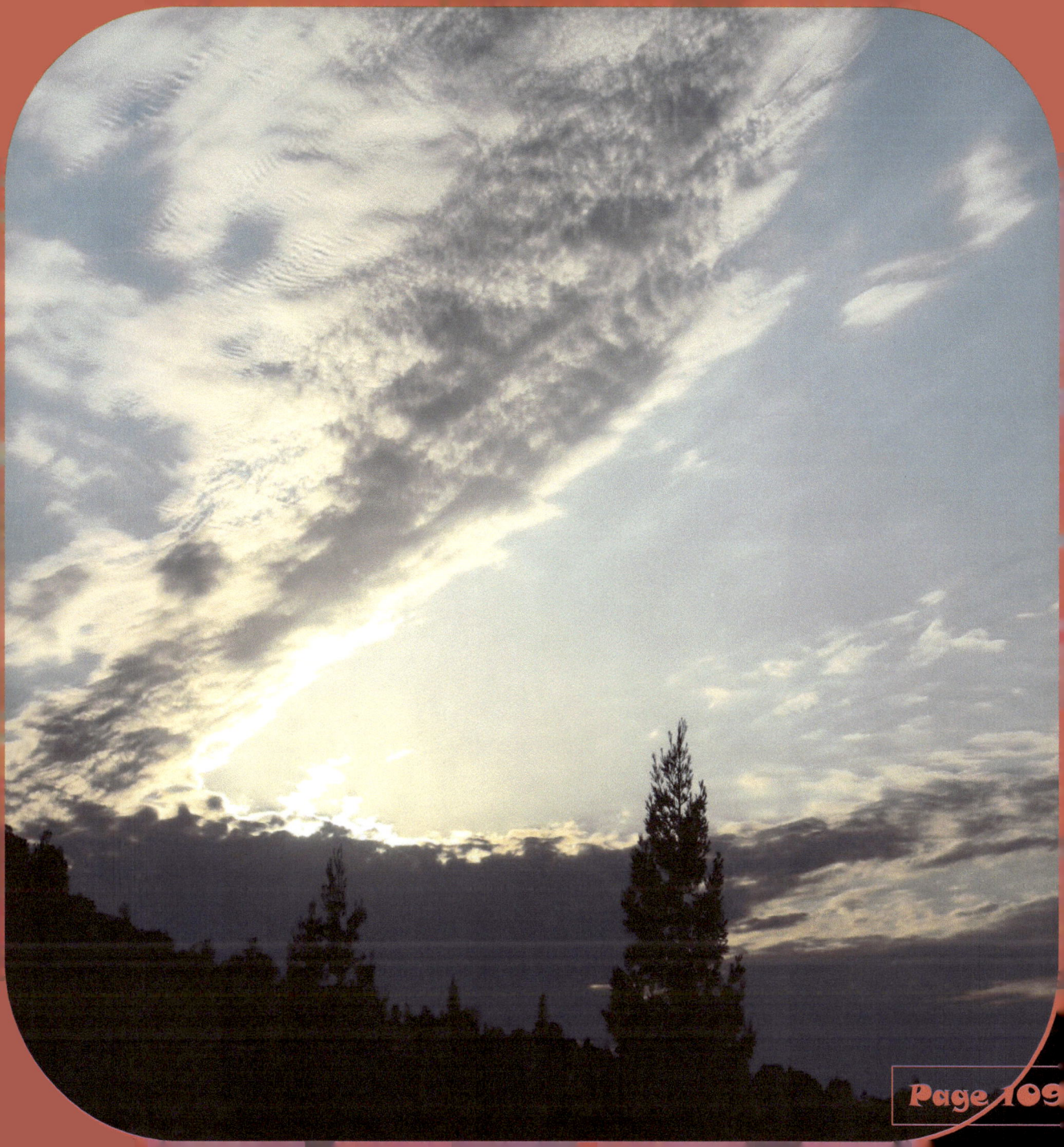

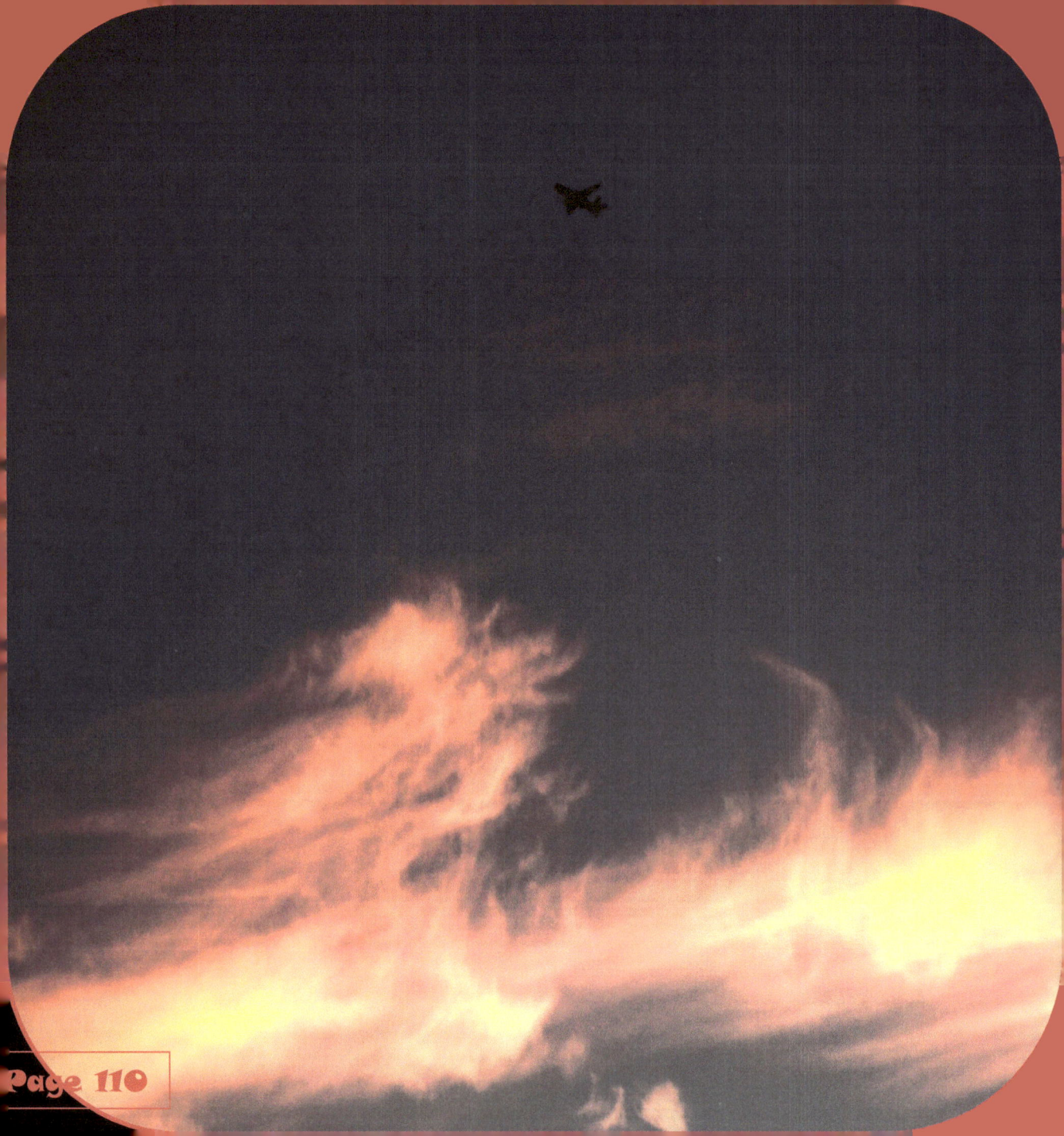

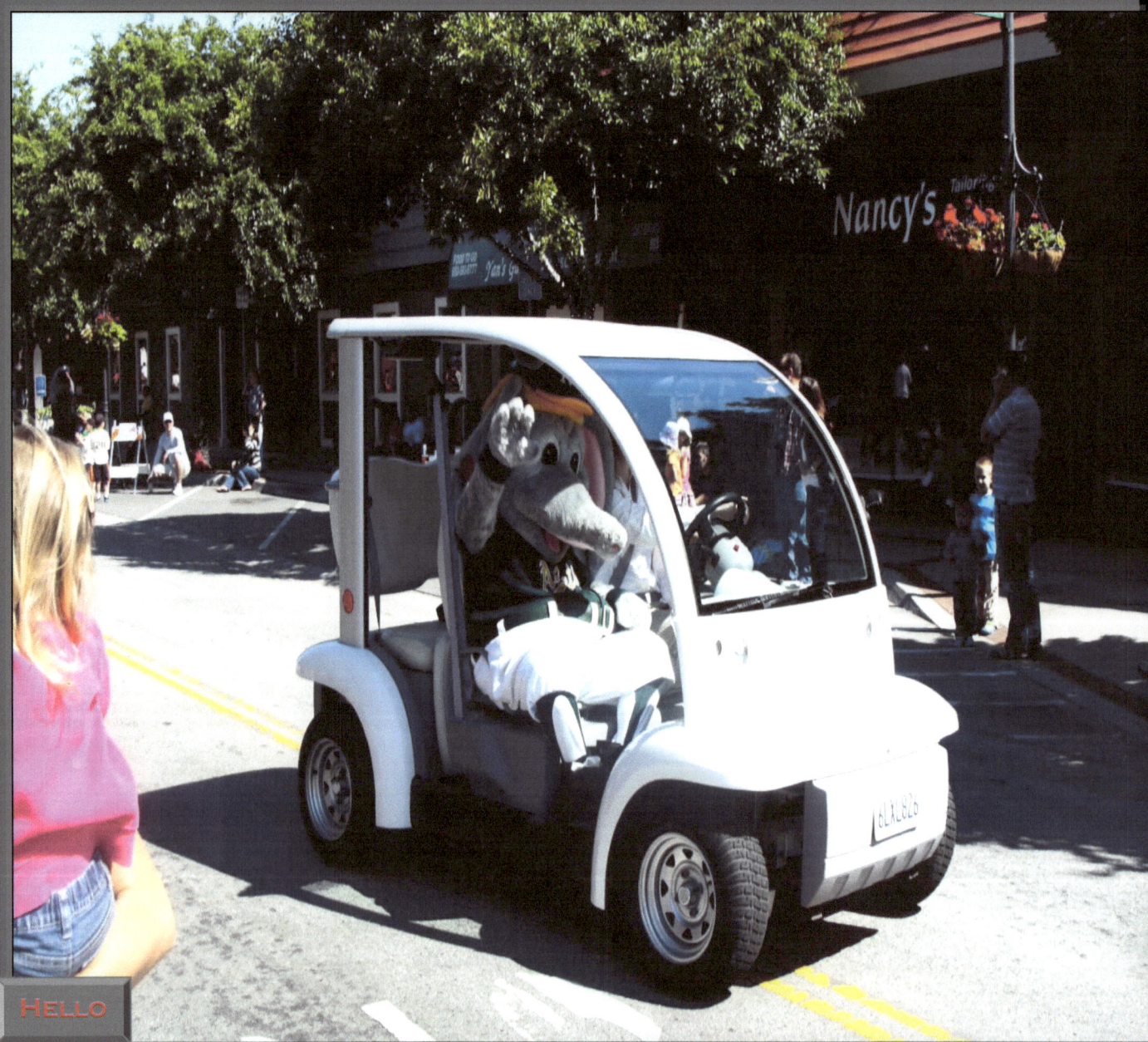

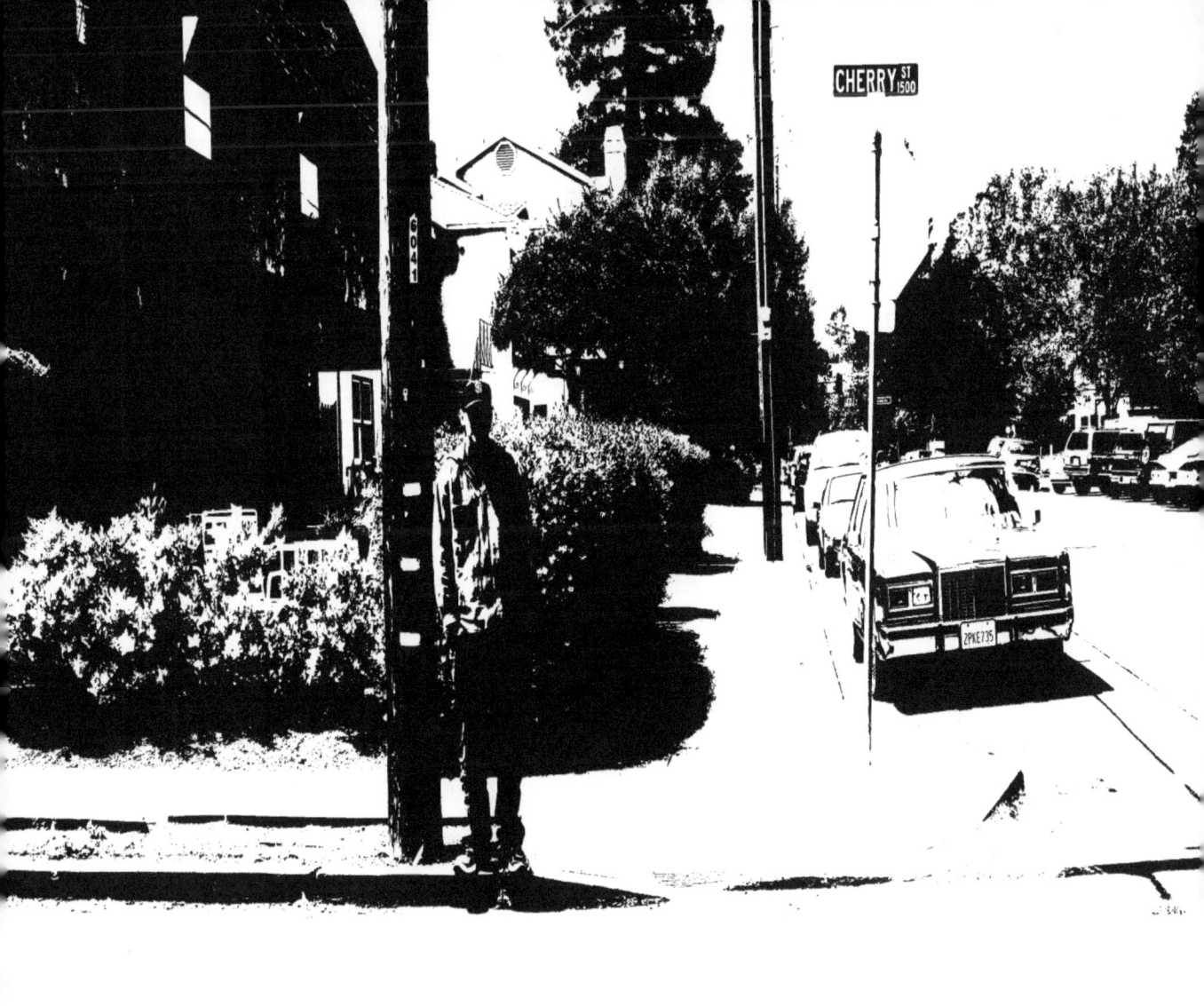

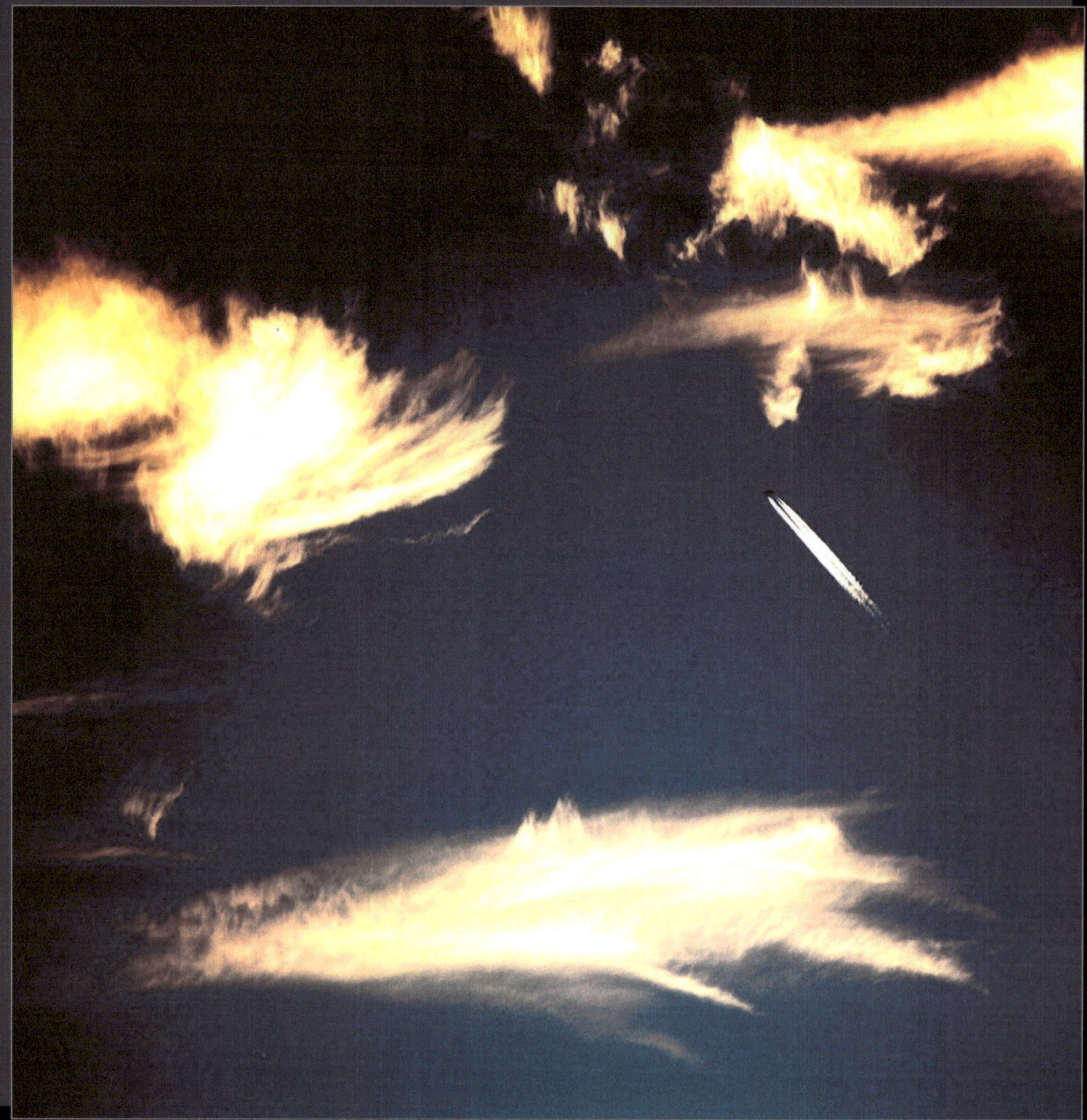

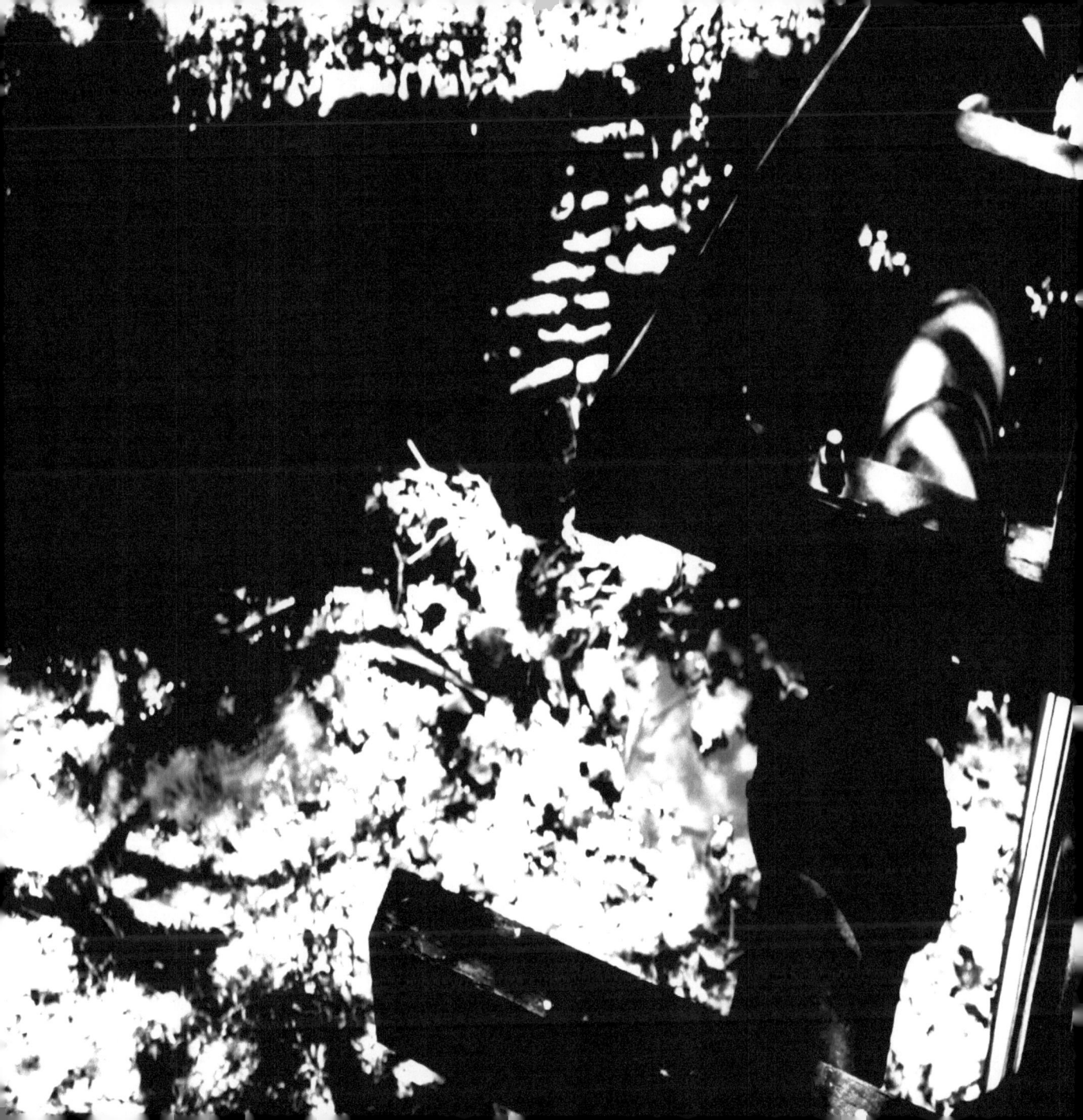

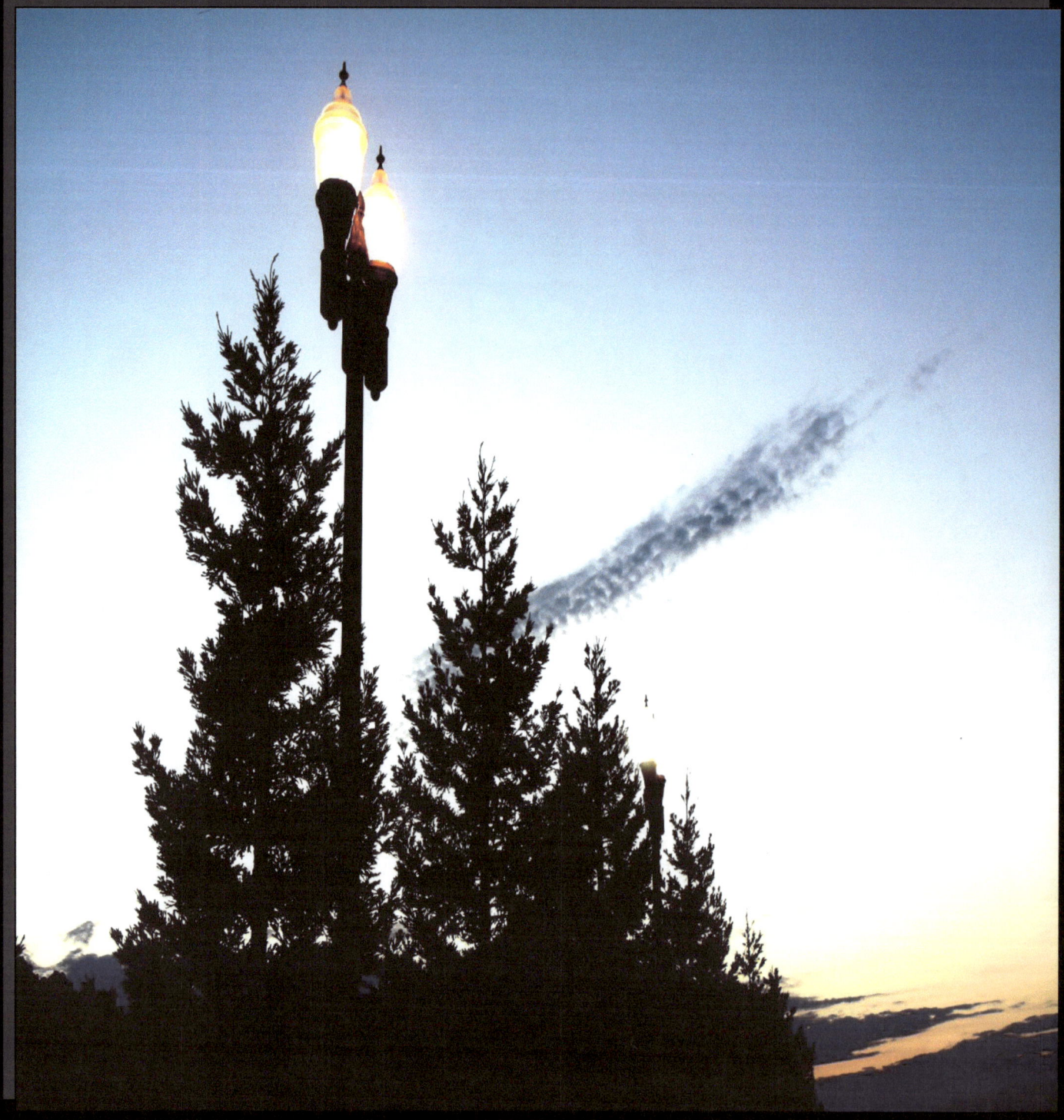

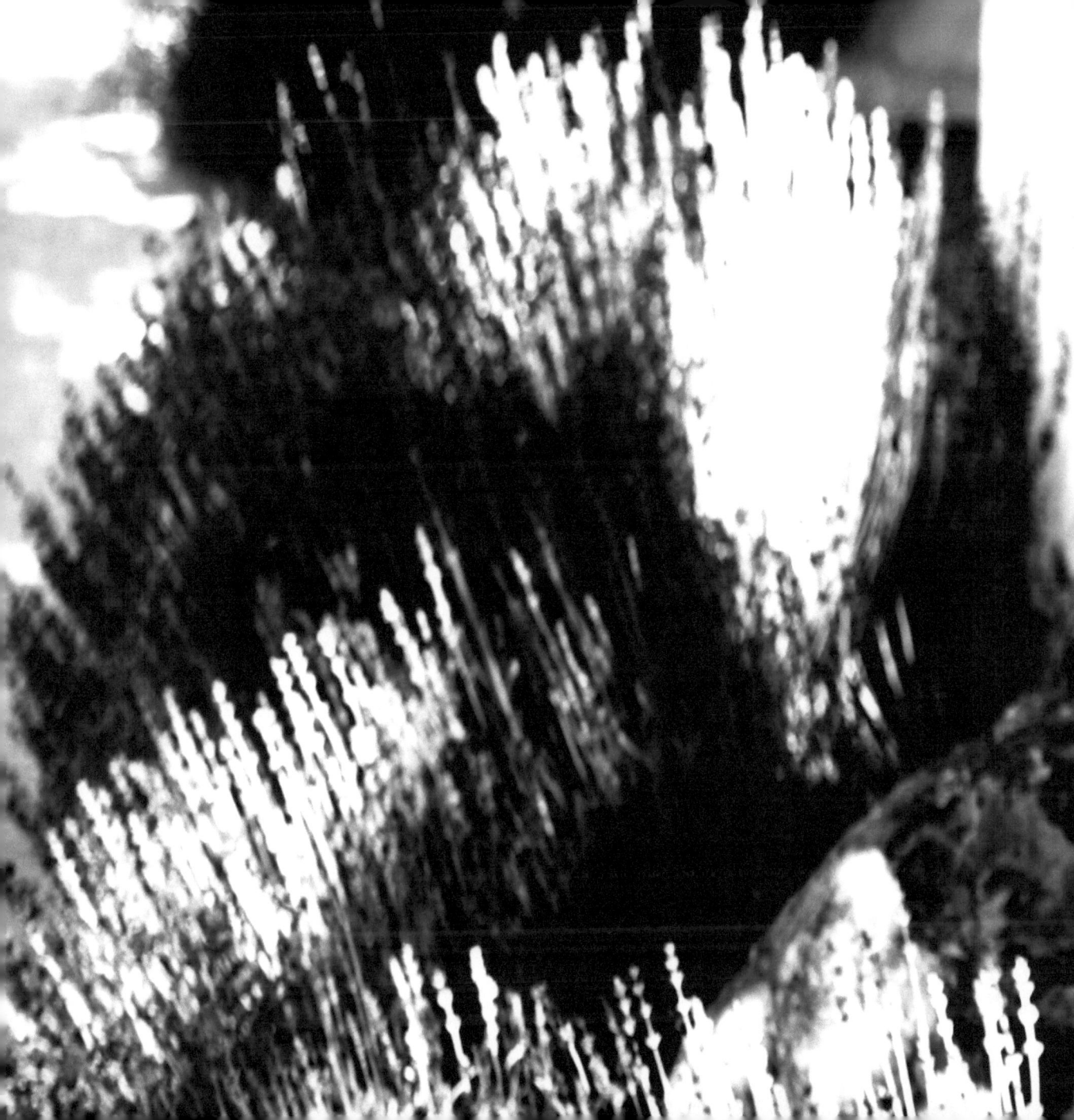

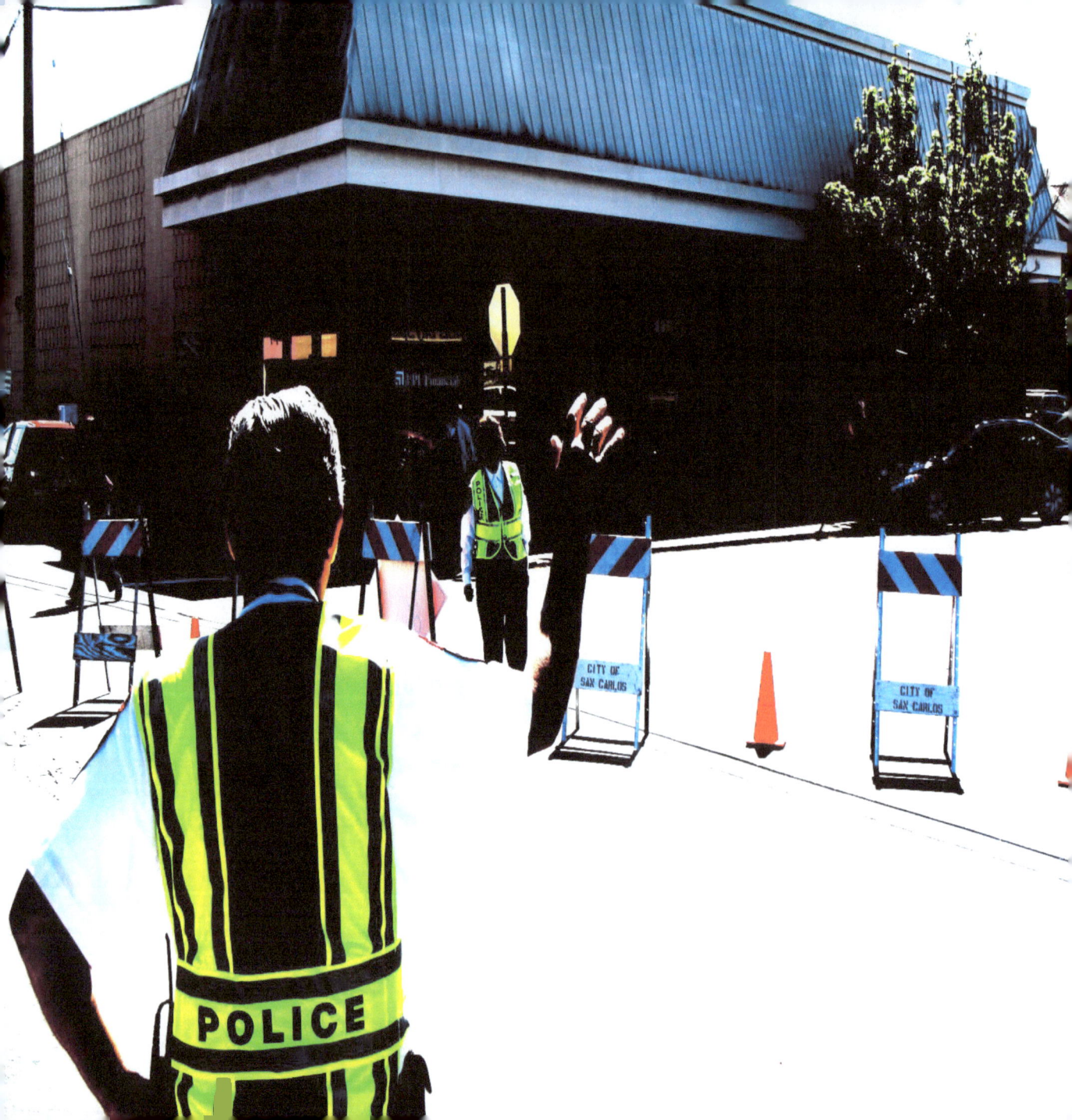

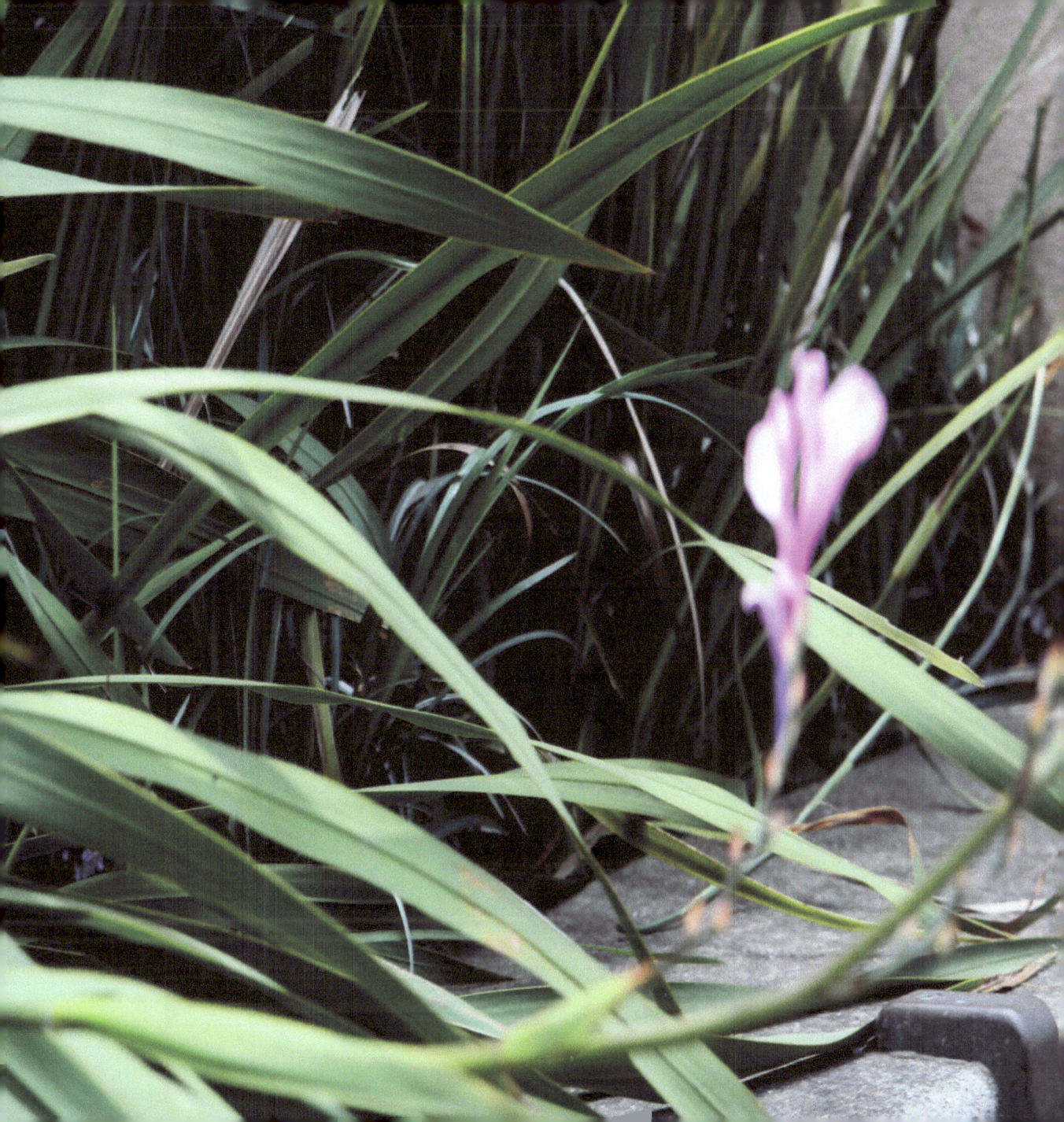

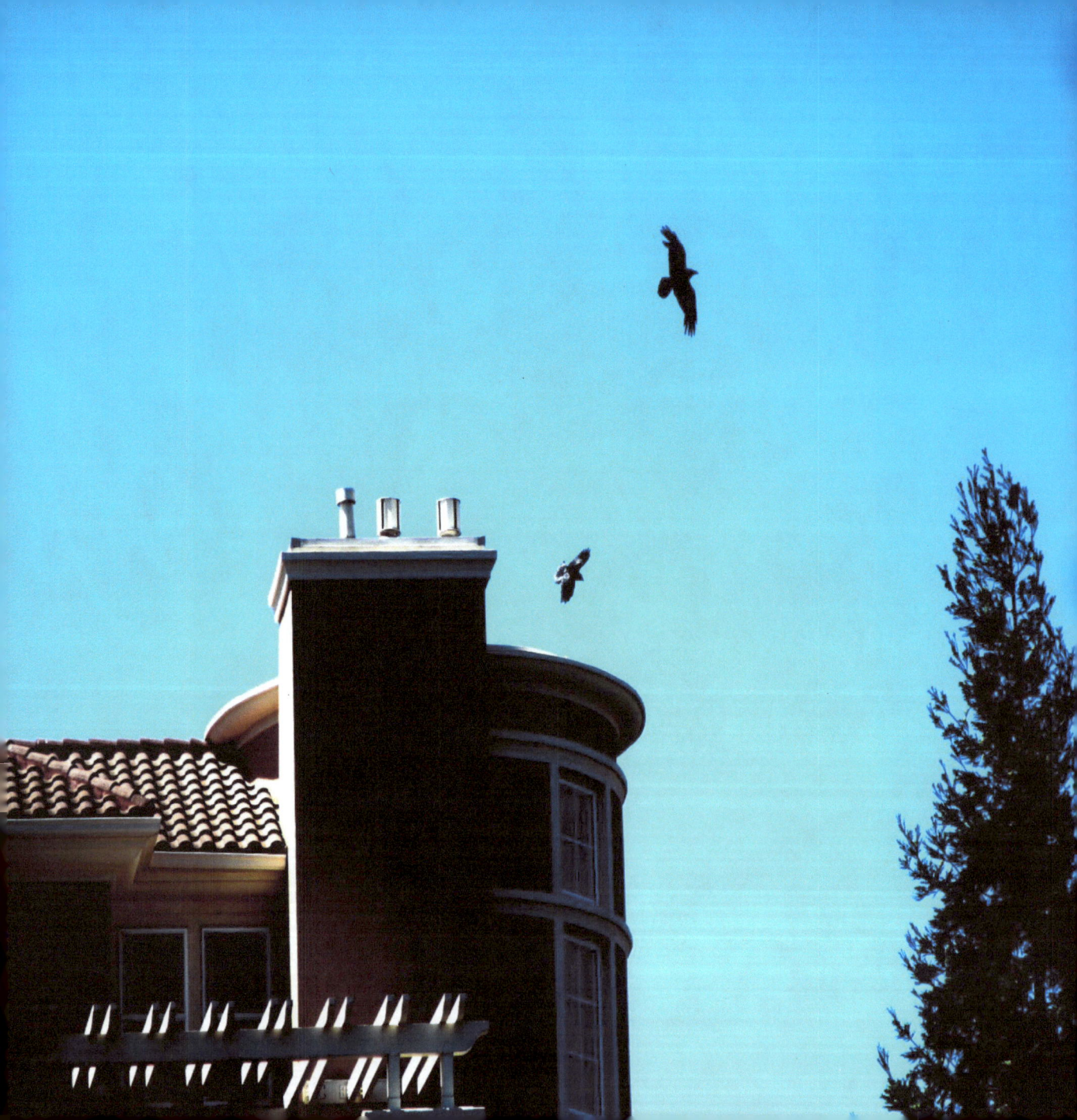

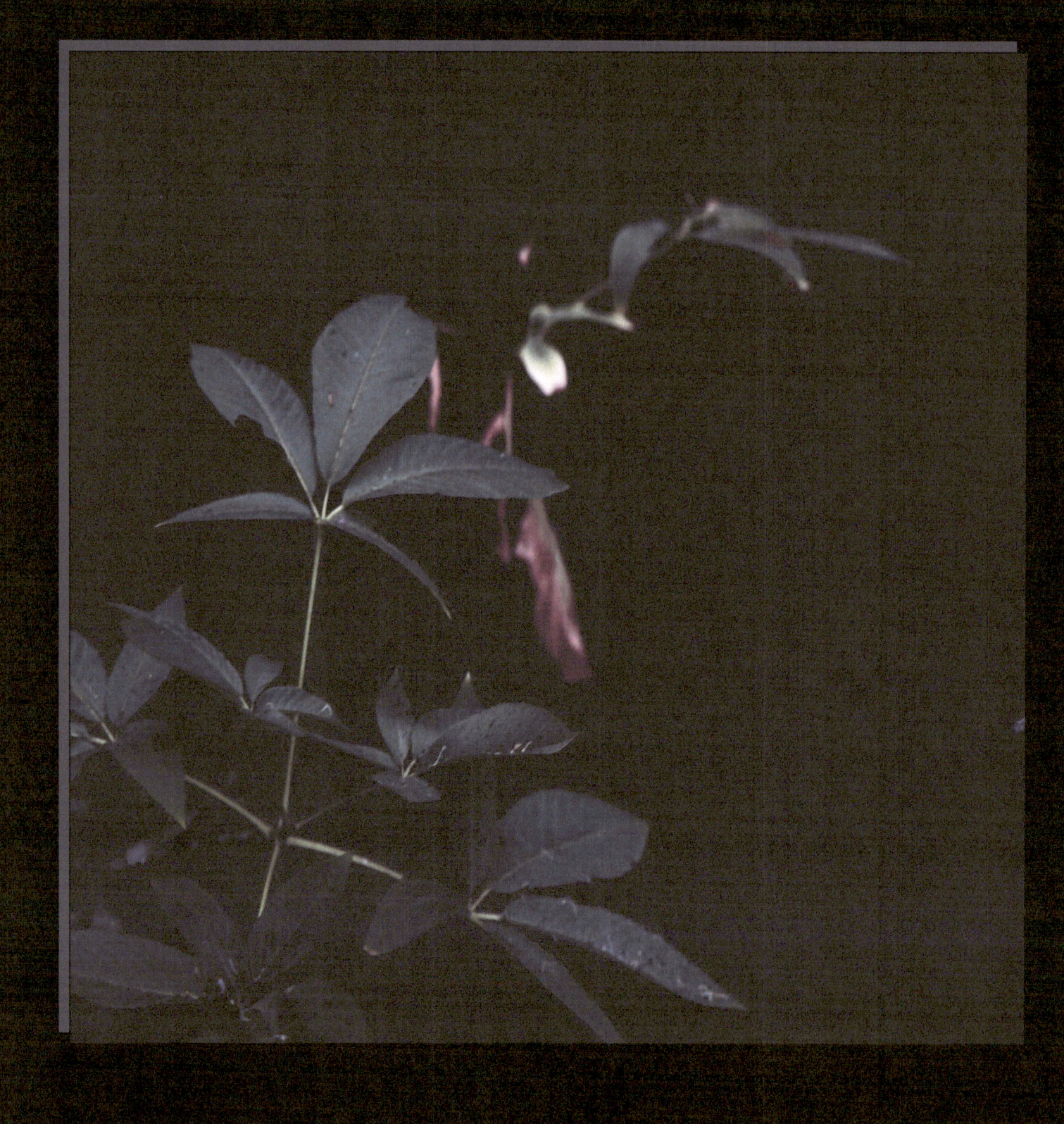

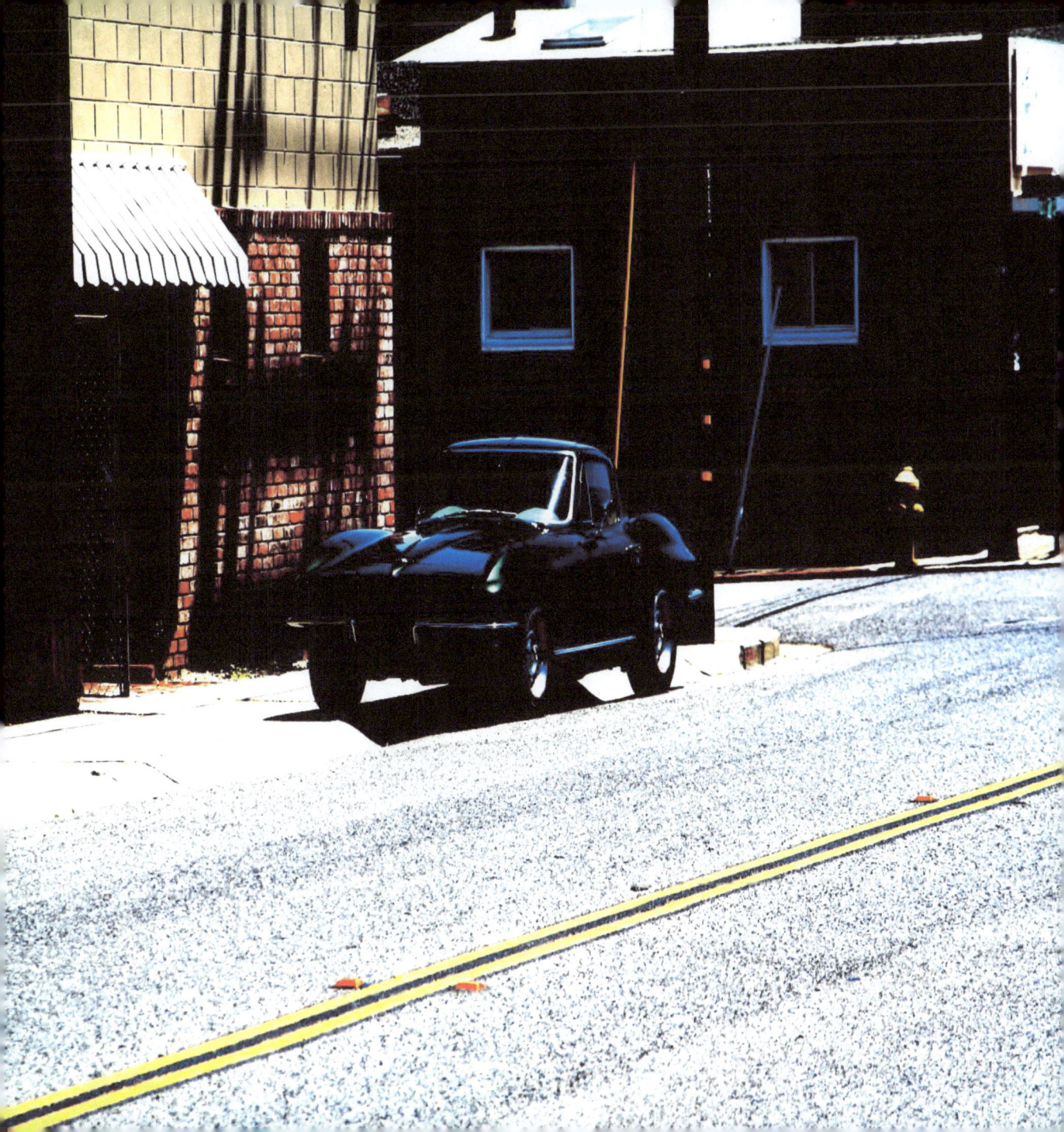

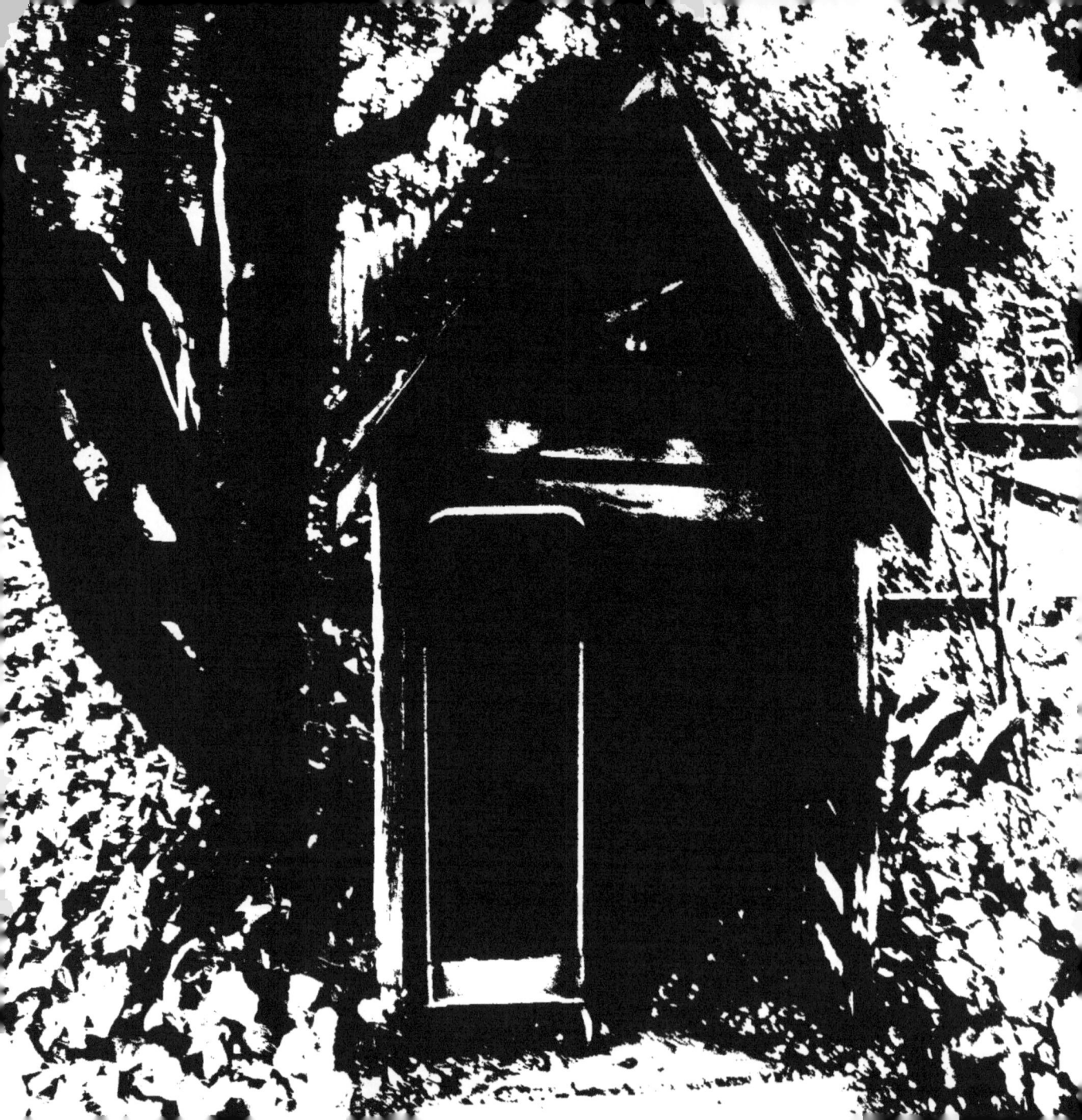

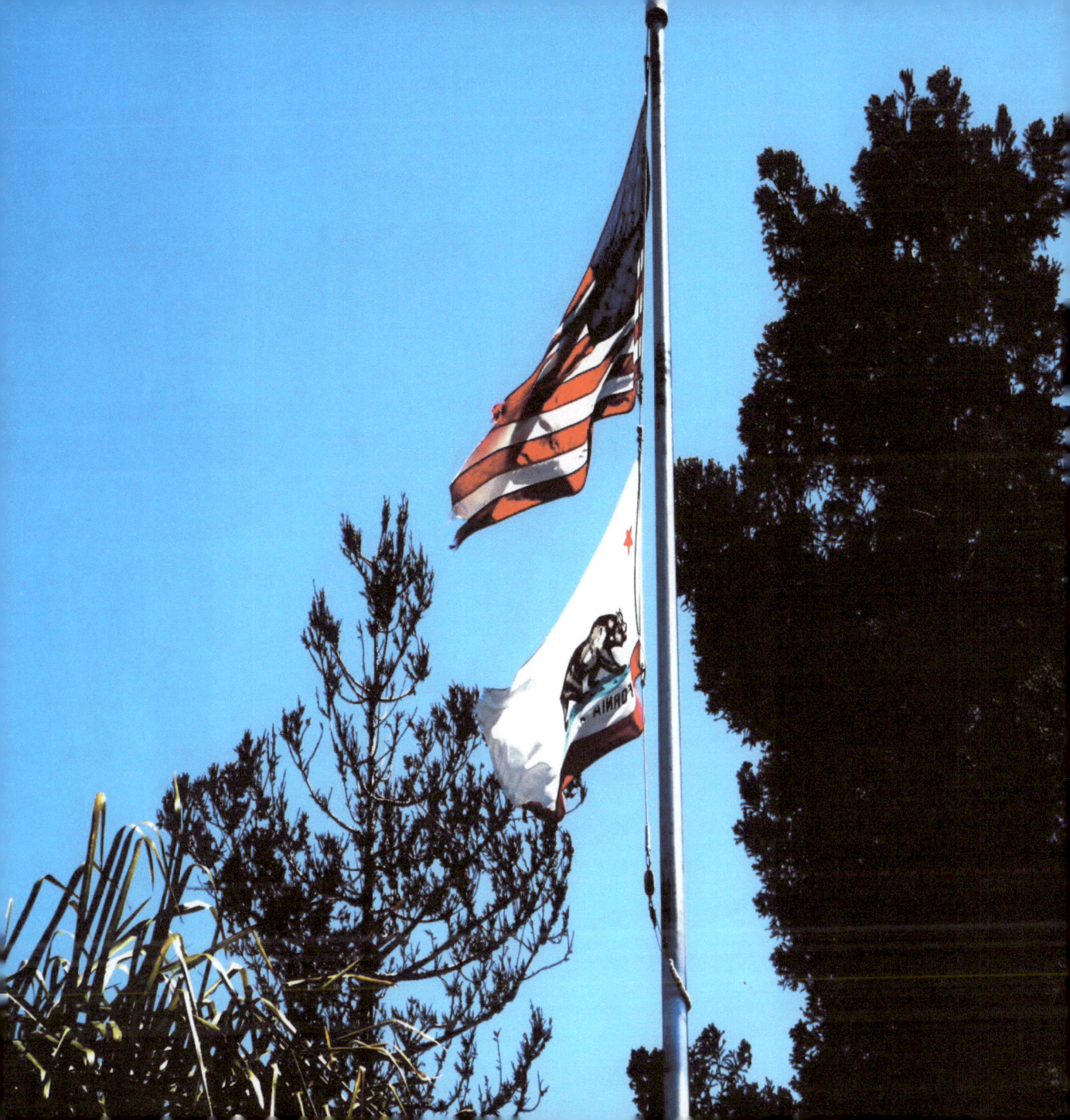

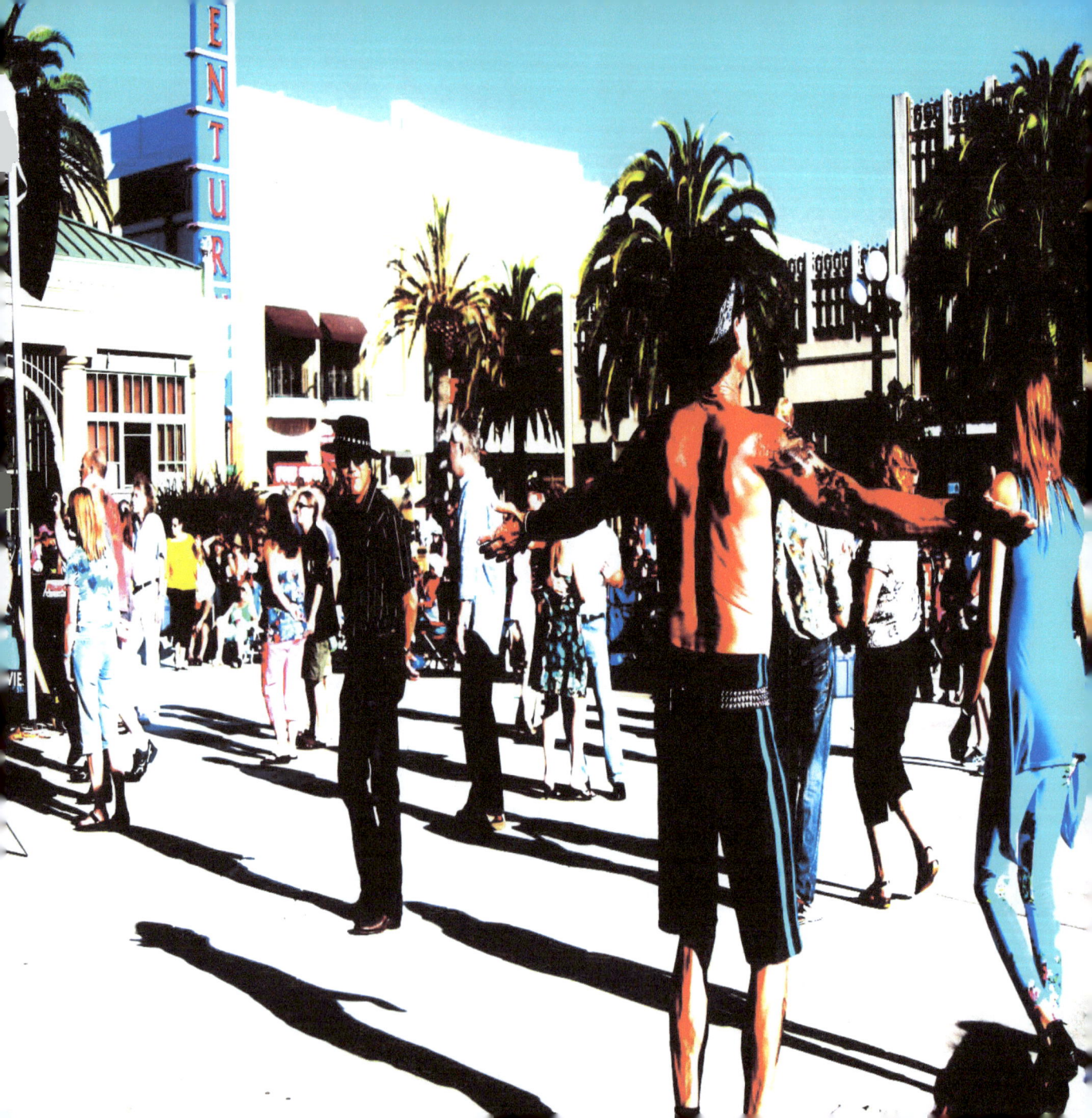

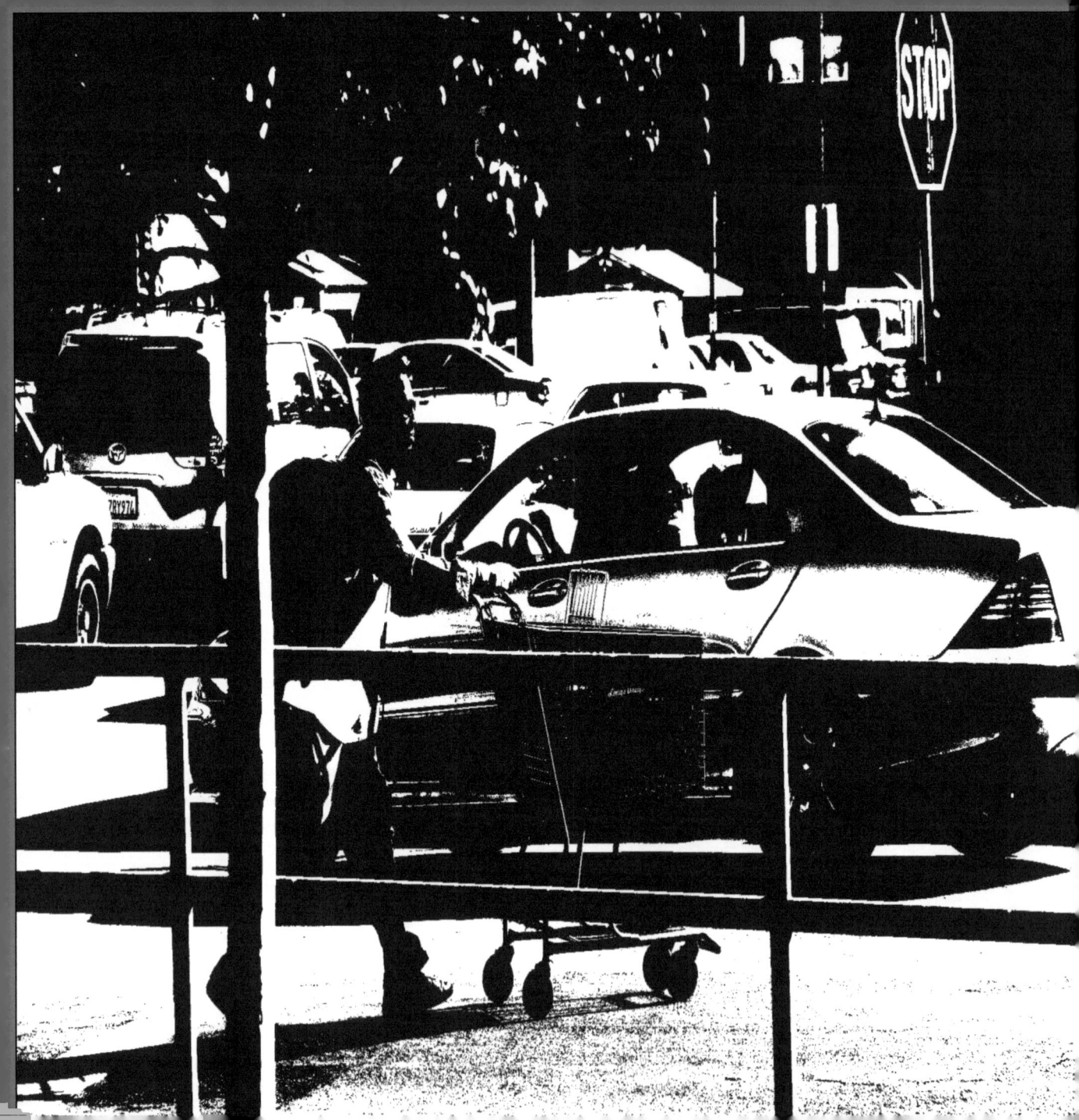

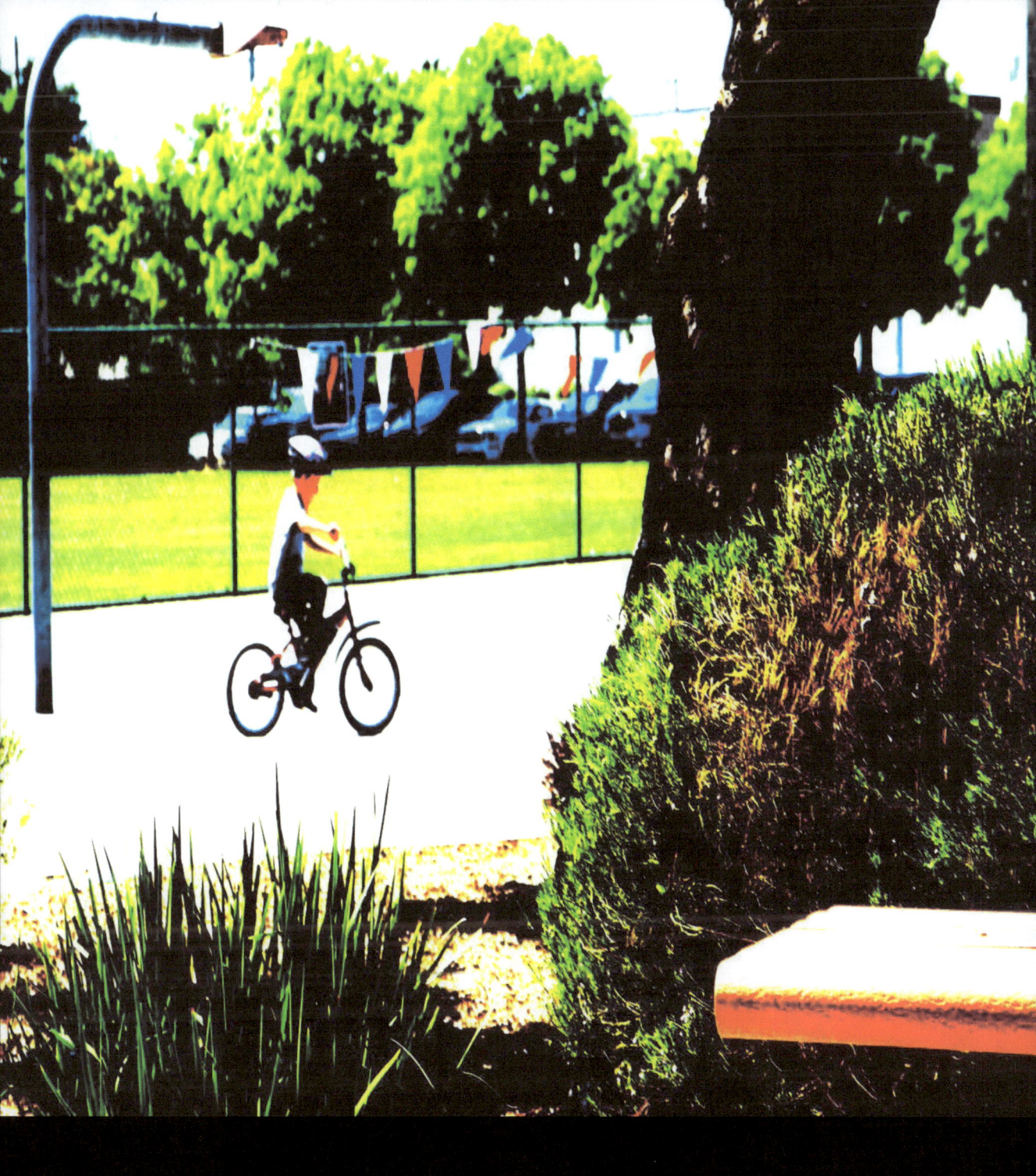

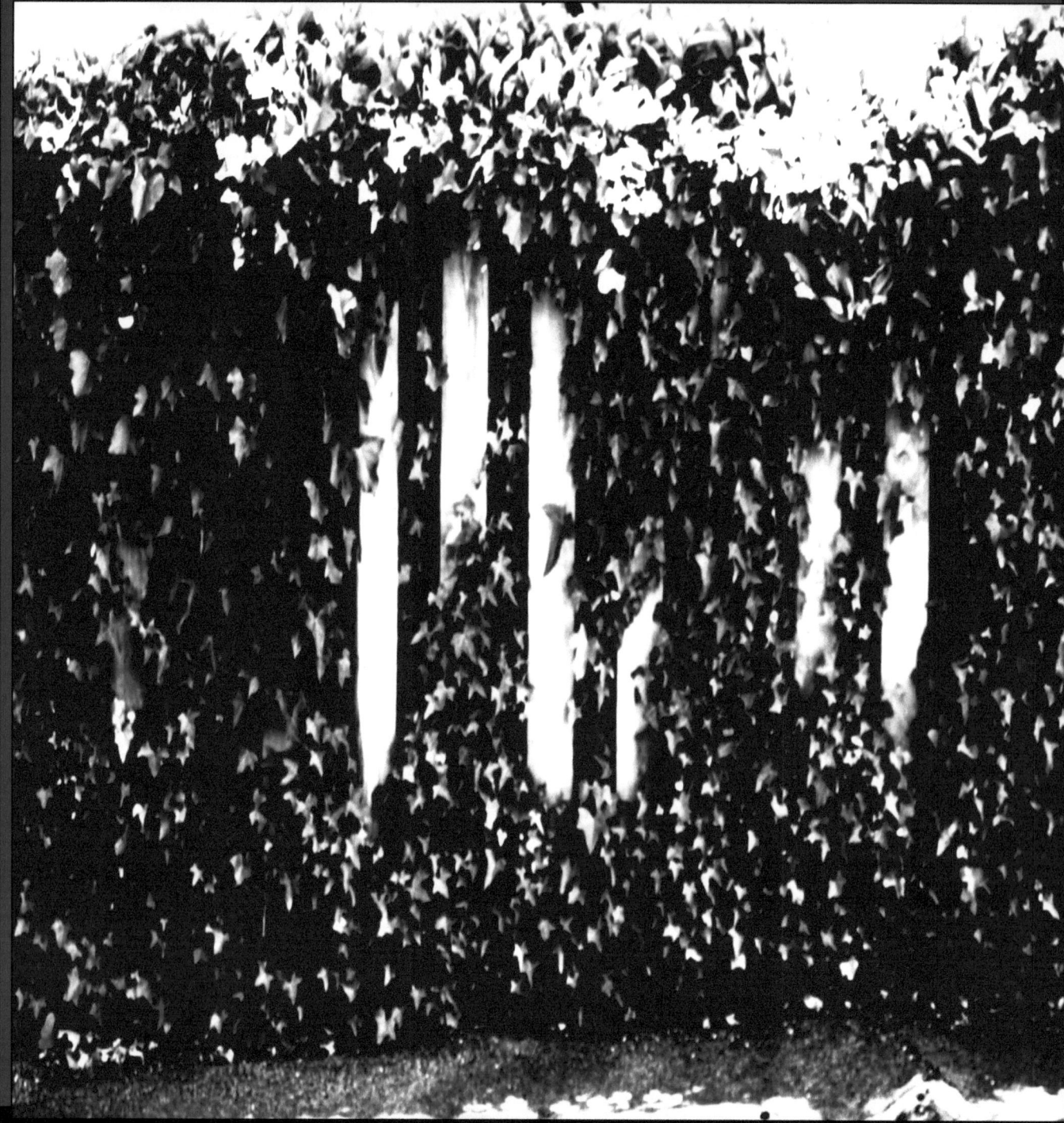

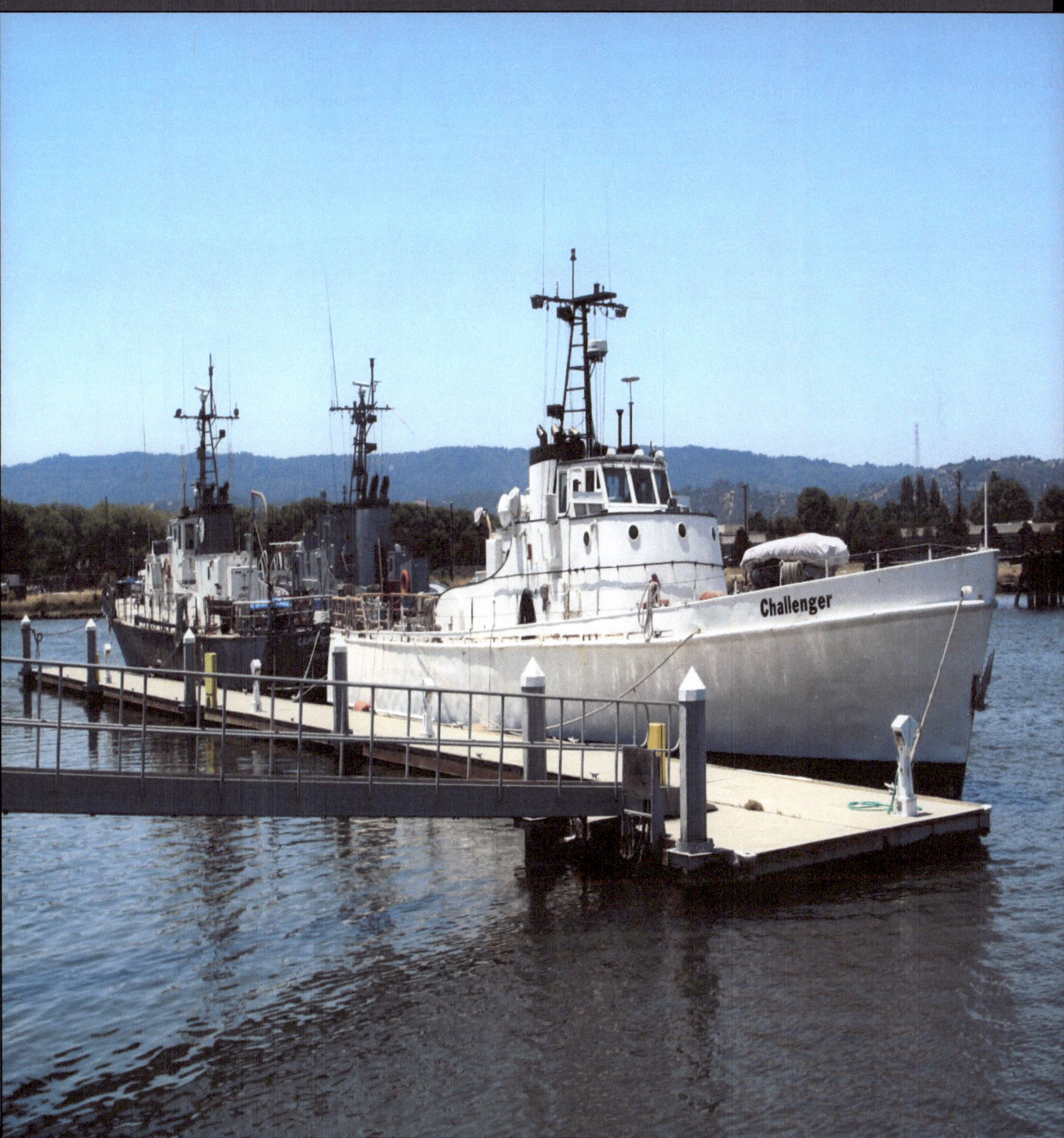

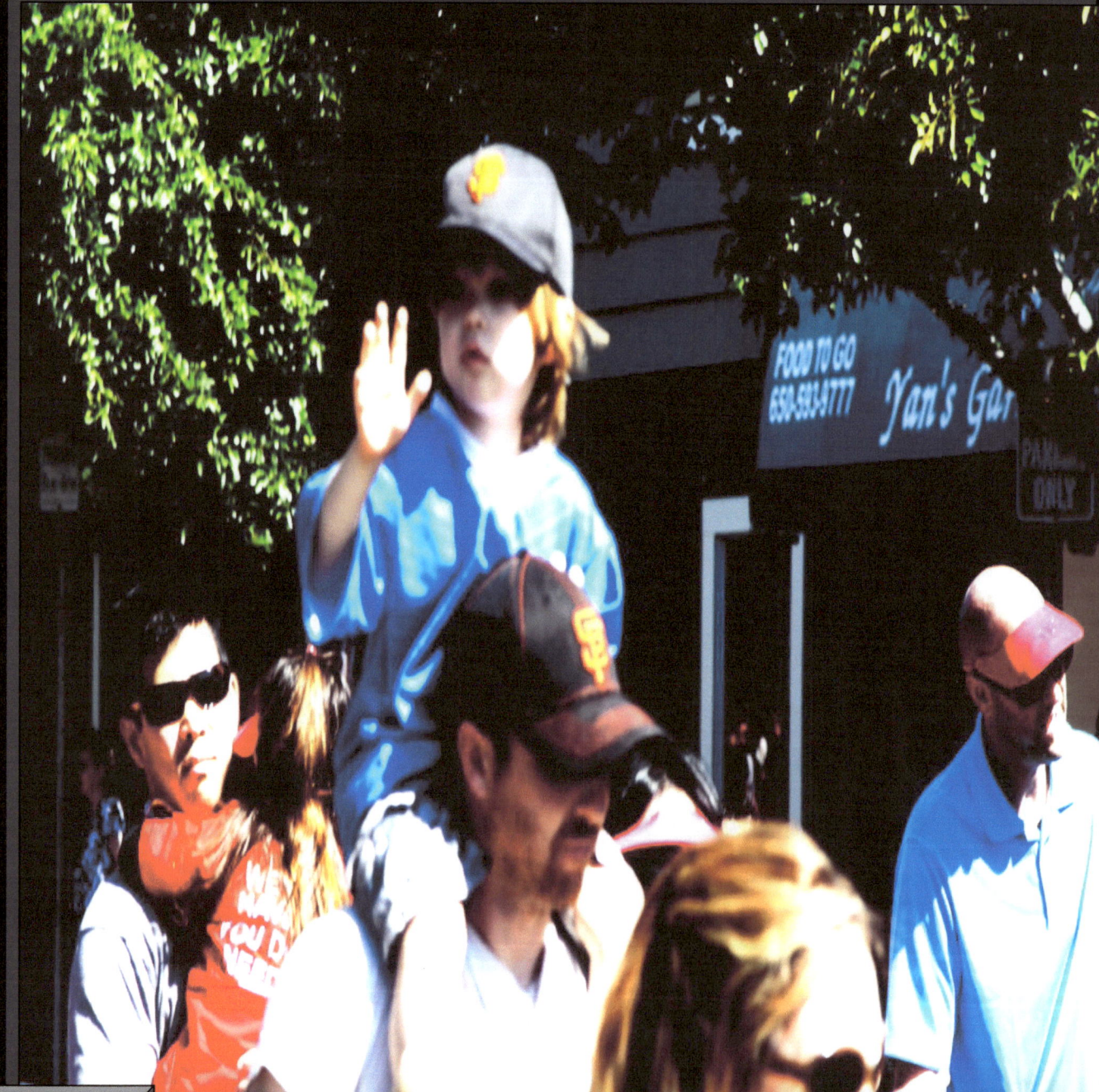

GOODBYE

GRATITUDES & SALUTATIONS

First to all involved,Thank you for your positive thoughts and pats on the back without whom...Well I still would have done it but with less motivation and determination.Chris my Cloud man and camera dude.Rick who allowed me computer usage. Juan(soft speaking John)and Carlos (Short Gaucagamolian)my brothers, and spiritual inspiration from all at Eaton Hall,Thank You Much and Much Thanks.

A few mentions on Johns Page,if you've ever seen the movie "The Untouchables" with Kevin Cosner and Robert Deniro when Al Capone by Deniro has the family at a round table he takes a baseball bat and beats to death this one wiseguy...hence, John Bracci the actor my friend.About Street Church the photograph on page 32-this is held every Monday and Wednesday nights in Redwood City,California.If it touches your heart you can help by volunteering or donating to Streetlife Ministries contact; David Shearin,Executive Director at email david@streetlifeministries.org or on the web at www.streetlifeministries.org or telephone at (650)716-6624

The Dude who did this; Greg Mills grew up in Washington State next to the mighty Columbia river,always a true adventurer.A Rock and Roll Disc Jockey at age 15,also fought forest fires,aTaxi Disptcher,a Carpenter after Hurricane Katrina, an Entertainment Director and a Publisher at age 25.He created an Ad Campaign while with Auto Trader Magazines in Seattle in 1989 in which he is "Promoman" at age 26.Created and Produced "Community Business Voice"in 1993 in Spokane,Wa. On KSBN Business Radio 1230 am at age 30.He has been a Newspaper and Travel Publisher with 25 years of Photography throughout the western U.s. and Canada.Now calling San Francisco home yet still traveling shooting Photographs.You can visit him at www.promoman69.wix.com/spiritwind and leave a message from there.

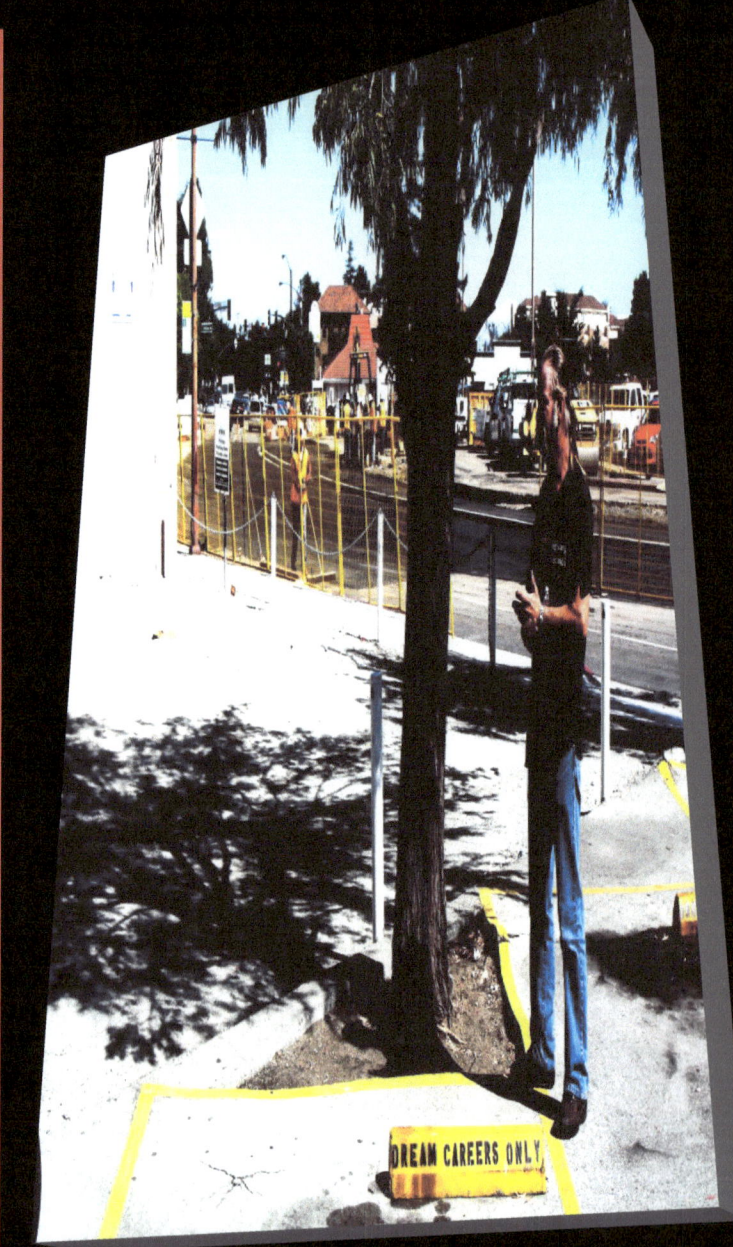

www.ingramcontent.com/pod-product-compliance
Lightning Source LLC
Chambersburg PA
CBHW050718180526
45159CB00003B/1070

9780615881997